COGNITIVE-BEHAVIORAL THEORIES OF COUNSELING

ABOUT THE AUTHOR

Dr. Marty Sapp is a Professor of Educational Psychology at the University of Wisconsin–Milwaukee. He earned his Ed.D. in Educational Psychology at the University of Cincinnati, and his substantive interests are cognitive-behavioral therapies, hypnosis, research methods and designs, measurement, and anxiety disorders.

Dr. Sapp is a licensed psychologist and Fellow of the American Psychological Association. In addition, he has published five books and authored more than forty-five journal articles. Moreover, he is an editorial board member of the *Journal of Rational-Emotive and Cognitive-Behavior Therapy,* and he has served on the following editorial boards: *Multiple Voices for Ethnically Diverse Exceptional Learner, Cognitive and Behavioral Practice, Journal of Counseling and Development,* and *Journal of Mental Health Counseling.* Finally, he has served as a reviewer for the following journals: *The Journal of Counseling Psychology, The Counseling Psychologist,* and *Educational Foundations.*

COGNITIVE-BEHAVIORAL THEORIES OF COUNSELING

Traditional and Nontraditional Approaches

By

MARTY SAPP

*Professor
Department of Educational Psychology
(Counseling Area)
University of Wisconsin–Milwaukee*

CHARLES C THOMAS • PUBLISHER, LTD.
Springfield • Illinois • U.S.A.

Published and Distributed Throughout the World by

CHARLES C THOMAS • PUBLISHER, LTD.
2600 South First Street
Springfield, Illinois 62704

This book is protected by copyright. No part of
it may be reproduced in any manner without
written permission from the publisher.

© 2004 by CHARLES C THOMAS • PUBLISHER, LTD.

ISBN 0-398-07498-4 (hard)
ISBN 0-398-07499-2 (paper)

Library of Congress Catalog Card Number: 2004041181

With THOMAS BOOKS *careful attention is given to all details of manufacturing and design. It is the Publisher's desire to present books that are satisfactory as to their physical qualities and artistic possibilities and appropriate for their particular use.* THOMAS BOOKS *will be true to those laws of quality that assure a good name and good will.*

Printed in the United States of America
GS-R-3

Library of Congress Cataloging-in-Publication Data

Sapp, Marty, 1958–
   Cognitive-behavioral theories of counseling :
traditional and nontraditional approaches / by Marty Sapp.
     p. cm.
   Includes bibliographical references and index.
   ISBN 0-398-07498-4 – ISBN 0-398-07499-2 (pbk.)
   1. Cognitive therapy.   I. Title.
   RC489.C63S275   2004
   616.89′142–dc22
                                      2004041181

To my students

PREFACE

Cognitive-Behavioral Theories of Counseling: Traditional and Nontraditional Approaches is designed for clinicians who are interested in traditional and nontraditional cognitive-behavioral approaches to psychotherapy. Some readers may be aware of traditional behavioral approaches such as neo-behaviorism, applied behavior analysis, cognitive-behavioral theory, social learning theory, personal constructs psychotherapy, and multimodal theory; however, there are several nontraditional cognitive-behavioral approaches to psychotherapy theory, such as the following: Adlerian theory, transactional analysis, and reality therapy. Nontraditional cognitive-behavioral personality theories did not develop from academic schools of behavioral thought, nor are they associated with the largest behavioral organization–the American Association for the Advancement of Behavior Therapy.

Cognitive-behavioral theories are the strongest paradigm within the fields of psychotherapy and psychology. Even though many academic writers emphasize theoretical eclecticism, many theories of psychotherapy are epistemologically incompatible; nevertheless, a clinician can be eclectic within a general paradigm or classification of theories, such as cognitive-behavioral. Therefore, this book emphasizes to the clinician to be eclectic within the broad cognitive-behavioral umbrella, without haphazardly attempting to integrate opposing theories.

In summary, books that present clinicians an in-depth discussion of both traditional and nontraditional cognitive-behavioral approaches to theories of psychotherapy have not been heretofore available. Finally, this book emphasizes the current framework of psychotherapy and psychology-cognitive-behavioral theories.

ACKNOWLEDGMENTS

It took several individuals to bring this text into press. First, I would like to thank the students on my research team. Second, I offer thanks to the University of Wisconsin–Milwaukee School of Education word processing pool for typing this entire manuscript. Moreover, I thank Dr. Walter Farrell at the University of North Carolina at Chapel Hill. In addition, I offer thanks to my University of Cincinnati connections: Dr. Patricia O'Reilly, Dr. Judith Frankel, Dr. Marvin Berlowitz, Dr. Purcell Taylor, the late Dr. David L. Johnson, and Dr. James Stevens. I offer special thanks to Dr. Stevens, because he taught me how to embrace the quantitative aspects of being a psychologist. Finally, thanks also go to Mariana Gómez. In closing, comments or discussions concerning this text–both positive and negative–are encouraged. My address is The University of Wisconsin-Milwaukee, Department of Educational Psychology, 2400 E. Hartford Avenue, Milwaukee, Wisconsin 53211. My telephone number is (414) 229-6347, my e-mail address is sapp@uwm.edu, and my fax number is (414) 229-4939.

CONTENTS

Preface .... *Page* ix

Chapter
1. PSYCHOTHERAPY RESEARCH 1
   Psychotherapy Effectiveness 1
   Meta-analysis 8
   Effect Size Measures for Traditional Cognitive-Behavioral
      Therapies 11
   Summary 15

2. CRITERIA FOR CRITIQUING TRADITIONAL AND
   NONTRADITIONAL COGNITIVE-BEHAVIORAL
   THEORIES OF COUNSELING 18
   Precision and Testability 18
   Multicultural Counseling 23
   Major Cultural Groups within the United States 24
   Racial Prejudice Hidden within the Brain 29

3. ADLERIAN PSYCHOTHERAPY 32
   Chapter Overview 32
   Biological Sketch 33
   Freud versus Adler 34
   Key Concepts 37
      Organ Inferiority 37
      Lifestyle 38
      Masculine Protest 39
      Striving for Superiority 40
      Phenomenology 41
      Individual Psychology 41
      Fictional Finalism 42
      Social Interest 42
      Defense Mechanisms 43
      Children's Actions 44

Compensation 45
　　　Teleology 45
　　　Private Logic 45
　　　Family Constellation 46
　　　Birth Order 46
　　Therapeutic Process 48
　　　Therapeutic Goals 48
　　　Stage One: Establish an Empathic Relationship 49
　　　Stage Two: Help Client Understand Lifestyle,
　　　　Beliefs, and Feelings 49
　　　Stage Three: Help Client Develop Insight 52
　　　Stage Four: Help Client Commit to Change and
　　　　Initiate Alternatives to Current Behavior 53
　　　Level III Skills or Action Strategies 53
　　　Role of Therapist 55
　　　Therapeutic Relationship 56
　　　Multicultural Applications and Limitations 56
　　　Critique 56
　　Summary 58

4. BEHAVIOR THERAPY 65
　　Chapter Overview 65
　　Approaches to Behavior Therapy 66
　　　Applied Behavior Therapy 66
　　　Cognitive-Behavioral Therapy 68
　　　Social Learning Theories 71
　　　Multimodal Behavioral Therapy 72
　　Common Characteristics of Behavior Therapies 72
　　Anxiety Disorders 73
　　Therapies Based on Principles of Classical Conditioning 75
　　Therapies Based on Extinction 77
　　Therapies Based on Instrumental or Operant Conditioning 78
　　Self-Control Procedures 82
　　Eye-Movement Technique 87
　　Applications of Progressive Relation Techniques 88
　　　Transcript 88
　　　Debriefing 89
　　Guided Imagery Transcript 90
　　　Debriefing 91
　　Psychological Hypnosis 91
　　Hypnosis as Adaptive Regression 94
　　Cognitive-Behavioral Hypnosis (CBH) 95
　　CBH Transcript 95
　　　Debriefing 96
　　Therapeutic Process 96

        Therapeutic Goals 96
        Role of Therapist 96
        Therapeutic Relationship 97
        Multicultural Applications and Limitations 97
        Critique 97
     Summary 98

5. FAMILY OF SOCIAL LEARNING THEORIES 103
     Chapter Overview 103
     Miller and Dollard's Social Learning Theory 103
     Rotter's Social Learning Theory 104
     Locus of Control 105
     Interpersonal Trust 106
     Bandura's Social Learning Theory 107
     Therapeutic Process 108
        Therapeutic Goals 108
        Role of Therapist 108
        Therapeutic Relationship 108
        Multicultural Applications and Limitations 109
        Critique 109
     Summary 110

6. RATIONAL-EMOTIVE BEHAVIOR THERAPY 112
     Chapter Overview 112
     Historical Developments of REBT 112
     Major Psychological Influences 113
     Key Concepts 113
     Two Basic Human Disturbances 116
     Psychological Interactionism 116
     Three Psychological Insights 116
     Expanded ABCs of REBT 117
     The Nature of Emotions 117
     Hurt 119
     Irrational Jealousy 119
     Disrupting Clients' Irrational Beliefs 120
     Therapeutic Process 122
        Therapeutic Goals 122
        Role of Therapist 122
        Therapeutic Relationship 123
        Multicultural Applications and Limitations 124
        Case Example: Applying REBT with an African American
           Adult Male 125
     Summary 126

7. MULTIMODAL BEHAVIOR THERAPY 129
   Chapter Overview 129
   Key Concepts 129
   Structural Profiles 130
   Coping Imagery 131
   Cognitions 131
   Bridging 132
   Tracking 132
   Therapeutic Process 134
      Therapeutic Goals 134
      Role of Therapist 134
      Therapeutic Relationship 134
      Multicultural Applications and Limitations 135
      Critique 136
   Summary 136

8. COGNITIVE THERAPY 138
   Chapter Overview 138
   Key Concepts 139
      Depression 139
   Cognitive Therapy and Other Therapies 143
   Personality Theory 144
   Learned Helplessness and Depression 144
   Cognitive Distortions 147
   Cognitive Model of Depression 147
   Depression Checklist 148
   Therapeutic Process 150
      Therapeutic Goals 150
      Treatment 151
      Role of Therapist 152
      Therapeutic Relationship 153
      Multicultural Applications and Limitations 154
      Critique 154
   Summary 156

9. COGNITIVE-BEHAVIOR MODIFICATION 159
   Chapter Overview 159
   Key Concepts 159
   Therapeutic Process 162
      Therapeutic Goals 162
      Role of Therapist 162
      Therapeutic Relationship 162
      Multicultural Applications and Limitations 162
      Critique 163
   Summary 164

10. **PERSONAL CONSTRUCTS PSYCHOTHERAPY** 165
    Chapter Overview 165
    Key Concepts 165
    Kelly's Corollaries 167
    Emotions 168
    Action Strategies 168
    Therapeutic Process 169
        Therapeutic Goals 169
        Role of Therapist 170
        Therapeutic Relationship 170
        Multicultural Applications and Limitations 171
        Critique 171
    Summary 172

11. **TRANSACTIONAL ANALYSIS** 176
    Chapter Overview 176
    Biographical Sketch 176
    Developmental Perspective of Human Nature 177
    Structural Analysis 179
    Transactions 181
    Analysis of Psychological Games 184
    Script Analysis 186
    Bernian or Traditional Transactional Analysis Approach 187
    Gouldings' Redecisional Theory 189
    TA and Family Therapy 189
    Other Action Strategies 190
    New Developments within Transactional Analysis 192
    Therapeutic Process 192
        Therapeutic Goals 192
        Role of Therapist 193
        Therapeutic Relationship 193
        Multicultural Applications and Limitations 193
    Summary 195

12. **REALITY THERAPY** 199
    Chapter Overview 199
    Biographical Sketch 199
    A Nondeterministic View of Human Nature 200
    Applications to Mental Health 203
    Therapeutic Process 204
        Therapeutic Goals 204
        Role of Therapist 205
        Therapeutic Relationship 205
        Characteristics of Reality Therapy 205
        Eight Steps of Reality Therapy 206

  Eight Characteristics of an Effective Plan .206
  Fourteen Principles of Reality Therapy 208
  Multicultural Applications and Limitations 208
   Critique 209
  Summary 211

13. SUMMARY 213

 References 215
 Index 239

COGNITIVE-BEHAVIORAL THEORIES OF COUNSELING

Chapter 1

PSYCHOTHERAPY RESEARCH

PSYCHOTHERAPY EFFECTIVENESS

How do we know that psychotherapy is effective? Bergin and Garfield (1994, pp. 31–66) found that all forms of psychotherapy were effective. However, various forms of psychotherapy differ in terms of effect sizes. Bergin and Garfield used **meta-analysis,** a technique that summarizes the effect sizes of several studies to show that psychotherapy was effective. When psychotherapy groups are compared to control groups, psychotherapy has an overall ***d* effect size** of .70 (Sapp, 1997a, 1999, 2002). In addition, clients undergoing psychotherapy are better off than the 79 percent of clients receiving no treatment. Some theorists such as Kirsch (1990) and Kirsch and Lynn (1999) believe that psychotherapy is mostly a **placebo effect,** or an **expectancy effect** and they base their position partially on automaticity theory.

Kirsch and Lynn's (1999) notion of **expectancy** comes from a group of behavioral theories called **social learning theories.** For example, Miller and Dollard, Rotter, and Bandura developed social learning theories (Sapp, 1997a). Neal Miller and John Dollard were the first theorists to use the term **social learning theories.** They took tenets from Clark Hull's theory of learning and extended it to reflect social and cognitive perspectives. Hull believed that **drives** (reinforcement) energized all behavior; however, they do not direct behavior; and he stated that there were two types of drives—primary and secondary. **Primary drives** are physiological needs such as food, clothing, and shelter; in contrast, **secondary drives** are associated, or acquire reinforcement value by being associated with primary drives. For example, money, diamonds, pearls, and stocks are some examples of secondary drives. **Cues** determine how people respond to drives. For example, if one were having dinner at a prestigious restaurant and did not know which fork to use while eating, one could observe others and determine from the social cues which fork to use. According to Dollard and Miller's social learning theory, social cues are learned through a trial-and-error method. In essence, Dollard and Miller proposed a drive reduction theory in that reinforcement involves drive reduction. It is worth noting that Dollard and Miller were one of the first groups of theorists to attempt to combine psychoanalytic theory with behavioral theory, and their notion of drive reduction has the same meaning as it does within Freud's theory. Finally, Dollard and Miller's theory influenced the theories of Rotter and Bandura.

Rotter's social learning theory was the second development within the area of social learning. Rotter included more of a cognitive emphasis with his theory. Rotter's theory has four basic constructs: behavior potential, reinforcement value, expectancy, and psychological situation.

Behavioral potential is the potential for behavior, and it is the probability that a given behavior will occur in a situation, if it is reinforced. Reinforcement value is a client's preference for one reinforcer over another, and expectancy is a belief that a certain behavior will produce a certain reinforcer (Sapp, 1997a). The **psychological situation** is the context in which behavior occurs. Rotter's theory can be summarized as Behavior Potential = Function of (Expectancy and Reinforcement Value). This formula states that behavior potential is a function of the interaction of expectancy and reinforcement value; therefore, a client's subjective perception, not external reality, determines his or her behavior potential. Finally, Rotter stated that behavior has to be interpreted within the social context of the client, and one does not want to give too much influence to dispositional factors.

Bandura's social learning theory was the third development within the area of social learning. Even though Bandura started his career as a traditional behaviorist, he found that operant and classical conditioning could not explain complex behaviors. He found that clients who had requisite skills for certain behaviors could extend their repertoire of skills by observing a therapist perform specific behaviors. What is interesting about Bandura's notion of observational learning, learning by observing, is that the public assumes that modeling will occur if there is a model; however, there is an important ingredient for successful modeling—the client has to accept the model. This point is often missed by popular psychology books and individuals within the media.

In summary, Bandura's theory is a social-cognitive-behavioral one, and he stated that behavior is determined by the complex interaction of personal, behavioral, and situational factors-**reciprocal determinism.** Moreover, reciprocal determinism explains why clients think, feel, and do the things that they do.

Recently, Kirsch and Lynn (1998) and Wegner and Wheatley (1999), presented a **sociocognitive theory of automaticity.** According to Bargh and Barndollar (1996), the following four conditions are necessary and sufficient for cognitive processes or behavioral actions to be **automatic** (Bargh and Gollwitzer, 1994):

1. The cognitive process of behavioral action is outside of the client's awareness.
2. The cognitive process or behavioral action cannot be prevented; therefore, the cognitive process or behavioral action is uncontrollable or unstoppable.
3. The cognitive process or behavioral action does not require cognitive resources to become initiated; that is, the client does not have to think about the cognitive process or behavioral action for it to be initiated.
4. The cognitive process or behavioral action does not require volitional effort to become initiated; therefore, the cognitive process or behavioral action is unintentional or nonvolitional.

Kirsch and Lynn's (1998) theory was influenced by several social cognitive theorists (Bargh, 1994; Bargh & Barndollar, 1996; Libet, 1985; Bargh & Gollwitzer, 1994; Dixon, Bruent, & Laurence, 1990; Dixon & Laurence, 1992; Lynn, 1992; Lynn & Rhue, 1994) and Kirsch's (1990, 1997) response expectancy theory. Kirsch and Lynn proposed that all routinized behaviors are automatic. The reader may be aware that theories such as **classical conditioning** describe responding as automatic (Pitsch, Sapp, & McNeely, 2001). For example, if a puff of air (unconditioned stimulus) is blown into one's face, the automatic response is to blink (unconditioned response). Moreover, a sudden loud noise tends to produce automatic startle responses. In addition, Van Den Hout and Merckelbach (1991) presented a persuasive argument that clients are genetically prepared to respond to certain conditioned responses, and that classical conditioning is not just the simplistic cue to respond, but clients' anticipations about the probable relationship between stimuli (Sapp, 1997a). In summary, this neo-Pavlovian theory states that clients can respond to automatic and intentional responses.

Kirsch and Lynn's (1998) theory is also influenced by Norman and Shallice's (1986) model. Norman and Shallice stated that all behavior is initiated automatically, and this happens through hierarchically organized interactive sensory motor **schemata.** Readers may remember that Bartlett (1932) and Piaget (1926) were the first to describe the concept called schemata. Schemata are composed of four interconnected concepts: cognitive structure, cognitive propositions, cognitive operations, and cognitive products (Granvold, 1994). **Cognitive structure** is how information is mentally stored in the brain or mind; **cognitive propositions** are the content stored with cognitive structures. **Cognitive operations select,** encode, and retrieve information. **Cognitive products** are the results of information processing, and they are self-cognitions, self-judgments, self-expectations, and self-conclusions. Finally, schemata serve as the basis for attributing actions as automatic.

According to Norman and Shallice (1986), two complementary systems control the initiation of actions. The lower system is called **contention scheduling** and it handles routine actions and does not require attentional or conscious control or effort. The **supervisory attentional systems** control novel tasks and nonroutinized behaviors (Woody & Farvolden, 1998).

Clearly, with Norman and Shallice's (1986) two-tier model, volition is connected with the supervisory system, and this model is similar to Hilgard's (1994) **neodissociation model of nonvolitional hypnotic responding.** Hilgard explains automatic hypnotic responding through a **dissociation theory.** Actually, before Hilgard developed his theory, Jean Marie Charcot (1825–1893) and his student, Pierre Janet (1859–1947), presented a dissociation theory of hypnosis. They believed that dissociation was more likely to happen when a client was exposed to extreme psychological stress or trauma. According to their theory, when clients experience extreme stress or trauma, there is a tendency for ideas and behavioral patterns that normally associate to become dissociated or separated.

Hilgard's (1994) theory differs from Charcot's and Janet's in that he presented an incomplete theory of dissociation among cognitive systems, and his theory is based on cognitive psychology. Specifically, his theory has the following assumptions: (a) there is a central processing unit, called the executive ego, that evaluates activities; and (b) the executive ego has several hierarchical subsystems below it that govern cognitive functions. Hilgard suggested that automaticity within hypnosis is the result of a combination of dissociation among the executive ego and the cognitive subsystems and the erection of an amnesic or communications barrier among the dissociated parts. Woody and Farvolden (1998) modified Hilgard's theory, and they presented a dissociated control theory of hypnotic automaticity; however, they did not believe that automatic hypnotic responding was the result of an amnesic barrier; rather they believed it was the result of hypnosis weakening control of the frontal lobe brain functions, which results in a dissociation of brain functions (Woody & Sadler, 1998).

Kirsch and Lynn (1998) argued that **response expectancies** determine clients' subjective feelings of automaticity, and that response expectancies are self-confirming and they tend to generate the subjective and physiological substrates of automaticity. To illustrate, Kirsch (1999; 2000) found that the placebo-induced expectancies could produce changes in asthma, anxiety, depression, panic, sexual arousal, tension, heart rate, blood pressure, dermatitis, and bronchial constriction. In essence, according to Kirsch and Lynn, automaticity is the result of response expectancies; therefore, when a client expects to experience automaticity, he or she can modify his or her expectancy for that response and it can occur as a result of response expectancy modification.

Kirsch and Lynn's (1998) position on automaticity theory explains one facet of automaticity, especially within the area of hypnosis. For example, Barber (1999; 2000), within the area of hypnosis, describes positively set clients as having positive motivations to perform well in experiences during hypnosis and have positive expectancies. Moreover, these clients are able to think with and imagine the suggested phenomena. In essence, these clients are conforming, trusting, and imaginative (Sapp, 2000; Spiegel & Connery, 1982). However, Barber described two other types of clients–amnesic prone and fantasy prone. Barrett (1990, 1996) found that certain clients had amnesia for hypnosis, and these clients had amnesia during their daily lives. Barber described these clients as amnesic prone. Moreover, Barber described a third type of hypnotic clients that he termed fantasy prone, and unlike the positively set clients and amnesic-prone clients, have a long history of make-believe and fantasy, vivid memories dating back to the age of three, and the ability to use their minds to affect their bodies. In summary, the fantasy-prone clients have well-developed fantasies, and they use their fantasies to live interesting lives.

In conclusion, Kirsch and Lynn's (1995; 1998) theory is too simplistic to explain all the features or mechanisms of automaticity. This is due to the fact that automaticity is a multivariate construct as opposed to a univariate or a common factor construct like some response expectancies. Automaticity includes, but is not limited by, suggestions, dissociation, fantasy proneness, and response expectancies. As Pashler (1998) pointed out, automaticity is a theory, not a fact; however, Kirsch and Lynn appear to assume that it is a fact. Finally, research will determine if theories of automaticity will provide empirical data that complement theories of counseling and psychotherapy.

Lambert and Bergin (1994) found that the average d effect size for placebo control groups was .42, which is a small effect size. Kirsch and Lynn (1999) even argued that antidepressant medications are placebos. The concept of placebo comes from expectancy theory, or the notion that expectations lead to change. Clearly, there is a placebo component to medications as well as psychotherapy; however, Hamburg (2000) voiced disagreement with this position. He reported methodological problems with placebo-control trials. For example, placebo-control trials of antidepressant medications are biased against antidepressants. Moreover, participants vary greatly in such studies, and drug effects are reduced or canceled out completely because of participants' individual differences. Hamburg concluded that the most effective antidepressants produce response rates of 60 percent, and that participants who are the most likely to respond are those with moderate-to-severe depression. If Kirsch and Lynn's thesis were correct about placebos, if one could increase the response expectancies of clients with moderate-to-severe depression, then depression would decrease as a result of the placebo effect. Finally, there are fairly conclusive data that certain forms of hypnosis are correlated with changes in brain functions that are independent of placebo effects (Woody & Bowers, 1998).

META-ANALYSIS

Some questions the reader should have would include: What is meta-analysis? And what are effect sizes? The reader is familiar with traditional literature review, where a researcher or scholar summarizes studies within an area. Well, **meta-analysis** is a mathematical or quantitative method for summarizing or synthesizing the literature within an area into one overall value.

Many of my colleagues within counseling psychology assume that this is a new statistical technique; however, it is not new. For example, Cohen (1977) was one of the first researchers to describe meta-analysis and a related technique called power analysis (Sapp, 2002a). Cohen described the basic effect size measure, the statistic that is summarized, which is an analog to the t-tests for two group means. The reader may remember from elementary statistics that the t-test for two group means is the difference between two group means (the difference between the averages of two groups) divided by the standard error (the standard deviation squared for each group divided by the appropriate group size). The reader can consult Sapp (1999, 2002a) for a detailed discussion on how to calculate the t-test for two independent groups. Essentially, the t-test determines if two group means are statistically significantly different. Within meta-analysis, the d effect size is the difference between two means divided by the standard deviation (the amount of variability, Cohen, 1977; Sapp, 1997a, 2002a). One of the problems with the d effect size is that the standard deviation can be from the control group posttest measure; it can be the pretest standard deviation for the control group, or it can be some weighted standard deviation that involves the treatment and control groups. Finally, the d effect sizes are averaged, and the result is an overall effect.

Even though meta-analysis is a quantitative technique, many of my colleagues within counseling psychology confuse it with statistical significance testing. **Statistical significance** testing attempts to reject or fail to reject the **null hypothesis** (the population means do not differ greater than one would expect by chance). In contrast, meta-analysis addresses **practical significance,** or the degree to which the null hypothesis may be false (Sapp, 1997a, 1999, 2002a).

Cohen (1977) provided the following rough guidelines for interpreting the d effect size: $d = .2$ **small effect size,** $d = .5$ **medium effect size,** and $d = .8$ **large effect size.** Wolf (1986) cautions practitioners from blindly interpreting effect sizes as small, medium, and large. One must interpret effect sizes within a given professional area.

There is another **effect size** called *r*, and it was described by Rosenthal (1984). The reader may remember that *r* is the **Pearson product-moment correlation coefficient.** Mathematically, *r* is the **covariance,** the amount two variables vary co-varies, divided by the number of pairs times the product of the standard deviation for each variable. Again, the reader can consult Sapp (1997a, 1999, 2002) for the formula for the Pearson product-moment correlation coefficient. Like Cohen (1977), Rosenthal provided the following rough guidelines for *r*: ***r* = .1 small effect size, *r* = .3 medium effect size, and *r* = .5 large effect size.** There is an interesting point that must be made about performing arithmetic operations on *r*. Arithmetic operations cannot be performed on *r* because as the population correlation coefficient gets further and further from zero, the distribution of *r* becomes skewed, and Fisher (1928) developed a transformation of *r*. Arithmetic operations have to be performed on these transformed values of *r,* and Fisher's transformations of *r* can be found in Sapp (1997a).

In summary, there are over 40 different measures of effect and some are standardized differences like Cohen's *d* or in correlation form like *r*. Finally, effect sizes can be presented as corrected and uncorrected measures (Sapp, 2002a).

Thompson (2002) has made a number of recommendations for social sciences research. First, he recommended that researchers put confidence intervals around reliabilities like coefficient alpha. Readers may remember, as Sapp (2002a) stated, that reliability is a function of test items and reliability measures the consistency of test items. Thompson defined a confidence interval as an interval among an infinitely large set of intervals for a given parameter in which 95 percent of the intervals would capture the population parameter.

Confidence intervals around reliability indices require a noncentral distribution—which allows one to a perform power analysis, or the probability of rejecting a false null hypothesis (no treatment effect). Fortunately, SPSS can calculate noncentral distribution for reliabilities, and unlike centralized distributions, which have a mean of zero, noncentralized distributions have a mean of some hypothesized value, and noncentralized distributions are skewed (Bird, 2002).

Fan and Thompson (2001) provided the following SPSS code for reliability confidence intervals:

```
Reliability variables = v1 to v3/
  scale(TOTAL) = v1 to v3/
  statistics = corr cov/summary = means var total/
  icc = model(random)  type(consistency)  cin = 95  testval = .70/
  model = alpha.
```

The following are the complete control lines on SPSS for the example from Fan and Thompson:

> Title 'Crocker2.sps********'.
> Data list free/person item score
> Begin data.
> 1 2 1
> 7 4 6
> 3 1 1
> 3 2 5
> 7 4 4
> 7 4 6
> 5 3 4
> 3 2 2
> 2 1 1
> 0 1 2
> end data.
> list.
> reliability variables item score/
>   scale(Total) = item score/
>   statistics = corr cov/summary = means var total/
>   model = alpha.

The following are the results from this analysis:

Intraclass Correlation Coefficient

Two-Way Random Effect Model (Consistency Definition):

People and Measure Effect Random

Single Measure Intraclass Correlation = .7473*
95.00% C.I.:   Lower = .4414   Upper = .9222
$F = 1.2340$ DF = (9, 18.0) Sig. = .3351   (Test Value = .7000)

Average Measure Intraclass Correlation = .8987
95.00% C.I.:   Lower = .7033   Upper = .9726
$F = 2.9617$ DF = (9, 18.0) Sig. = .0239   (Test Value = .7000)

*: Notice that the same estimator is used whether the interaction effect is present or not.
Reliability Coefficients: 3 items
Alpha = .8987   Standardized item alpha = .9417

The reader should notice several things from the output from SPSS. First, coefficient alpha is .8987. And the 95 percent confidence interval is .7033, .9726. While .7033 is the lower limit of value of the confidence interval, and the .9726 is the upper limit or value for the 95 percent confidence interval. Moreover, testing the hypothesized value for coefficient alpha of .7000 against the calculated value of coefficient alpha of .8987 did differ significantly because F = 2.9617 and the probability level is .0239. It is recommended that the reader run this analysis with sample data in order to get the intuitive feel for interpreting the computer output.

In addition, Thompson has challenged the use of statistical significance testing within the social sciences, likewise, Sapp (1997a, 2002a) poignantly stressed the same point. Readers should be aware that statistical significance only allows one to determine if a relationship is significantly greater than zero, and it does not ensure replicability, nor does it control for threats to internal validity (Sapp, 1999).

Internal validity is the judgment applied by a researcher to determine if an independent variable caused a change on a dependent variable. Theoretically, random assignment or randomly assigning participants to groups initially controls for all threats to internal validity.

Moreover, Thompson, like Sapp (1997a, 1999, 2002a), recommended that researchers provide effect size measures and reliability indices for their data. In addition, he recommended confidence intervals for effect size measures. Unfortunately, this process is an iterative one that involves noncentral distributions and readers who are interested in SPSS programs for calculating such intervals can consult (Bird, 2002; Smithson, 2001). For a nominal fee, Professor Geoff Cummings, at La Trobe University in Australia, has developed software that runs under the Excel program, which can be downloaded from the following website: http://www.latrobe.edu.au/psy/esci.

In summary, Thompson suggested that researchers provide effect size measures for their data and that they calculate reliability indices for their data. In conclusion, Thompson is suggesting that researchers think meta-analytically and not in the mindless way of applying statistical tests of significance.

EFFECT SIZE MEASURES FOR TRADITIONAL COGNITIVE-BEHAVIORAL THERAPIES

Cognitive-behavioral therapies are eclectic groups of techniques that combine strategies from cognitive and behavioral psychology. Albert Ellis is the grandfather of cognitive-behavioral therapy within the area of clinical psychology; whereas Aaron T. Beck is a prominent figure for cognitive therapy within the area of psychiatry. **Traditional forms of cognitive-behavioral therapies** developed from academic psychology or were embraced by academic psychology.

TABLE 1-1
HIGHEST AVERAGE EFFECT SIZE MEASURES FOR TRADITIONAL
COGNITIVE-BEHAVIORAL ORIENTATIONS

Orientation	Effect size d	Effect size r	Number of studies
Behavioral therapy	1.06	.48	214
Hypnotherapy	1.82	.68	475
Systematic Desensitization	1.05	.47	475
Implosive therapy	.68	.33	475
Behavior modification	.73	.35	475
Cognitive-behavioral therapy	1.13	.50	475
Cognitive therapy	1.00	.46	214
Self-control strategies	1.01	.46	214
Biofeedback	.91	.42	214
Covert-behavioral	1.52	.61	214
Flooding	1.12	.50	214
Relaxation therapy	.90	.42	214
Reinforcement	.97	.45	214
Modeling	1.43	.59	214

In contrast, **nontraditional forms of behavioral therapies** did not develop from academic psychology and they were not embraced by academic psychology. Effect sizes for the traditional cognitive-behavioral orientations are found in Table 1-1. **Behavioral therapy** is a collection of techniques to change behavior. **Hypnotherapy** is the therapeutic use of hypnosis to change behavior. Hypnosis parallels guided imagery, biofeedback, and progressive relaxation. In essence, it is a therapeutic process between a therapist and a client in that the client receives suggestions that have physiological effects. Hypnosis can lead to behavior change, and there are several approaches or styles of hypnosis.

Systematic desensitization is an imagination technique that pairs relaxation with anxiety-evoking stimuli. **Implosive therapy** is also an imagination-based technique that is similar to flooding but uses psychoanalytic connotations with the imagery scenes. **Behavior modification** is the use of behavioral techniques to modify or change behavior. **Cognitive-behavioral therapy** is a blend of cognitive and behavioral psychology, and it contends that a client's problems are the result of faulty belief systems. Cognitive therapy is a form of cognitive-behavioral therapy that was developed by Aaron Beck. The goal is to change clients' cognitive distortions. **Self-control strategies** are procedures that the client implements himself or herself, such as self-monitoring, self-reinforcement, self-punishment, bibliotherapy, self-hypnosis, and so on. **Biofeedback** is the use of computers and other technologies to provide clients with feedback about physiological processes, such as blood pressure, heart rate, body temperature, and so on. **Covert behavioral therapy** is an imagination technique that uses aversive stimuli to desensitize

TABLE 1-2
HIGHEST AVERAGE EFFECT SIZE MEASURES FOR NONTRADITIONAL
COGNITIVE-BEHAVIORAL ORIENTATIONS

Orientation	Effect size d	Effect size r	Number of studies
Adlerian	.71	.34	375
Transactional analysis	.67	.33	475
Reality therapy	.75	.35	21

clients to anxiety. **Flooding** is an imagination or in vivo real-life-based technique that leads to the extinction of unlearning of behaviors.

Relaxation therapy is the use of progressive relaxation or muscle-tension exercises or guided imagery to produce relaxation. **Reinforcement** is a procedure that leads to an increase in behavior. Finally, modeling is a social learning technique that uses models to model and change certain behavior. Table 1-1 has the highest average effect size measures for the traditional cognitive-behavioral orientations. The reader should notice that cognitive-behavioral therapy has a d effect size of 1.13, which is a large effect size. And there are 475 studies to support this statistic. Hypnotherapy has a d effect size of 1.82—again a large effect size measure. Moreover, cognitive therapy has a large d effect size measure of 1.00 with 214 studies to support the overall effect. Of the traditional cognitive-behavioral techniques, implosive therapy has a medium effect size of .68. In contrast, flooding, a technique that is similar to implosive therapy, has a large d effect size of 1.12. One of the appeals of cognitive-behavioral therapy is that most of the techniques have large effect sizes.

Effect sizes for the following nontraditional cognitive-behavioral orientations are found in Table 1-2. Adlerian therapy is a precursor to traditional cognitive-behavioral approaches to psychotherapy. This is a cognitive-behavioral and analytic form of psychotherapy. Most of the theories discussed in this text were influenced by Adlerian psychotherapy. **Transactional analysis** is a nonacademic form of cognitive-behavioral therapy that did not develop from academic or traditional forms of behavior therapy. Generally, with this form of psychotherapy, one will not see references to classical and operant conditioning, but an analysis of a client's ego states, which is a behavioral way to operationally defining Freud's constructs of the personality—id, ego, and superego; however, transactional analysis refers to these as the child, adult, and parent ego states. Unlike Freud's psychoanalysis, transactional analysis is a humanistic-existential form of psychotherapy that stresses that clients can choose and change even when experiencing strong environmental and social forces. **Reality therapy** also did not develop from academic psychology, and it has aspects of humanistic existential therapy and behavior modification. **Choice theory,** a recent development within reality therapy, teaches clients that they create their reality with their own brains or minds.

Moreover, clients are taught to take personal responsibility for their behavior or actions, and clients are taught to take action in order for changes to occur.

Table 1-2 has the highest average effect size measures for nontraditional cognitive-behavioral therapies. For the nontraditional cognitive-behavioral therapies, or therapies that did not develop from academic psychology, Adlerian therapy has a d effect of .71, which is indicative of a medium effect size. This statistic was based on 375 studies. Transactional analysis, another nontraditional form of cognitive-behavior therapy, has a d effect size of .67, another medium effect size measure. Finally, reality therapy has a d effect size of .75, which rounded, is approximately .80—indicative of a large effect size; however, there are only 21 studies used for this effect size.

Table 1-3 has 95 percent confidence intervals for highest average d effect sizes for various forms of psychotherapy along with their power values. These confidence intervals were calculated with software found in Smithson (2003). This table provides more information than Tables 1-1 and 1-2. For example, it is clear that short-term dynamic therapy and reality therapy both have low power values. Stevens defined power values greater than .70 as adequate and values greater than .90 as excellent. The reason short-term dynamic therapy and reality therapy have low power values are because of their small sample sizes. With a sample size of about 100, normally power is not an issue. The reader should also notice that short-term dynamic and reality therapy both have zero included within their confidence intervals which suggests that the null hypothesis was not rejected and the negative values within these intervals also suggest that both therapies can produce negative effects or harm; however, clearly any form of psychotherapy can produce negative effects, especially treatments with high effect sizes.

To summarize, both short-term dynamic therapy and reality therapy have confidence intervals that include zero and the confidence intervals around d provide more information than the single point estimates of d.

Cognitive-behavioral therapy had a lower limit of .4677 (about a medium effect size) and an upper limit of .6614, again a value that reflects a medium effect size. Hypnotherapy had a lower limit of .8025 large effect size and an upper limit of 1.0163, again a large effect size.

Dynamic/humanistic therapy, Person-centered therapy, and Gestalt therapy all had lower confidence limits in the lower ranges, with dynamic/humanistic therapy with a lower limit of .0648—which is the lowest for the humanistic therapies.

In terms of cognitive-behavioral therapies with upper limits with values of .8 or greater, only hypnotherapy, covert-behavioral, modeling, and reality therapy had upper limits with high d effect sizes using confidence intervals.

Clearly, Table 1-3 provides more information about effect sizes for various forms of psychotherapy and values of d are more meaningful when the upper

TABLE 1-3
CONFIDENCE INTERVALS FOR HIGHEST EFFECT SIZES FOR VARIOUS FORMS
OF PSYCHOTHERAPY WITH POWER VALUES

Orientation	Effect size d	Estimated t-values	95% Confidence interval for d	Power values	Number of studies
Short-Term Dynamic Therapy	.71	1.81	−.0451, .7483	.41	26
Psychodynamic	.69	7.52	.2523, .4374	1.00	475
Dynamic Eclectic	.89	9.69	.3505, .5392	1.00	474
Adlerian	.71	6.87	.2502, .4589	1.00	375
Dynamic/Humanistic	.40	2.93	.0648, .3354	.83	214
Person-Centered	.63	6.10	.2111, .4185	1.00	375
Gestalt	.64	6.97	.2274, .4118	1.00	475
Transactional Analysis	.67	7.30	.2424, .4272	1.00	475
Behavioral Therapy	1.06	7.75	.3861, .6723	1.00	214
Hypnotherapy	1.82	19.83	.8025, 1.0163	1.00	475
Systematic Desensitization	1.05	11.44	.4287, .6206	1.00	475
Implosive Therapy	.68	7.41	.2474, .4323	1.00	475
Behavior Modification	.73	7.95	.2717, .4575	1.00	475
Cognitive-Behavioral Therapy	1.13	12.31	.4677, .6614	1.00	475
Cognitive Therapy	1.00	7.31	.3571, .6413	1.00	214
Self-Control Strategies	1.01	7.39	.3624, .6469	1.00	214
Biofeedback	.91	6.66	.3140, .5956	1.00	214
Covert-Behavioral	1.52	11.12	.6072, .9116	1.00	214
Flooding	1.12	8.19	.4151, .7034	1.00	214
Relaxation Therapy	.90	6.58	.3087, .5899	1.00	214
Reinforcement	.97	7.09	.3424, .6258	1.00	214
Modeling	1.43	10.46	.5642, .8645	1.00	214
Reality Therapy	.75	1.72	−.0722, .8083	.38	21

d: population effect size for the t-test for independent two groups and $t = (\sqrt{N/2})d$ and $d = 2t/\sqrt{N}$. According to Stevens (2002), power $> .70$ is adequate and $> .90$ is excellent.

and lower limits of population parameters are estimated. To reiterate, in general, cognitive-behavioral therapies tend to have large d effect size values, but confidence intervals suggest that true population parameters vary from the d point estimates and most forms of cognitive-behavioral therapies have upper confidence limits within the medium effect size ranges.

SUMMARY

There are many factors that determine the effectiveness of a given form of treatment. Smith, Glass, and Miller (1980) found that any form of counseling was more effective, on average, than untreated control groups. This suggests that all forms of psychotherapy have effects sizes greater than **zero,** since zero would indicate **no effect.** Smith et al. also found that group therapy is just as effective as individual therapy. Sapp (1999) reported that some of the factors that influence the outcome of psychotherapy are client-therapist factors, client factors, therapist factors, and treatment factors (Frank, 1986).

A good client-therapist treatment alliance is correlated with positive treatment gains (Gendlin, 1986; Marziali, Marmar, & Krupnick, 1981). Moreover, higher levels of intelligence are correlated with better therapy outcomes. In addition, marital status is correlated with therapy outcome. For example, psychological problems are highest among separated and divorced individuals, followed by single persons and widows and widowers (Bootzin, Bower, Zajonc, & Hall, 1986).

In terms of therapist factors, the more experience a therapist has, the greater the chances are that a client will not drop out of therapy and will experience positive outcomes.

Finally, as Paul (1967) pointed out, what treatment and by whom under what conditions is effective for which kinds of clients with what kinds of specific concerns is an important question for psychotherapy outcome research.

Glossary of Key Terms

Automaticity. The theory that states at the moment of activation all behavior is automatic, or does not require thought.

Behavioral therapy. Theories that are based on changing behavior or things that people do.

Classical conditioning. A theory of learning that is emphasized by some forms of behavioral therapy. The term conditioning means learning, and classical conditioning is the conditioning of reflexes.

Cognitive-behavioral therapies. Therapies that work on changing thoughts and behaviors.

Drives. A term used by the psychologist Hull as a synonym for reinforcement.

Expectancy. A term employed by social learning theorists to note that expectancies influence behavior.

Effect size. A quantitative method of measuring the effects of counseling or psychotherapy.

Meta-analysis. A quantitative method of summarizing the effect sizes of several quantitative studies.

Neodissociation. A theory of hypnosis that states that hypnosis is an altered state of consciousness.

Nontraditional forms of behavioral therapies. These are forms of behavioral therapy that did not develop from academic departments of psychology.

Null hypnosis. A statistical hypothesis that states that there is no treatment effect.

Placebo effect. A term from social learning theory that emphasizes the influence of expectations on behavior.

Statistical significance. The rejection of the null hypothesis (no treatment effect), and the assumption of the alternative hypothesis (there is a treatment effect).

Practical significance. The significance of studies based on effect sizes.

r effect size. The correlation measure of effects, with ranges between -1.0 and $+1.0$, including 0. Zero would suggest no effect.

Traditional forms of cognitive behavioral therapies. Cognitive-behavioral therapies that developed from academic forms of cognitive-behavioral therapy.

Review Questions

1. How do psychologists know that cognitive-behavioral therapies actually make a difference?
2. What is meta-analysis, and how does it differ from a traditional narrative literature review?
3. What is the difference between cognitive-behavioral theories of counseling and nontraditional cognitive-behavioral approaches?
4. What are social learning theories and what have they offered to psychotherapy effectiveness?
5. What is the sociocognitive theory of automaticity?
6. What is the Norman and Shallice's theory of automaticity?
7. Briefly describe the neodissociation model of nonvolitional hypnotic responding.
8. Describe schemata theory.
9. When social learning theorists state that all forms of psychotherapy are just placebo effects, how do the data by Lambert and Bergin (1994) challenge this assumption?
10. Are there any problems in stating that one form of cognitive-behavioral therapy is consistently superior to others?

Chapter 2

CRITERIA FOR CRITIQUING TRADITIONAL AND NONTRADITIONAL COGNITIVE-BEHAVIORAL THEORIES OF COUNSELING

The goals of psychotherapy are to describe and predict the behavior of clients. Clinicians often forget that a theory is a systematic way of describing why clients do what they do. Moreover, a **theory** is an overall framework for understanding clients. In addition, theories are made up of constructs or concepts that can be operationally defined, or defined in measurement terms. A theory connects constructs through unifying themes. Without theories, the area of psychotherapy would consist of isolated parts without a common thread. Another reason theories are important is that they permit researchers to test hypotheses and to revise or change hypotheses. In summary, theories are important for the science of psychology and for the practice of psychology.

Sapp (1997a) and Ryckman (1989) provided the following seven criteria for evaluating theories of psychotherapy: comprehensiveness, precision and testability, parsimony, empirical validity, heuristic value, applied value, and multicultural application and limitations.

A **comprehensive** cognitive-behavioral theory would have to explain human development from birth through death. Many of these theories do not adequately explain how clients or why clients become disturbed. In summary, a comprehensive cognitive-behavioral theory must account for a wide range of data.

PRECISION AND TESTABILITY

Precision refers to the operational definition of variables. For example, within social sciences methodology, independent variables and dependent variables are often used to explain the relationship between variables. By the way, a variable is any factor that can change.

For example, any form of cognitive-behavioral therapy would be a variable, or more specifically an independent variable. Within psychotherapy, **independent variables** are forms of psychotherapy or forms of treatment. And they have at least two levels-one can give the therapy or not give it. **Dependent variables** are the results of the measures for independent variables; they are the presumed effect, while the independent variables, moderator control, and suppressor, influence the dependent variables. **Moderator variables** moderate the relationship between an independent variable and dependent variable. For example, motivation and level of intelligence are important variables to consider within the area of psychotherapy.

Control variables are held constant, within a research context, so they do not affect the results. For example, if a researcher was investigating reducing anxiety, he or she would want to hold constant anxiety—that is find clients with high levels.

Suppressor variables are independent variables that suppress or obscure the relationship among interdependent variables, because they are correlated with other independent variables, but uncorrelated with the dependent variables. Within a regression context, a statistical technique that deals with predicting variables, Pedhazur (1997) described their counterintuitive concept with the following example:

Suppose 3 variables have correlations as follows:

$$r_{12} = .3 \quad r_{13} = .0 \quad r_{23} = .5$$

If variable 1 is the dependent variable, clearly it is not correlated with variable 3; however, variables 2 and 3 have a correlation of .5; nevertheless, variables 1 and 3 are not correlated; hence, the correlation between these two variables is 0. Now, the semipartial correlation also called the part correlation can be denoted as $r_{1(2.3)}$. This notion says that variable 3 has been partialed out from variable 2 but not from variable 1; in other words, this is the correlation between variables 1 and 2 with variable 3 held constant from variable 2 and not variable 1. The semipartial correlation is as follows:

$$r_{1(2.3)} = \frac{.3 - (.0)(.5)}{(1 - .5)^{1/2}} = \frac{.3}{(.75)^{1/2}} = \frac{.3}{.866} = .35$$

The reader should notice that the correlation between variables 1 and 2 increases from .3 to .35 when variable 3 has been partialed out from variable 2 but not from variable 1. In addition, Stevens (2002) provided the following example to illustrate a suppressor variables:

$$r_{yx1} = .60 \quad r_{yx2} = .0 \quad r_{x1x2} = .50$$

Note that y is the dependent variable and x_1 and x_2 are predictors of y or independent variables. The formula for the semipartial correlation is the following:

$$r_{y1.2(S)} = \frac{r_{yx1} - r_{yx2}r_{x1x2}}{(1 - r_{x1x2})^{1/2}} = .693$$

Again, the reader should notice an increase in predictive power of predictor $1(x_1)$ from .60 to .693. It is not uncommon for suppressor variables to have a negative regression coefficient and a regression coefficient is a number that shows how values of an independent variable or predictor variable are connected with values of a dependent variable or criterion. This value is a part of what is called a regression equation. The formula for a regression equation is as follows:

$$y' = a + bx + e$$

where y' is the predict dependent variable, x is the independent variable, a is the y intercept, e is the error term, and b is the regression coefficient or slope. In summary, when several variables are intercorrelated and negative regression coefficients exist, their variables may be suppressor variable.

Lancaster (1999) cited the earliest study of suppressor variables or effects, which occurred during World War II as an attempt to predict pilot success. Researchers used mechanical ability, numerical ability, spatial ability, and verbal ability to predict pilot success. Interestingly, when verbal ability was added to a regression equation, an equation to predict pilot success, the accuracy of the overall model increased; nevertheless, verbal ability had almost a zero correlation with pilot ability; verbal ability was a suppressor variable. Why did verbal ability increase the utility of the overall regression model? First, verbal ability was required to read the instructions and it was needed to take the paper-and-pencil tests. Second, verbal ability removed the measurement artifact variance from the mechanical, numerical, and spatial ability scores (Thompson, 1992). Finally, Lancaster (1999) provided the following concrete example of suppression and how the squared multiple correlation R^2 increases to 1.0, perfect prediction. Lancaster described a two predictor case – that is two predicts x_1 and x_2, and one dependent variable denoted by y. The correlation of y with predictor one (x_1) was $-.707106$, the correlation of y with the second predictor (x_2) was 0, and the correlation of the two predictors was $-.707106$. He provided the following formula for finding the beta weight (b):

$$\beta = [r_{yx1} - (r_{yx2})(r_{x1x2})]/1 - r_{x1x2}^2$$

The b, or beta weight for the first predict is the following:

$$\beta_1 = [(.707106 - (0)(-0.707106)]/1 - (-0.707106)^2$$
$$= [(.707106 - (0)(-0.707106)]/1 - .49999$$
$$= .707106/.50001$$
$$= 1.41$$

The beta weight for the second predict (b_2) is as follows:

$$\beta_2 = [r_{yx2} - (r_{yx1})(r_{x1x2})]/1 - r_{x1x2}^2$$
$$= [0 - (.707106)(-0.707106)]/1 - .49999$$
$$= [0 - (-.5)]/.5$$
$$= 1.0$$

And he provided the formula for the multiple correlated squared (R^2) as the following:

$$R^2 = (\beta_1)(r_{xy1}) + (\beta_2)(r_{yx2})$$
$$R^2 = 1.41\,(.707106) + (1.0)(0)$$
$$= 1.0 \text{ (rounded to one decimal place)}.$$

In summary, suppressor variables are not easy to detect, but with regression research it is important to study the following: zero order correlations, they are correlations of each X variable with each Y variable; standardized beta weights or coefficients, or beta weights with a common mean and standard deviation, structured coefficients, which are the correlations of a predictor with a dependent variable divided by the multiple regression equation (Sapp, 2002a; Vogt, 1999; Thompson, 1992). In closing, suppressor variables are elusive but important variables within research.

The reader should notice that the semipartial correlation crystallizes the relationship between variables 1 and 2. Within a multiple regression context (two or more predictors for a criterion), simple correlations cannot determine the usefulness of correlations. Even when a researcher conducts a randomized study, it is possible that intervening variables could affect the results. Unlike independent variables and dependent variables, **intervening variables** are theoretical variables that cannot be seen, measured, or manipulated.

Once a clinician or researcher is aware of these variables, it is possible to operationally define them and to turn them into moderating variables. For example, with cognitive-behavioral therapies, learning is an important factor to consider; however, learning is a theoretical construct or intervening variable that can be operationally defined into a moderating variable.

To summarize, **precision** is the relationship between independent variables and dependent variables, and testability is the testing of hypotheses of a theory-based on some criterion that can be verified.

Parsimony is the notion that the best theories are concise, economical, or have few concepts. For example, theories that include unnecessary concepts lead clinicians and researchers far afield. In conclusion, clinicians and researchers prefer theories that only use the number of concepts that are necessary to describe the phenomenon that is under investigation.

Empirical validity is related to precision and testability. Empirical validity suggests that a theory is based on hypotheses that can be verified using data such as observations or questionnaires. The notion of validity is complex within the area of counseling psychology and psychotherapy. Unlike what many clinicians and researchers believe, **validity** is a measure that is the function of test items-not instruments (Sapp, 2002a). Specifically, **validity** is simply that the test items measure what they are supposed to measure. There are many forms of validity and the interested reader can refer to Sapp (2002a) for a detailed discussion. The simplest way to determine validity is to correlate the items from two instruments, and the result is a validity coefficient. Sapp (2002a) stated that structural equation modeling is the most effective way to explore the validity of test items. Specifically, **structural equations modeling** is based on testing the hypothesis that a sample covariance or correlations matrix differs from a population covariance of correlation matrix. The reader should note that the concept of validity is a complex issue and within psychology certain instruments are assumed to be valid and they are given a stamp of approval, but test items from instruments are seldom valid under all conditions. This is especially the case in terms of various cultural groups (Hernstein & Murray, 1994).

Heuristic value suggests that a given theory has stimulated other theorists, clinicians, and researchers to conduct studies or investigations. Inadequate theories can also stimulate researchers to conduct studies; however, heuristic theories tend to lead to fruitful areas of investigations. For example, the new technique called eye movement desensitization-reprocessing (EMDR), a desensitization procedure developed by psychologist Francine Shapiro to treat traumas, has stimulated many researchers to try to determine the mechanism underlying this new technique (Sapp, 1997a).

Applied value means that a theory can be applied within a clinical setting to solve clients' problems. Each clinician has to determine if a given theory is useful within his or her environment or clinical setting. For example, a clinician has to determine if techniques from a given theory can be applied within his or her setting. Within multicultural settings, the concept of applied value becomes more complex in that various cultural groups differ in how they may respond to techniques of psychotherapy.

Since the United States is a multicultural country, cognitive-behavioral theories must be evaluated with a multicultural context. Unfortunately, many traditional theories of counseling such as psychoanalysis were based on upper-class white clients. Cognitive-behavioral theories of counseling can be tested for multicultural applications by asking which cultural groups, such as African American, Hispanic, Asian, Native American, and so on, could benefit from a specific form of cognitive-behavioral therapy. Moreover, another question is what are the limitations of specific cognitive-behavioral therapies to various minority groups? A clinician must deliberate with regard to the utility of cognitive-behavioral therapies to minority groups.

In summary, it is doubtful that any one cognitive-behavioral therapy will have high ratings with all of the criteria; however, these criteria do provide a framework for evaluating cognitive-behavioral theories of counseling. It is important for clinicians to keep these criteria in mind when reading the theories that follow in the succeeding chapters.

MULTICULTURAL COUNSELING

Axelson (1993) pointed out that the goal of **multicultural counseling** is to include all the cultures that make up the United States, and this includes gay, bisexual, and transgender groups as well. Many readers may not be aware that **social class** is a factor that must be considered when counseling clients. For example, the **middle class social strata** is the core class structure in the United States. Some values and aspects of the middle class are hard work, competition, and self-expression. In addition, the middle class has certain language, values, behaviors, lifestyles, and core values associated with it. **Culture** is a social personality structure. And as Axelson stated, it involves language, sanctions, values, gender identity, family constellation, ethnic and racial identity, and acculturation. Moreover, culture can be seen as a social structure, social system, and social organization. Likewise, culture is defined by rules that guide social structures like marriage, patriarchy, matriarchy, nuclear family, and extended family. The American Psychological Association ethical principles endorse the concept of multicultural counseling, and multicultural competence has been endorsed by the organization. Finally, any practitioner working within the United States needs to know about multicultural counseling and the various cultural groups within the United States.

MAJOR CULTURAL GROUPS WITHIN THE UNITED STATES

Many Americans are not aware of their own cultural identity. For example, there are few Americans who are not immigrants to the United States. Within the racial group that identify themselves as white, subgroups include Anglo-Saxons, which comprise the following groups: English, Celtics, Welsh, Scottish, Northern Ireland Irish, Swedes, Norwegians, Danes, Finns, Germans, Dutch, and Appalachians. White ethnics include the following: Southern and Eastern Europe, Ireland Irish, Italians, Sicilians, Poles, Austrians, Hungarians, Czechs, Greeks, Portuguese, Russians, and Yugoslavs. Jews, Mormons, and Amish are considered socioreligious ethnic groups. Blacks include Africans, African Americans, West Indians, and Haitians. The term Spanish/Hispanic is confusing in the United States because it includes individuals from Mexico, Puerto Rico, Cuba, Spain, Central America, and South America. Spanish/Hispanic individuals within their countries have racial categories, but once they come to the United States, they are put into one racial category. Perhaps, Latino or Latina is an alternative term to Hispanic. There are about 263 tribes of American Indians or Native Americans within the United States, and the Navajo tribe is the largest group. Interestingly, Eskimos, Aleuts are considered to be Native Americans. Finally, the Asian/Middle Eastern category includes people from Asia as well as the Middle East such as Iranians, Egyptians, Turks, and Pakistani. The following groups will be discussed in the following section: Anglo-Saxon Americans, White Ethnic Americans, Black Americans, Native Americans, Hispanic Americans, and Asian Americans.

Sapp (1997a) stated that Anglo-Saxon Americans formed the foundations for many of America's values, and they were the first group to migrate to America. When one thinks about values such as competition, individualism, and hard work, these values can be traced back to the Anglo-Saxon. These individuals came primarily from England and Germany. During 400 and 500 A.D., the German tribes drove out the English in England. These early white Americans were Protestants, and sometimes they are referred to as White Anglo-Saxon Protestants (WASP's).

It was not until the period of between 1820 and 1929 that northern and western Europeans such as the Swedes, Danes, Norwegians, Finns, Dutch, and Germans immigrated to the United States. Germans were the largest group, followed by Italians.

Appalachian Americans are individuals who now live in the Appalachians Mountains, which includes parts of Georgia, Alabama, Kentucky, Maryland, Mississippi, New York, North Carolina, South Carolina, Tennessee, Virginia, and West Virginia. Most Appalachian Americans are white. Before the 1950s, coal mines offered a means of employment for Appalachian Americans, but during the 1950s when coal mines closed, the economic structure for these people collapsed. Unlike Anglo-Saxon Americans, Appalachian Americans did not want nor did they seek governmental or bureaucratic structures. Their basic values were dependence on family members and simple lifestyle.

White ethnic Americans include individuals from southern and eastern Europe, which includes Austria, Hungary, Czechoslovakia, Greece, Southern Italy, Sicily, Poland, Spain, Portugal, Russia, and Yugoslavia. Between 1880 and 1920, these groups arrived in America in large numbers, and they were primarily Catholic (Axelson, 1993).

According to Axelson, between 1880 and 1910, more than 4 million Italians from Southern Italy and Sicily entered America. This group valued family and the expense of individual achievement and few Italians entered college. Unfortunately, Axelson stated that this was one of the most illiterate ethnic groups to come to America.

Most Polish Americans came to the United States between 1880 and 1920, and similar to the Italians, they were indigent, illiterate, and lacked political power. Many of the Midwestern states such as Michigan, Illinois, Indiana, and Pennsylvania have many Polish descendants, but some hid their identity by learning English and Anglo-Saxoning their last names.

Jewish Americans were the last white ethnic group to come to the United States, and unlike Italian Americans and Polish Americans, many were professionals, and used educational achievement to combat anti-Semitic practices during the early part of the twentieth century.

Most of the Africans who immigrated to the United States were slaves, even though a few were indentured servants. Axelson described the history of three groups of blacks in America: (1) freed blacks, (2) emancipated slaves, (3) blacks from the West Indies. It may be hard for some readers to imagine, but blacks and whites were legally segregated until about the 1960s. For example, there were separate restaurants, hotels, swimming pools, and so on for blacks and whites. One benefit of segregation was that blacks were able to establish economically sound communities, and this laid the foundation for what is now the black middle class. Blacks immigrating from the West Indies make up about 1 percent of the total black population in the United States, and the first generation was poor and settled in the Harlem area of New York City. The second generation of West Indians was upwardly mobile, but the Haitians, the newest black immigrants, are extremely poor and they may not be accepted by African Americans or white Americans.

It was not until 1865, that the United States Constitution abolished slavery (13th Amendment), and it was not until 1868 (14th Amendment) that equal protection was provided to everyone under the law. The 15th Amendment of 1870 provided all persons the right to vote; however, but as alluded to earlier, it was not until the 1960s that the United States started desegregating

America. Even with a few amendments to the United States Constitution, African Americans were held under subservience by a variety of tactics; for example, the rise in many vigilante and hate groups such as the Ku Klux Klan. These groups used extreme tactics to control African Americans such as lynching and post-facto racial segregation (Marger, 2000, 2003). Actually, segregation originated in the North as a means of disenfranchising African Americans, and as a means of keeping them within their places. Even during the twenty-first century, African Americans still appear to be affected by the aftermath of slavery, racial prejudice, and social discrimination.

For example, Herrnstein and Murray (1994) have argued that IQ differences between blacks and whites are due to genetic factors. Specifically, Herrnstein and Murray have perpetuated racial, ethnic, and gender stereotypes about intelligence (Sapp, 2002a). Many Americans are not aware that African Americans are divided into at least three strata: middle class, made up of white-collar and skilled blue-collar individuals; working class, consisting of semiskilled individuals; and the lower class, consisting of unskilled workers. Most of the attention within the United States tends to focus on lower class African Americans—where there are high poverty rates, high welfare rates, and low educational attainment. Moreover, there is a host of problems such as high rates of teenage pregnancies, high crime rates, and extremely high dropout rates from schools, and so on. Clearly, when individuals refer to "the inner city and central city" the reference is often to African Americans at the lower strata of American society.

In 2001, a more recent act of possible racial prejudice is the death of an African American police officer who was shot and killed by fellow police officers while he was off duty. In Providence Rhode Island, Patrolman Cornell Young was mistakenly shot and killed by two fellow police officers, when, while off duty, he tried to break up a fight at a local restaurant. Obviously, Patrolman Young had pulled his gun when he saw another man was brandishing a gun. Apparently, the patrolman thought that the other on duty police officers recognized him. Unfortunately, the officers did not recognize him and they fatally shot him in the head, stomach, and chest. What is even more striking about this case is that patrolman's father was a high-ranking officer within the Providence police force. This stirred controversy because critics believed that Young was killed because he was African American. This notion that there is built-in and automatic discrimination will be addressed later within this chapter when evidence is presented that supports that prejudice may lie within the brain.

Many other minorities often forget that Native Americans are the ethnic minorities within the United States. And, like African Americans, this is a very diverse group. And also, very similar to African Americans, this group has had several synonyms such as American Indians, Native Americans, Original

Americans, and Native People. When Europeans came to America, they thought America was India, and they referred to Native Americans as "Indians." Native Americans were also exterminated because earlier European explorers wanted their land, and these early settlers used various measures to take Native Americans' land. For example, the exposure to European diseases, wars, starvation, moving Native Americans to reservations, and attempts at assimilating Native Americans within white American culture almost eliminated this minority group from the United States. The Indian Removal Act of 1830 had the devastating effect of destroying Native American culture by the federal government. This act relocated Native Americans to reservations. Unfortunately, life on reservations has also been devastating for Native Americans. For example, on reservations, unemployment often exceeds 30 percent; poverty affects about one-half of the residents; alcoholism and school drop out rates are high (Sapp, 1997a; Axelson, 1990, 1993; Marger, 2000, 2003). The Indian Gaming Regulatory Act of 1988 provided Native Americans with a means toward economic development with legalized gambling. Finally, even with the new gaming laws, most Native Americans still experience high rates of unemployment and poverty.

Hispanic or Latin Americans are increasingly becoming the largest minority group within the United States. See Table 2-1 with the U.S. Census data. Actually, about one out of every four persons in the United States is a minority. Latinos are persons from Latin, Central, and South America. Like African Americans and Native Americans, Latin Americans are a very diverse group. The common denominator among these groups is the Spanish language. Marger (2000, 2003) argued that Latin Americans are an "in-between" status minority. They are an ethnic group that is between European American groups and African Americans. Mexican Americans are a racially diverse group and, often, within Mexico, racial distinctions are more a function of social class and cultural differences than of physical characteristics. In addition, Puerto Ricans are also an in-between racial group with African, European, and Indian ancestry. Puerto Ricans cover the entire hue spectrum, and like Mexican Americans, racial classifications are often a function of social class and culture. Within the United States, Cubans are the least racially diverse group, in that most Cubans are seen as "white." Even the pattern of discrimination directed toward Latin Americans has not been as severe as those directed toward African Americans and Native Americans. Overall, Latin Americans remain poor and are at the bottom ladder of American socioeconomic strata. Cuban Americans appear to have more social access than Mexican Americans, and Puerto Rican Americans appear to be at the lowest socioeconomic level.

Like African Americans, Native Americans, and Latin Americans, Asian Americans are a very diverse group (Marger, 2000; Sue & Sue, 1990; Sapp, 1997a). This group includes Chinese, Filipino, Japanese, Asian Indians,

TABLE 2-1
U.S. CENSUS DATA

Subject	Number	Percent
RACE		
Total population	281,421,906	100
One race	274,595,678	97.6
White	211,460,626	75.1
Black or African American	34,658,190	12.3
American Indian and Alaska Native	2,475,956	0.9
American Indian	1,865,118	0.7
Alaska Native	97,876	0
Both American Indian and Alaska Native	1,002	0
American Indian or Alaska Native, not specified	511,960	0.2
Asian	10,242,998	3.6
Asian Indian	1,678,765	0.6
Chinese	2,432,585	0.9
Filipino	1,850,314	0.7
Japanese	796,700	0.3
Korean	1,076,872	0.4
Vietnamese	1,122,528	0.4
Other Asian category	1,061,646	0.4
Two or more Asian categories	223,588	0.1
Native Hawaiian and Other Pacific Islander	398,835	0.1
Native Hawaiian	140,652	0
Samoan	91,029	0
Guamanian or Chamorro	58,240	0
Other Pacific Islander category	99,996	0
Two or more Native Hawaiian or Other Pacific Islander categories	8,918	0
Some other race	15,359,073	5.5
Two or more races	6,826,228	2.4
Two races including Some other race	3,001,558	1.1
Two races excluding Some other race, and three or more races	3,824,670	1.4
Two races excluding Some other race	3,366,517	1.2
Three or more races	458,153	0.2
HISPANIC OR LATINO		
Total population	281,421,906	100
Hispanic or Latino (of any race)	35,305,818	12.5
Mexican	20,640,711	7.3
Puerto Rican	3,406,178	1.2
Cuban	1,241,685	0.4
Other Hispanic or Latino	10,017,244	3.6
Not Hispanic or Latino	246,116,088	87.5
RACE AND HISPANIC OR LATINO		
Total population	281,421,906	100
One race	274,595,678	97.6
Hispanic or Latino	33,081,736	11.8
Not Hispanic or Latino	241,513,942	85.8
Two or more races	6,826,228	2.4
Hispanic or Latino	2,224,082	0.8
Not Hispanic or Latino	4,602,146	1.6

Koreans, Vietnamese, Cambodians, Hmong, and Laotian. In fact, Asian Americans in some ways are more diverse than even Latin Americans, in that not a common language nor a common religion is shared. Currently, within the United States, Chinese, Filipino, and Asian Indian are the largest Asian groups. Marger (2000, 2003), and Sue and Sue (1990) both have argued that Asian Americans are not model minorities, but they are often used as a standard for other minority groups; however, in reality, Asian Americans experience high poverty rates and various forms of discriminations like other minority groups.

The Hmong are the most recent Asian group to enter the United States. As many as 160,000 Hmong are within the United States, and they tend to be concentrated in Wisconsin, Minnesota, and California. And like other Asian groups, they speak a variety of dialects. Moreover, there are Hmong in China, Thailand, and Laos. Hmong have been persecuted by communists in Thailand. Their culture is agrarian with religious beliefs based on animism, which includes Shamanism and other supernatural philosophies. Hmong, as a people, are refugees, and many of the Hmong within the United States are refugees from Laos. After the Vietnam War, the North Vietnamese government attempted to exterminate the Hmong because they had helped the CIA fight wars in Laos. In summary, Asian Americans are diverse groups and they have experienced racial discrimination just like other minority groups. Marger (2000) concluded that within the United States, the ideology reflects Anglo cultural preferences, and that the American hierarchy consists of three tiers: white Protestants of various national origins at the top; white Catholics and Jews of various nationality, along with Asian Americans in the middle; and Latin Americans, African Americans, and American Indians at the bottom part of the hierarchy.

RACIAL PREJUDICE HIDDEN WITHIN THE BRAIN

As previously discussed, African American Patrolman Young was killed by fellow officers in Providence, Rhode Island. Why would officers kill one of their own? And is prejudice located somewhere within the brain? Is prejudice an automatic response to social and cultural pressures? Dasgupta, McGhee, Greenwald, and Banaji (2000) and Nosek and Banaji (2003) using the Implicit Association Test (IAT), a reaction time measure to black and white faces, found a strong automatic positive evaluation of white Americans and a consistently negative evaluation of African Americans. What is very interesting about this study is that about 50 percent of the African Americans also had a negative evaluation of other African Americans. These researchers showed that once a person learns certain stereotypes through associations to various cultural groups, these associations tend to bias an individual toward certain social groups (Baldwin, Critelli, Stevens, Russell, 1986).

For example, an individual may be consciously tolerant toward minority groups but, due to the automatic response to social and cultural cues, respond in a very prejudice way that is essentially automatic and nonconscious. For example, the African American Patrolman who was gunned down was probably killed because he was a black police officer responding to an off-duty call. Clearly, the officers who shot him did not react in a conscious way, but there are many cultural and social stereotypes that are associated with blacks, especially black males in America. Apparently these officers reacted in the way that they were conditioned culturally to do within the United States, and they responded with extreme fear and overreaction. Since research shows that there is an automatic preference for white faces, clearly, the opposite is also true, there is an automatic negative reaction to black faces. Anderson and Phelps (2000) and Broks (2000) showed that the amygdala of the brain is associated with the processing of emotional properties that we assign to social groups within the United States. Cultural influences affect people at all levels, which includes the brain; nevertheless, what is not known is what will IAT research show or predict in the real world. For example, does it matter if a police officer has a high IAT score? Or is a police officer with a high IAT score more likely to shoot someone who is black than a police officer with a low IAT score.

Finally, these questions have not been researched, and readers who are interested in completing the IAT may do so at the following web site: buster.cs.yale.edu/implicit/ or at www.tolerance.org/hidden_bias/index.html. In closing, Nosek and Banaji have demonstrated that, on the average, there is an implicit preference for whites over blacks, younger individuals over older individuals, and males over females. This research suggests that there is automaticity in responding to stereotypes and that there may be dissociation between implicit and explicit social attitudes, and this may explain how Patrolman Young was killed by other police officers. In summary, automaticity, dissociation, and the amygdala combined with social stereotypes offer some explanations for racial prejudice.

Glossary of Key Terms

Dependent variables. The measurement variable, or the variable that changes as a result of the independent or treatment variable.

Empirical validity. The validation of a study through observations and other forms of data. The term validity means that items of a test measure what they purport to measure, and empirical suggests that qualitative and quantitative are employed.

Independent variables. Independent variables are variables that have at least two levels, and within psychotherapy, these are the treatments. There are a variety of independent variables such as control, moderator, suppressor, and so on. Theoretically, independent variables can or should cause a change on the dependent or measurement variable.

Multicultural counseling. A term that emphasizes all the cultures that make up a nation.

Review Questions

1. What are the goals of psychotherapy?
2. Describe how the criteria can be used to critique any scientific theory.
3. Describe the term multicultural counseling.
4. Describe the major cultural groups within the United States.
5. When some cognitive-behavioral theorists say that all problems are a matter of perception, how does this concept fail to address discrimination, homophobia, culture, sexism, and racism?
6. In terms of culture, what is the assumed hierarchy within the United States?
7. What are the implications that racial prejudice may be hidden within the brain?

Chapter 3

ADLERIAN PSYCHOTHERAPY

CHAPTER OVERVIEW

Adler's theory, Individual Psychology, is an analytic, behavioral, and cognitive form of psychology and psychotherapy. Individual Psychology is derived from the Latin individuum, which means indivisible or undivided. Individual psychology is a holistic unified form of psychology. One could perhaps classify individual psychology as a heavily cognitively-based theory and therapy, also with a heavy behavioral orientation, but without terminology from classical or traditional behavioral therapy. Adlerian therapy is an action-oriented Level III theory of psychotherapy, and these theories are designed to move a client toward change. In contrast to some traditional behavioral approaches, Alderian psychotherapy is an idiographic approach that is based on the study of individual cases and not group approaches or nomothetic approaches. Nomothetic approaches tend to be based on group analyses such as means, standard deviations, and other group averages and inferential statistical measures (Corsini & Wedding, 1989).

Sapp (1997a) stated that Individual Psychology is a forerunner to cognitive-behavioral theories of counseling. In fact, it predated the cognitive-behavioral movement of the late 1960s and early 1970s. Moreover, Adler was a subjective and socially oriented theorist (Mosak & Maniacci, 1999). Mosak and Maniacci (1999) stated the following seven contributions of Adler:

1. The confluence of drives (Adler, 1908).
2. The transformation of drives into opposites (Adler, 1908).
3. The projection of one's drive onto another (Adler, 1908).
4. The relationship between the aggression drive and anxiety (Adler, 1908).
5. Defense mechanisms as safeguards of the ego (Adler, 1912, 1983).
6. The ego-ideal concept (1912, 1983).
7. Ego psychology (Colby, 1951).

Philosophically, Adler was influenced by Kant, Nietzche, Vaihinger, Goethe, Shakespeare, and the Bible.

Long before many areas were popular as social and public policy issues, Adler addressed them, and nine of these issues were the following:

1. At-risk children and students (Adler, 1930, 1935, 1963, 1983).
2. The rights of women (Adler, 1978).
3. The rights of women to have abortions (Adler, 1978).
4. Adult education (Hoffman, 1994).
5. Teacher training (Adler, 1924, 1929).
6. Community mental health and family counseling clinics (Adler, 1929).
7. Experimental public school education (Birnbaum, 1935; Hoffman, 1994; Spiel, 1956).
8. Short-term and brief forms of psychotherapy (Maniacci, 1996).
9. Family education and family counseling (Sherman & Dinkmeyer, 1987).

One can clearly see that Adler had a strong influence on many areas, and he is seen as the father of self-help programs (Mosak & Maniacci, 1999). In addition, Adler influenced the following 14 approaches and or areas:

1. Existential psychotherapy (Frankl, 1983).
2. Person-centered psychotherapy (Frankl, 1983).
3. Transactional analysis (Berne, 1961).
4. Rational emotive behavior therapy (Ellis, 1973).
5. Cognitive therapy (Beck, 1976).
6. Family therapy (Minuchin, 1974).
7. Group therapy (Yalom, 1980).
8. Extensions and adaptations of psychoanalysis such as Karen Horney (1941) and Harry Stack Sullivan (1953, 1964).
9. Social Adaptations of psychoanalytic theory such as Erich Fromm (1941), Victor Frankl (1983), and Rollo May (1983).
10. Gestalt psychotherapy (Corsini & Wedding, 2002).
11. The self-psychology of Kohut (1971, 1977).
12. Object relations theory and psychotherapy (Kernberg, 1975). Borderline personality (Kernberg, 1975).
13. The integrationist and constructionist views of Guidano and Liotti (1983).
14. Founder of phenomenology (Adler, 1913/1962).

BIOLOGICAL SKETCH

Adler was the second of six children, born February 7, 1870 to a middle class Jewish family who lived in Penziq, Austria, a suburb near Vienna (Mosak &

Maniacci, 1999). As a child, Adler had rickets, was very sickly, and suffered spasms of the glottis. At the age of three, his younger brother died in bed next to him (Mosak & Maniacci). Adler was extremely affected by his birth order as a child. For example, he was in competition with his brothers and used his illnesses to gain the sympathy of his mother, and throughout childhood and adolescence, he was attempting to overcome feelings of inadequacy and feelings of inferiority (Bottone, 1957).

During his school years, Adler started as a poor student and had to repeat mathematics several times, but eventually he compensated and rose to the top of his class. Graduating in 1895, Adler studied medicine at the University of Vienna. In 1897, he married Raissa Timofeyena Epstein. Raissa was a Russian, devout socialist and feminist, and was politically active throughout their marriage (Schultz, 1981, 1990; Schultz & Schultz, 1992).

When Adler was treating performers from local circuses, he started to see how career choices affected how performers compensated within their bodies. Specifically, many of these individuals were viewed as sideshow freaks, and Adler believed that their bodies also represented or presented this same picture. In essence, Adler was beginning to formulate ideas about career choice, and he has influenced **vocational psychology.**

Adler did not come to the United States until 1926 at 56 years of age; however, he quickly learned English, gave lectures, and published in English. And, in 1935, he permanently came to the United States to avoid the fascists who had came to power in Austria (Mosak & Maniacci). In 1932, he lectured worldwide and accepted a position as the first chair of medical psychology at Long Island Medical College, and served as a visiting professor at Columbia University. While he was on a walk during a lecture tour in Aberdeen, Scotland, on May 28, 1937, Adler died of heart failure.

Rudolf Dreikurs, a psychiatrist, who studied with Adler in Vienna, continued Adler's work in Chicago. His colleagues, Bernard Schulman and Harold Mosak, and Adler's children, Alexandra and Kurt, continued the work of Adler. Even though Adler was well received in America, the prevailing Zeitgeist of the time was behaviorism in the universities and psychology departments and psychoanalysis monopolized psychiatry. Finally, readers who want a detailed biographical sketch of Adler's life can consult Ansbacher and Ansbacher (1964), Orgler (1963), Bottome (1957), Ellenberger (1970), and Stepansky (1983).

FREUD VERSES ADLER

Freud based his theory on the early neuronal theory of the 1800s, and this neuronal theory stated that energy could move from one neuron to another.

Freud theorized that at birth a certain area of the mind is sealed off, called the psyche and contained psychic energy that could move though the body. This notion was the basis for his famous psychosexual stages of development that was based on the movement of energy from the mouth, anus, and genitals. There are many misconceptions and inaccurate beliefs about Freud and psychoanalysis. First, Freud was not a psychologist, he was a psychiatrist; nor did he invent the concept of the unconscious. Actually, Gustav Theodor Fechner (1801–1887) found a relationship existed between the mind and body by demonstrating that the amount of sensation one feels-conscious experience, depends on the amount of stimulation experienced or received-unconscious experience. Essentially, Fechner showed that the unconscious sensations of threshold existed by using a method of psychology called **psychophysics.**

Another inaccuracy is that Freud created the first school of psychology. Actually, **Wilhelm Wundt,** a German psychologist, started psychology in 1879 in Leipzig, Germany. His school of psychology was called structuralism. Wundt used **introspection,** a method that subjectively analyzed images, sensations, and feelings to analyze conscious experiences. Moreover, between 1920 and 1930, **functionalism**–the second school of psychology, was founded by an American psychologist, William James. James broadened psychology to include child development, animal behavior, abnormal behavior, religion, and so on. The third school of psychology started around 1910 with Max Wertheimer, a German psychologist. Wertheimer founded **Gestalt psychology,** which means whole or pattern. Gestalt psychology was in conflict with structuralism, which wanted to study the elements of conscious experiences. The Gestalt psychologists thought that the whole was greater than the sum of the parts; hence, objecting to the **structuralists** who wanted to break human experiences into parts. Even though it is apparent that Frits Perls borrowed techniques from Gestalt psychology in order to develop his Gestalt psychotherapy, the two terms are not synonymous, because Gestalt psychology was an experimental form of psychology and Gestalt psychotherapy is an applied form of psychotherapy (Sapp, 1997a).

The reader, who may consider that Freud started psychotherapy, only need to consult Corsini and Wedding (2002), who pointed out that several individuals conducted psychotherapy before Freud developed his psychoanalysis. For example, Joseph Breuer had developed a talking cure before Freud developed psychoanalysis, and Franz Anton Mesmer (1734–1815), an Austrian physician, had practiced hypnosis before Freud was born (Wallace, 1993).

In contrast to Freud who attempted to reduce clients into id, ego, and superego, Adler tended to be holistic. Whereas Freud emphasized sex and aggression and the motivating factors, Adler emphasized a variety tasks of life such as work, social, sexual, self, and spiritual; therefore, life consists of making contributions to work, relating to others, forming intimate relationships, learning self-acceptance, and exploring physical dimensions (Corey, 2001, 2002). In contrast to psychoanalysis, which is pessimistic, Individual Psychology is optimistic by stressing the concept of **equipotentiality** of growth. This concept suggests that there is an ever-lasting process for growth; so unlike Freud, Adler was convinced about the effects of age on a client's ability to change; therefore, clients can change at any age. Moreover, Freud emphasized a dangerous unconscious that was sealed out at birth, but Adler emphasized more conscious activity and **soft determinism.** Adler avoided reifying the conscious and unconscious and viewed both as adjectives, not nouns. **Freud's determinism** assumed that early childhood experiences determined in a causal sense adult experiences and adult personality development. In contrast, Adler emphasized choice and a form of **soft determinism** that stressed influences, not causes, probabilities and possibilities, and not laws and givens. Freud was interested in facts and certainties, but Adler was interested in clients' beliefs about facts. Mosak and Maniacci noted that even though Edmund Husserl is often credited as the founder of phenomenology when he published his book, *Ideas: General Introduction to Pure Phenomenology* (1913), Adler had discussed phenomenology a year earlier in his book, *The Neurotic Constitution* (1912). The concept of **phenomenology** suggests that clients are in a process of becoming, and this is the foundation of **Rogers' Person-Centered psychotherapy.** Moreover, phenomenology is a client's subjective orientation, and this orientation is primarily cognitive and based upon clients' beliefs. Phenomenology provides clients with worldviews or cognitive maps of how to view the world, people, situations, and circumstances. Clients tend to draw conclusion, not from facts or reality, but from their world views, which are subjective views. Finally, phenomenology includes everything that makes up a client's inner world. Within contemporary cognitive theory, the notion of **constructivism** has become popular, and this notion is in line with Adlerian therapy that suggests that clients actively construct their reality and are not passive participants within an environment.

In contrast to Freud's intrapsychic, Adler based his theory on **social psychology,** or the notion that clients live within a social field or social context. Freud viewed problems as existing within the individual, hence the term **intrapsychic conflict.** Even though a client can be conditioned to respond to conditions that no longer exist, the client can choose to stop responding once conditions change; this is the notion of choice and soft determinism. While Adler embraced a social psychology view of humans, he realized that not all problems are social and that problems can exist within individuals. When a client has an intraindividual problem, when he or she engages with others, the problem can become a social problem if the client whines or complains and others become involved with the client. Freud saw the **transference relationship** as necessary for psychoanalysis; in contrast, Adler did not emphasize the transference relationship, since Adlerian therapy is educational and does not involve the deep analysis and interpretation of clients' unconscious influences from the past. Freud viewed humans as basically bad, whereas Adler took a neutral position, where clients are neither good nor bad, but have the choice to perform bad acts and the choice to perform good acts. In terms of dreams, Freud viewed them as the royal road to the unconscious; in contrast, Adler viewed dreams from a future or current orientation.

Masson (1984) was critical of how Freud developed the Odedipal complex and Electra complex. Through archival data, Masson found that Freud had a long communication with Wilhelm Fliess, where Freud discussed that he was convinced that many of his adult female clients were sexually abused as adults and were sexually abused as children by adults. This notion that Freud had that children were molested sexually was referred to as **Freud's seduction theory.** Masson claimed that due to the Victorian era, Freud modified his seduction theory or **hypothesis** by reporting that children's reports of sexual activity with their parents were just simply unconscious fantasies. Therefore, Masson proposed that Freud created both the Oedipal complex and Electra complex to diffuse the impact of sexual molestation that his female clients were reporting. Finally, Arlow (2002) has assumed that these allegations by Masson cannot be substantiated because Arlow believed that Freud would have not changed the seduction hypothesis to avoid extreme social pressure.

KEY CONCEPTS

Organ Inferiority

Adler defined organ inferiority as an inherit weakness of an organ or organ system. This suggests that individuals can be affected not just by biological factors, but they can also be affected by prenatal factors. Organ inferiority can lead to compensation at three levels: **somatic, sympathetic,** and **psychic.** For example, an individual born with a dysfunctional leg may compensate beyond normal by developing extreme competence with that leg. At a sympathetic level of competence, the person may compensate so that others give little attention to the leg. Finally, the individual may show extreme compensation by becoming outstanding in sports (Mosak & Maniacci).

Furthermore, when Adler formulated the concept of organ inferiority in 1908, he viewed it as imagined or actual physical dysfunction or disability that causes feelings of inadequacy. These feelings are based on perceptions and distorted data that influence lifestyle development. Finally, these feeling of inferiority are not objective feelings, but ones based a subjective worldview.

Lifestyle

Lifestyle is a client's way of being, feeling, thinking, and means of striving toward goals. The lifestyle or style of life is a socio-cognitive blueprint for a client's personality, view of self, self-concept, and orientation to life. Some other synonyms for lifestyles are psyche, personality, character, and ego. Adler, like Freud, believed that the lifestyle was shaped by the age of six, and it is based upon the client's family constellation, private logic, and community interest or social interests. It describes how one adapts to the difficulties of life. Lifestyles may support a certain position at one point in a client's life, but later may not be applicable. For example, depressive symptoms may get a client sympathy and pity as a child, but during adulthood, may cause others to be repelled by the client.

The important thing for clients to learn is how to adapt to circumstances and not to respond to conditions as though they were constant. Adaptability means being able to deal with issues of change, and if the client's lifestyle does not prepare him or her for change, the result can be an experience of trauma. Alder viewed the lack of application of common sense as a cause of trauma. For example, one may hold the following beliefs:

"I know I should work, but I am tired."
"I am lonely, but I am afraid to meet people."

The "yes, but" attitude supports the symptoms of private logic and does not support common sense. In essence, common sense is not followed, but ignored, and private logic or faulty perceptions are endorsed. Adler asked at least two questions about symptoms: first "Who is most affected by your symptoms?" Second, "What would be different if you did not have your symptoms?" The reader can clearly see that common sense takes into account others, and it is high in community interests and social feelings.

Stated somewhat differently, emotional problems occur when a client abandons common sense and follows private logic. Furthermore, common sense is the sensible thing to do. For example, some common sense attitudes could be:

"Eat, when hungry."
"Work to earn money for survival."
"Seek social interests."

Private logic supports clients' personal biases and they are noncommon sense based, and they are irrational, illogical, and distorted beliefs. Examples of private logic may be the following: "I know I should eat, but I do not have the time." "I know I should sleep, but I have work to do." Berne with his theory of Transactional Analysis had referred to these as "yes, but" statements to suggest that they are based on games that clients play with themselves and with others.

Moreover, lifestyle can involve mistaken beliefs about the world, people, and the self. For example, mistaken beliefs may be the following: "There are only winners and losers," "I will never find anyone to love me." "Things must always go my way." "Life owes me happiness." "I cannot tolerate misfortune." "People are dangerous." "Women cannot be trusted." "All men are the same." "Things will never change." An Adlerian would view the previous statements as distorted statements or perceptions within one's lifestyle.

Mosak (1971) described the following five lifestyles: getters, drivers, victims, controllers, and good ones. These lifestyles or personality types are similar to the work of Horney (1945, 1950). Horney described three typologies for dealing with inner conflicts, moving toward others, moving against others, and moving away from others. Getters have a low degree of social interest and they attempt to get what they want without any exchange. Drivers are characterized as workaholics or work addicts, and their primary aim is to achieve or attain something, without considering the social implications. The greatest thing that drivers fear is free time, and they remain busy achieving things. Victims suffer for the sheer reason of suffering, and they use their minds to make suffering as likely as possible. Controllers fear the unexpected and they attempt to control all aspects of their lives with certainty; however, often they are not prepared for physical disability, mental disability, or death. Good ones have a social sense of being superior by being brighter, holier, more moral, more right, more useful, and so on than anyone else.

In summary, none of these types are inherently bad, and seldom will one see pure types; however, if a lifestyle is destructive or does not depend on the person and the social situation, it may need to be changed. In closing, lifestyles can remain stagnant over time if they are not challenged and changed. Finally, lifestyles can become conditioned responses to stimuli that no longer exist.

Masculine Protest

In 1910, Adler developed the masculine protest concept, or how people deal with the overvaluation of masculinity. Men who endorsed the concept wanted to be "real men" or powerful. Likewise, women who overemphasize masculinity tend to overvalue masculinity by identifying with men, competing with men, and by overcompensating and eventually withdrawing. This overcompensating manifests itself by striving to be over or above others who are viewed socially as weak or inferior. Overcompensation are feelings that men or women attempt to compensate for by acting socially superior. In contrast to Adler, Freud viewed the masculine protest as nothing but penis envy, while Adler stressed the interpersonal processes. In contrast, Freud emphasized unconscious intrapsychic processes. At this point within Adler's career, it was clear that Freud and his followers saw Adler and his theory as an antithesis to psychoanalysis, and in 1911, Adler departed from Freud and his group and founded the Society of Individual Psychology. Originally, Adler entitled his society the Society for Free Psychoanalytic Research; however, he changed the name to Individual Psychology to stress the indivisibility and holistic nature of his theory. Interestingly, before Adler's resignation from Freud's society, he was Freud's personal physician and Freud had referred many patients to him. In reality, there are two periods of Adler's development. First, prior to World War I, he was a psychoanalyst; but after World War I, Adler became increasingly philosophical, social psychological, and educational. During Adler's association with Freud, there were weekly meetings called the Wednesday Evening Group for the Vienna Psychoanalytic Society. Colleagues discussed various aspects of psychoanalysis, and even though Adler attended these sessions, he had developed aspects of his theory before he had encountered Freud; therefore, in actuality, Adler was Freud's contemporary and colleague — not Freud's disciple or student.

Striving for Superiority

Adler viewed striving for superiority as the strongest motivating force for humans (Adler, 1937). Motivation, within an Alderian perspective, can be viewed as moving from perceived minus situations to perceived plus situations. Clearly, as Mosak and Maniacci documented, Adler gave various names to this movement throughout his writing. And they provided the following eight phases:

1. A real man.
2. A will to power.
3. Self-esteem.
4. Security.
5. Perfection.
6. Complexion.
7. Overcoming.
8. Superiority.

The first four phases characterize Adler's psychoanalytic phases, and the last four phases emphasized the social psychological nature of his Individual Psychology theory.

Striving for superiority does not mean wanting to be superior to another in an objective sense, but it is a move toward competence and mastery of the environment. Humanistic theorists use terms such as striving toward self-actualization or striving toward perfection, or striving for significance. All of these terms are comparable to striving for superiority. When clients have subjective feelings of being lesser than others, they can compensate and move toward an ideal self by striving for a significant place within a family, community, or society. Adler would even view attempts at suicide as attempts toward striving for significance. For example, the individual may believe that by attempting or committing suicide that he or she will receive the sympathy of others or punish others for not providing more attention. In addition, the person may inaccurately assume that suicide will increase his or her social worth. But as I point out to clients, social worth may be increased through one's death, but as far as we know, one will not be able to feel, so attempting suicide is not a constructive way to increase one's social significance.

Phenomenology

Phenomenology is a philosophical position that stresses that clients have an internal subjective world that affects their interactions with the outside world. This methodology and philosophy is the cornerstone of Humanistic and Existential forms of psychotherapy. It stresses the perceptions of clients by exploring clients' beliefs perceptions and facts. As previously stated, Freud was concerned with facts, but Adler was concerned with clients' beliefs about facts. For example, within a family, a client could be the first born (fact), and have the perceptions of being the baby within the family. Baby, from an Adlerian perspective, is a typology, and it can occur anywhere within the family constellation. A **Baby** likes to intertwine play and support and is not destructive unless the style is used in ways that are not constructive. In summary, phenomenology is the subjective perception of reality that is based upon beliefs and belief systems.

Individual Psychology

As previously stated, Individual Psychology is another name for Adlerian psychotherapy, and it stresses viewing a client holistically and as an indivisible unit that has intrapersonal, social, and environmental aspects; therefore, psychotherapy must explore a client's phenomenological view point, social context, and so on. Finally, the basic premise of Individual Psychology is that a client is indivisible, holistic, and needs to be understood in totality.

Fictional Finalism

The terms fictions and finalism have special meanings within Adlerian psychotherapy. First, the notion of **finalism** or **final cause** will be explored. The philosopher Aristotle discussed the concept of final cause, and he described four causes: material—what constitutes something or what something consists of, efficient—how something came about, formal—the effect of a cause or the shape or essence it takes, final—the purpose, reason, or sake of a cause. **Final cause** suggests that clients move toward goals; they attempt to belong; they attempt to be socially important; and they attempt movement. **Fictional goals** are what a client should or could accomplish in order to belong. Goals can be concrete or fictional, and long-term versus short-term. Fictional goals are subjective and they indicate what must be achieved such as perfection, power, fame, money, and so forth (Mosak & Maniacci). Furthermore, fictional finalism is the ideal image that clients have about the way things should turn out in their lives. This is a client's self-ideal about all the convictions in his or her lifestyle about what must be in order to achieve social significance. The danger with fictions is they often have perfectionistic underpinnings such as "When I am rich, everyone will adore me"; or, "I hope my death will hurt the family"; or, "I want to be the most sexually attractive person in the world." As Watts and Holden (1994) noted, **subjective final goal** or **guiding self-ideal** come closer to what Adler meant when he spoke about goals, but many writings within the area still use the term fictional finalism (Corey, 2001, 2002).

Social Interest

As Mosak and Maniacci pointed out, **community feeling** comes closer to what Adler meant by the term that is extensively used within the United States, social interest. From an Adlerian perspective, community feelings are viewed as an innate potential that needs to be developed (Mosak & Maniacci). Moreover community feeling, or social interest, is a construct within Individual Psychology. It suggests that an individual feels at home in the world, and that the individual has a sense of responsibility to the world. Moreover, this is the emotional bond that people have with each other and to the world in which they live. Social feeling is part of Individual Psychology's social-field theory. Furthermore, it takes into account phenomenology, the social environment, and the fact that people use social feelings as a means for survival. Adler thought that good emotional health was the result of positive social feelings and relationships that allow one to feel secure, accepted, and holistic.

Finally, Adler viewed all forms of emotional pathology as the result of a client not developing constructive and prosocial social feelings.

Defense Mechanisms

Adler viewed anxiety as a means to avoid meeting strivings, challenges, and not to accomplish anything. Here, anxiety can be used to prevent one from accomplishing something. For example, many people use fear to prevent themselves from making accomplishments and from attempting things. Anxiety is a safeguard mechanism against challenges to self-worth, and Shulman (1964) and Mosak and Maniacci described the following ten defense mechanisms: externalizing, blind spots, excessive self-control, arbitrary rightness, elusive confusion, retreat, contrition and self-disparagement, suffering, sideshows, and rationalization.

Externalizing is the blaming of others for one's problems. This is the basis of **attribution theory,** which states that people make an inferential cause about their behavior and the behavior of others. Clients, and humans, tend to make what is called the **major attributional error**—they are more likely to blame a person for a situational event, if the person is not them. Clients tend to underestimate situational explanations of behavior when the situation involves others. Cognitive-behavioral therapists, such as Ellis (2001), look at blame as the core to emotional disturbances and as a core schema, or the philosophy that guides behavior. **Blind spots** allow clients to see what they want to see and to avoid seeing what they do not want to take responsibility for, or they allow clients to overlook issues.

Excessive self-control is a striving away from being a human feeling and in the direction of a robot, and it can allow one to not deal with pain and, in some cases, happiness. **Arbitrary rightness** is similar to Berne's position of "I am ok" and "you are not ok." The client views himself or herself as right and others are arbitrarily viewed as wrong. Data and facts will not change the client's position, since his or her position is made up. **Elusiveness** and **confusion** permit a client to say a great deal, but the client cannot be held accountable for statements because of confusion. Moreover, often, the client cannot remember and cannot be held responsible for statements. **Retreat** is a life position that allows a client to withdraw and not to venture or risk anything nor gain or lose anything. Essentially, this style allows clients to distance themselves from social interactions and social situations. **Contributions** and **self-disparagement** is a pretense by a client to blame himself or herself without actually accepting responsibility. The client hopes that the more he or she blames oneself, the less others will attempt to blame him or her. **Suffering** is a lifestyle that can manipulate or justify suffering. Feigned suffering can be used to justify personal nobility – look how noble I am to suffer like this; I look forward to and deserve suffering. **Sideshows** are distractions from real issues within a client's life to sideshows or trivial matters. By focusing their attention on side issues, clients can avoid real problems. Finally, this is where clients use reasons to avoid accepting responsibility for defeat or bad behavior. For example, with the **sour grapes rationalization,** the client attempts to alleviate psychological pain by denying that he or she really wanted something. In contrast, with the **sweet lemons rationalization,** the client lessens anxiety by claiming that a negative outcome has positive aspects. In closing, Adler viewed defense mechanisms from a more common sense basis than did Freud.

Children's Actions

Since all behavior is **teleological** or purposeful and goal oriented, behavior can be explained in children's terms. Dinkmeyer, Dinkmeyer, and Sperry (1987), for example, described the following actions:

1. Attention seeking.
2. Struggle for power.
3. Desire to retaliate or get even.
4. Display of inadequacy or assumed disability.

Due to discouragement, children can seek attention. From an Adlerian perspective, this is a basic goal of children. For example, children, who seek attention, will do so even when it produces negative consequences. As Berne noted, negative attention is better than no attention at all. For children, excelling in school, fighting, being charming, and being annoying are all attempts at getting attention.

Resisting parents and struggling for power and superiority are a natural developmental process for children. Parent's requests are resisted, and even when children are defeated by their parents, the tendency to seize power becomes stronger with each battle children have with their parents.

Often adults, who are ruthless, as children sought retaliation as a means of being unlikable. Because they were hurt as children, these adults seek to hurt other as adults, especially parents, family members, and significant others. Within this personality structure, success or movement is seen with getting even and being ruthless, so the goals become being unlikable and seeking retaliation.

The actions of displaying inadequacy and appearing weak are indications of low self-esteem and a low self-concept. These children have been discouraged that their only sense of movement or action is to appear inferior, weak, and inadequate. These children do not want their parents to expect anything from them. Failure is a major problem for these children, but through appropriate modeling of how to view failing as a learning and self-enhancing experience, children who display these actions can learn to act differently.

Compensation

Compensation involves coping with a difficult task despite severe limitations. For example, if one breaks a leg, one must learn to function with a cast until the leg heals. Or if one becomes visually impaired, one would have to learn to function with the impairment. Within an Adlerian perspective, a deficit can be real, imagined, social, and physical. The ultimate form of compensation is striving for excellence and achievement, and by focusing on the things that one can do well, and by not focusing on things that one cannot perform well. Finally, one can also compensate by being the worst at a particular task. For example, this writer had a client who tested within the genius range in terms of intelligence, but he compensated by being the worst within his family at school. He made sure that his grades were as bad as they could be, and, often, he would not attend class, and he would spend hours debating his teachers to why what they were teaching was insignificant to his life. This client had internalized several messages from his parents. First, you do not have the mental discipline to achieve and, second, because your father did not achieve, you cannot do so either since this is part of a family value, the lack of success (Birnhaum, 1935).

Teleology

Within Individual Psychology, **teleology** deals with purposefulness and the force that guides self-ideal. Self-ideals organize and guide toward the direction of the future. Unlike psychoanalysis, which stressed unconscious causation, teleology stresses the continuity among the past, present, and future, but with more emphasis and anticipation for the future (Shulman, 1984).

Private Logic

Private logic was one of the concepts that helped Albert Ellis, Aaron Beck, and other cognitive and cognitive-behavioral theorists develop concepts like Ellis' irrational beliefs and Becks' cognitive distortions. Private logic is automatic nonconscious thoughts that form the bases for clients' lifestyles and philosophies of life. The reader should remember that nonconscious does not have any connection to the connotation that Freud gave the word unconscious (Sherman & Dinkmeyer, 1987).

An example of private logic could include a client assuming that his thoughts were the only correct ones, and that thoughts of others were always incorrect. The automatic process of private logic is cognitive, but often the client is not aware of the reasons for his or her private logic. Moreover, the process underlying private logic involves thinking, judging, analyzing, and interpreting. Clients lacking the insight that underlie their private logic can create false premises and dichotomous thinking about the client's life by such premises as good versus evil, moral versus immoral, masculine or feminine, love or hate, and so on (Shulman, 1985). Finally, as previously stated, clients need to learn how to distinguish private logic from common sense.

Family Constellation

Family constellation is the early environment within a family. For example, what are the family norms, values, expectations, hopes, and dreams? Were there alliances within the family, and, if so, how they did they operate? Were there favorite siblings within the family? Family constellation is a social and psychological description of a family's interactions. Parents can establish an atmosphere where children do not know what to expect. For example, at certain points parents can be authoritarian and at another time permissive. An inconsistent environment can create confusion for children who do not know what to expect or the position of their roles. It is common within the United States where things or material possessions become a replacement for family and human relationships. Often, parents will buy things for their children with the hope of not actually having to be a parent.

Inconsistency with family can lead to a variety of role shifts, where at one time a child is a victim, next a rescuer, and yet another time a persecutor. With constant role shifts, families can become chaotic and vacillate between order and disorder. Disorder can be the fighting, bickering, and constant disagreements.

Birth Order

One of the interesting areas of Adlerian work is the area of birth order, and Adler pointed out that one's perceptions, earlier recollections, and family constellation determined one's psychological position within a family. Many professionals often confuse a client's ordinal position within a family for a client's psychological position. In this regard, Alder was clear in stating that the actual ordinal position was not as important as the client's perception about that position. Birth order research is one area that could benefit from additional research and Simpson, Bloom, Newlon, and Arminio (1994) suggested using the following three questions when conducting such research:

1. How many children have you had?
2. What are the birth dates of your first four children?
3. What is the birth day of your last born child?

Simpson et al. (1994) stated that despite the number of studies researching birth order, many problems exist in the uniformity of the research, especially the research methodology. For example, many researchers have failed to compare birth order proportions of participants with actual parameters found in the United States population. Carefully collected statistics would allow researchers to more accurately research Adler's theory about birth order. Finally, Simpson et al. stated that it is now possible to develop accurate pictures of birth order proportion in the United States, especially with the elaborate census data that has been collected.

The first child, who is also the oldest child, is perceived as the original child within the family and whose position changes through the birth of another child. The first child tends to be hard working, achievement oriented, and dependable. How the first born handles other siblings can influence the family constellation, and if he or she can handle that more than one child within a family can be special—this will influence sibling interaction.

The second born often will strive in directions that are in competition and opposite of the first born. The factor that helps determine reactions of the second born are similar age and gender. When siblings are close in age and of the same gender, the tendency is greater for the perceived second born to move in an opposite direction of the first-born.

The middle child often feels left out of the family, since he or she is neither the first-born nor the last-born child. These children can feel that there is no one to deal with and they can rebel within the family. When families are chaotic, the middle child can serve as a negotiator for peace and actually hold the family together.

The youngest or last child can, but not always, become the baby. They often have the luxury of developing in ways that other siblings did not consider. Not growing up within a family becomes the family norm for the perceived baby. As previously stated, baby is more of a type than an ordinal position within a family. Sometimes perceived babies become drivers and attempt to catch up with other family members. In addition, babies strive for play and support, they love attention, and constant emotional support. With the last child, comfort becomes more important than responsibility, and they tend to be very social creatures.

The only child is characterized as pampered, and a miniature adult. Due to not having other siblings and only adults to interact with, he or she matures early and becomes competent as an adult. The only child does not learn the value of sharing, since he or she does not have to interact with siblings. It is not common for only children not to learn appropriate age-related social skills because most of their interactions are with their parents. In addition, the only child can grow to become pampered and dependent upon parents. Finally, as adults, these individuals can have difficulty not being the center of attention.

THERAPEUTIC PROCESS

Therapeutic Goals

Adlerian therapy is not a series of techniques (Biter, Christensen, Hawes, & Nicoll, 1998), and Mozdierz and Greenblatt (1994) urged again just attempting techniques in psychotherapy. In addition, research supports the fact than the client-therapist relationship, especially the one emphasized in Individual Psychology, is more significant than being the wild eclectic use of techniques. Dinkmeyer et al. (1987) pointed out that Adlerian therapy is a complicated and intricate intertwine of four objectives or four stages of a counseling process. The reader may recall that psychoanalysis also has four phases that were outlined by Arlow (2002), and these phases, which are overlapping, are opening phase, development of transference, working through, and resolution of transference. During the opening phase, the therapist obtains the client's case history, and free association is encouraged. This phase of free association can last anywhere from three to six months. Interestingly, one difference between short-term, dynamic therapy and traditional psychoanalysis, other than the amount of time or years used for therapy, is that short-term dynamic therapy does not generally use free association, and there tends to be stringent selection criteria for clients. The opening phase, along with the development of transference, represent the majority of therapy. Some argue that Freud's greatest discovery was transference. Transference is part of the therapeutic relationship in which clients project feeling and fantasies from the past onto the therapist. If a client can distinguish fantasy from fiction, it is possible than transference can be worked through, and that analysis leads to the working phase. When a client can resolve issues of transference, the termination of treatment can begin.

In contrast to the psychoanalysis, the following are the four phases of Adlerian or Individual Psychology (Dinkmeyer, 1987):

1. Establish an empathic therapeutic relationship with client.
2. Help client comprehend lifestyle, beliefs, feelings, and behaviors.

3. Help client develop insight.
4. Help client commit to change and initiate alternatives to current behavior.

Bitter et al. (1998) pointed that often therapy starts with an interview that assesses a client's strengths and weaknesses. In addition, therapists gather information about the client's family constellation and questionnaires can aid this process. Powers and Griffith (1987) is an excellent resource for life-style assessment.

Stage One: Establish an Empathic Relationship

Contracts can be used to spell out the goals that the client and therapist will collaboratively work toward. Within this form of therapeutic relationship, both the client and therapist are as equals working on agreed upon goals. Level I counseling skills are used during this phase such as reflecting feelings, and content, and permitting the client to feel understood. As done throughout therapy, the psychotherapist offers encouragement and stresses the client's strengths as opposed to weaknesses.

Stage Two: Help Client Understand Lifestyle, Beliefs, and Feelings

Using a holistic synthesis, the purpose of this phase is to show the client how one's lifestyle, perceptions, beliefs, and feelings fit within a chosen framework. The purpose of this stage is to show the client how his or her beliefs have influenced lifestyle development, and how beliefs can lead to feelings and how feelings can lead to actions. Interestingly, Ellis viewed beliefs, feelings, and behaviors from an interactional perspective, namely that all three occur simultaneously. Also, during this phase, **The Question** is proposed, a technique often used by solution-oriented therapists such as de Shazer (1991). de Shazer calls this the miracle question; for example, suppose a miracle happened to you overnight and that your problem was resolved. What would be different? How you know that your problem was resolved? Next, within de Shazer's solution-oriented therapy, clients are encouraged to act out what would be different despite the perceived problem. Often, solution-oriented therapy is a single-session form of therapy.

Adler developed **The Question** in (1935), and it explains the purpose that symptoms serve. For example, what would be different in your life if you did not have thoughts of suicide? Or, if you did not experience depression, how would your life be different. When Adlerians find that nothing would be different with physical symptoms, they suspect organic problems and seek medical consultation (Corey, 2001; 2004). Moreover, the skillful use of questions, a technique used by reality therapists, permits therapists to make a differential diagnosis.

In exploring a client's beliefs, they posed tentative questions such as "Perhaps you have developed inadequate social skills because intimate socialization was not encouraged within your family?" Moreover, Adlerians attempt to understand clients' lifestyles, which is the highest form of empathy or a Level II counseling skill. In addition, Individual Psychology practitioners try to understand clients' mistaken beliefs, which could include the following: "Life is totally out to destroy me. I have to please everyone. I cannot stand myself. Life has to treat me like someone special. I must have control and structure. I cannot stand free time. I have to stay preoccupied with something or I will go insane. Nothing unexpected should happen to me." During stage two, the therapist employs Level I and Level II counseling skills to communicate affect and beliefs to the client.

Also during phase two, Adlerians assess the client's family constellations, early recollections, dreams, and priorities. The family constellation could be assessed as follows: "Describe the siblings within your family? Were there any favorite siblings? If so, who were they? What is your perception of your parents and siblings when you were nine years of age? What is your perception of your birth order? How would you describe the personality of your family environment when you were growing up?" After information is gained about the family constellation, this information is communicated to the client to make sure that there is agreement. Summarization is the technique that Adlerians repeatedly employ to communicate what has been covered during the therapy sessions.

Some examples of assessing early recollections and dreams could be the following: "Can you remember a childhood dream that had special meaning to you? Can you describe a feeling connected with an early childhood memory? Are there any themes that run through your childhood memories?" As previously stated, dreams from an Adlerian perspective are not viewed as unconscious symbols of intrapsychic conflict, but are goal-oriented, purposeful behaviors. Moreover, dreams have a future reference in which a client can choose some future course of action. This view is in direct opposition to Freud's latent content (unconscious symbols) and manifest content (conscious recollections of dreams). Adlerians use tentative interpretations to discuss dreams with clients, and the reader can consult Fakouri and Hafner (1994) for a discussion of how early recollections can be employed as an assessment technique.

Clients' priorities are also assessed during stage two of psychotherapy. Dinkmeyer et al. (1987) listed the four following priorities: **comfort, pleasing,**

control, and **superiority.** Each priority can be the theme that determines clients' lifestyles. These priorities are not used to categorize clients, but they are used to understand client's goals.

Sapp (1997a) provided two questions to assess clients' lifestyle priorities. First, "What is the most important quest for you in terms of belonging?" Second, "What are some things you must avoid at any cost?" If a client's prime priority is to avoid stress and tension, his or her first priority could be **comfort.** If a client strives to avoid rejection, he or she may have a **pleasing priority.** Clients attempting to avoid humiliation may be using a **control priority.** Finally, **superiority priority** is when clients strive to avoid feelings of being unimportant and meaningless.

The **superiority priority** can manifest itself in a variety of ways. It is a striving to be socially superior to others at any cost, and it can be seen in clients who want to be the "most competent" "most right." Moreover, by seeking out others who are socially inferior, individuals with the superior priority can evoke feelings of guilt and feelings of inferiority from others.

The **control priority** expresses itself as control over oneself and control over others. Clients with a **primary priority** to control others will strive toward achievement as a way to evoke feelings of resentment and acquiescence from individuals they want to control. Moreover, clients attempting self-control seem restricted and "uptight" in social situations. Extreme control is used in contrast to creativity and spontaneity.

The **comfort priority** expresses itself as self-indulgence without any delay, and the hallmark of this priority is to get others to obtain what one wants without having to individually produce anything. These individuals try to avoid pain at any cost, and they tend to delay confronting problems and they attempt to avoid making decisions.

With the **pleasing priority,** one lacks respect and does not expect respect from others. These individuals are affectionately called "nice men and nice women." This priority occurs along an active-passive dimension. To illustrate, if one's primary priority is pleasing, one can actively seek out others to please, or one can passively submit oneself to others and hope for pity and help from others. The pleasing client can be assertive and appear self-righteous or take a passive stance as a victim or saint. In addition, controllers can be active in controlling others or passive when avoiding contact with others. This could be displayed as extreme self-control. Finally, as previously suggested, just as clients seeking comfort may behave actively like "spoiled children," they can also take a passive role and wait for others to serve them.

Adlerians do not try to change a priority that a client holds, rather they let a client see the penalty that is being paid for maintaining a specific priority. After a client sees the covert "only if" statements are only choices, he or she can change a primary priority. For example, a therapist may get a client to see the irrational nature of such statements as "Only if I had control of others would my life have meaning," or "Only if I please others will I feel a sense of belonging." If a therapist can get a client to alter the "only if" statement, he or she can experience growth and a wider range of choices.

Stage Three: Help Client Develop Insight

Unlike psychoanalysis, which has the goal of bringing unconscious material to conscious awareness, Adlerian psychotherapy attempts to help clients develop insight into their mistaken goals and self-defeating behaviors. As with stage one and stage two of Adlerian therapy, the therapist continues to use Level I and Level II counseling skills, and the therapist encourages the client to explore mistaken and/or faulty perceptions. At this point of therapy, the goal is to assist the client in understanding the purpose of his or her behavior and how particular goals can be translated into action. Confrontation is employed to show the client the nature of faulty thinking and beliefs, and the therapist starts to initiate Level III counseling skills. Dinkmeyer et al. (1987) offered the following list of basic mistakes and self-defeating behaviors:

1. Overgeneralizations. "All people are the same and there is no sense in trying to connect with people." These are conceptualizations that clients hold which go beyond sensory data and they have an explicit or implicit "all or every" meaning.
2. False or impossible goals of security. "I must please everyone in order to feel worthwhile. Only with total control of myself and others will I feel secure."
3. Misperceptions of life and life's demands. These can be delusions and distorted convictions such as the following: "Life is so shitty." "Why can't I get a break?" "I cannot tolerate life."
4. Minimization of denial of one's worth. "I am shit." "I do not deserve a fucking thing." "I am just a pussy." "How could anyone have interest in me? I am just a loser."
5. Faulty values. "I will get to the top anyway I can, and if I have to, I will destroy the world."

The reader should be aware that the therapist uses tentative interpretations, careful confrontation, and encouragement to assist the client in developing insight into faulty thinking and to understand how it is possible to surrender mistaken goals and to choose self-enhancing goals instead.

Stage Four: Help Client Commit to Change and Initiate Alternatives to Current Behavior

This is the Level III aspect of the therapeutic process, and although the therapist continues to employ Level I and Level II counseling skills, the client is encouraged to translate insight into action. Stage four is also called the reorientation phase, and there are at least eleven commonly employed strategies within this phase, which can be called Level III skills or action strategies (Dinkmeyer et al., 1987; Maniacci, 1996; Mosak, 1989).

Level III Skills or Action Strategies

First, **immediacy** involves the therapist describing to the client how he or she experiences the client at the moment. Since Adlerian therapists are aware that immediacy can enhance or injure the counseling relationship, immediacy is approached tentatively. The therapist provides to the client information about his or her verbal and nonverbal forms of communicating. When clients are congruent, both verbal and nonverbal communications will match.

Second, **encouragement** helps realize individual worth, and assets, and it fosters self-concept and self-esteem. This is a process that once it becomes internalized produces positive social interactions.

Third, **paradoxical intention,** also prescribing the symptoms or antisuggestions involves encouraging clients to increase their symptoms. For example, if a student is having difficulty passing examinations, a therapist—using paradoxical intention—could say, "See if you can fail each examination that you take." Paradoxical intentions are best used as experiments for specific periods of time. The therapist wants the client to learn something about the experience and not to feel manipulated. These techniques can allow a client to see the specific consequences of certain behaviors. Interestingly, Adler believed that in order for a client to maintain a symptom, he or she would have to fight to maintain it. Once a client stops fighting, he or she can be open to free choice and a wider range of possibilities. Readers should note that it is unethical to employ paradoxical intentions with clients who are severely depressed and suicidal since clients may act upon such suggestions. And, unfortunately, the therapist can be held legally liable for malpractice and an ethical violation of failing to protect a client from harm.

Fourth, **spitting in the client's soup** or **besmirching a clean conscience** comes from Adler's boarding school days where a student could get another's food by spitting on it. The therapist must determine the payoffs of a certain behavior and spoil the game by decreasing the benefit of the behavior within the client's eyes. For example, the writer once had a wife report during therapy to her husband, "You never touch me and I keep telling you, but you never respond." Here, the wife was expressing a desire to connect with her husband. So, this writer stated, "Perhaps, you would like to use your husband's touch as a means to feel connected with him." This writer used tentative interpretation to point the wife's desire for contact from her husband. Once the couple understood the purposes of each other's behaviors, they choose to change and their marriage improved greatly.

Fifth, **acting as if** is a creative technique in which a client is requested to act or behave in a way he or she does not believe is possible. Often, this writer uses role-playing or imagination techniques to assist the client in acting out or imaging the behaviors he or she would like to possess. For example, this writer had a client who lacked confidence in approaching women. Within several role-playing exercises, the client was asked to see himself having confidence and approaching women. Eventually, the client was given the homework assignment of acting as if he had confidence when approaching women in bars, at supermarkets, and on the streets, and within several weeks, he was no longer shy when approaching women and he developed self-confidence when he was in the presence of women.

Sixth, **catching oneself** is when a client understands that he or she will make mistakes when trying new behaviors and that therapeutic growth involves catching oneself when attempting to change a behavior. During earlier phases of therapy, a client may catch himself or herself too late and may feel discouraged. At this juncture of therapy, the therapist can point out that it is important to view setbacks as learning experiences, and it is important to learn to laugh at oneself and to realize that it takes time to avoid falling into self-defeating behaviors.

Seventh, **creating movements** are any tactics that can help a client to continue moving toward change. Such tactics appear to be the most beneficial when there is a strong client/therapist relationship. Sapp (1997a) reported creating movements with a client by showing surprise. For example, a client reported "When I date intimidating men, I feel discouraged, and I do not want to date again." Sapp replied, "Yes, I agree you should not date intimating men. Dating is meant to be a sharing encounter, not one based upon fear."

Eighth, **avoiding the tar baby** is the notion that the therapist should realize that no matter how self-defeating a client's behaviors may be, the client probably feels these behaviors are effective methods from his or her viewpoint, and it is important for the therapist not to fall into the trap of self-defacing or putting the client down during therapy.

Ninth, **push button technique** is where a client is instructed to imagine pleasant and unpleasant experiences, and the client is instructed to notice feelings associated with these experiences. The purpose is to show clients that feelings can be created through the thinking process, and it is the basis for rational-emotive imagery used within rational emotive behavior therapy.

Tenth, **task setting** and **commitment** are steps that clients have to take to ensure that they choose tasks that they strongly endorse. The reader should note that commitment is an important ingredient within reality therapy. Tasks should be specific, attainable, and measurable. It is best that clients perform tasks for a specific time, so that they will know that they are not signing up for tasks for life. Thus, they may be more committed to undertaking tasks.

After clients choose tasks, they have to be committed to performing them, and feedback from tasks can provide the client with useful therapeutic information about one's ability to handle failure, feedback, and how quickly one can revise a task and try again.

Eleventh, **terminating** and **summarizing** are used throughout the therapy process, but at this juncture of the counseling process, it is useful for putting limits on the counseling relationship. Many inexperienced therapists have difficulty terminating a counseling session, so carefully structuring the counseling session can help to prevent the client from bringing up new material during the end of a counseling session. Clearly, the client should have an idea of the length of time of a counseling: forty-five to fifty minutes for adults and adolescents and twenty to thirty minutes for children. When clients bring up new material or major material toward the end of a session, it can be useful to state that this will be a good place to start during the following week. The conclusion of the counseling session involves the client summarizing what he or she had gotten from the counseling session. The therapist could say, "We have covered several issues during this session, can you summarize in your own wording what you got out of this session."

Role of Therapist

The Adlerian therapist uses Level I, Level II, and Level III counseling skills and comprehensively assesses the client's level of psychological functioning. For example, information about the client family constellation, lifestyle, early recollection, and dreams are gathered by the therapist. According to Mosak and Maniacci, Adlerian therapists reported from a survey that therapy generally lasts four to six months or from sixteen to twenty-four sessions. Even though Alderian therapists conduct long-term therapy when it is indicated, often therapy is brief. Finally, Individual Psychology is analytic, behavioral, and cognitive, although therapists tend to focus primarily on cognitive aspects of therapy.

Therapeutic Relationship

The therapeutic relationship is viewed as a collaborative one; however, unlike Rogers' person-centered therapy, Adlerians therapists do not view the therapeutic relationship as necessary and sufficient to bring about therapeutic changes. Adlerians believe that insight translated into action is the process in which change occurs.

Multicultural Applications and Limitations

Clearly many cultural groups such as Asians, Latinos, African Americans, and American Indians could benefit from Adlerian therapy, since it has a community feeling and a social interest. One difficulty that some of these minority groups have is trying to adjust to the individual nature of American society. Generally with the United States, the individual tends to have more rights than a community. Furthermore, the United States tends to value competition and individual achievement. These values may be at odds with some cultural groups and Alderian therapy could reinforce an aspect of some minority cultures that may not be entirely benefited within the majority society. For example, the majority society tends to emphasize personal responsibility and not communal responsibility nor community achievement.

Critique

COMPREHENSIVENESS. Some Adlerian therapists assume that lifestyle is everything and that lifestyle is all. Moreover, Adlerian therapy tends to be descriptive and predictive. It would be useful to know the details of what actually predicts certain lifestyles. For example, Adlerians are good at telling what to do with clients, but issues like schizophrenia and other complicated mental issues have not been adequately addressed, except Shulman's (1984) work on schizophrenia. When one compares Individual Psychology with the comprehensiveness and depth of psychoanalysis, clearly, Freud provided greater detailed discussion of early childhood than did Adler. Moreover, the psychoanalysis and ego-psychologist Erikson covered human development into old age, and Adler was not clear about his conceptions about development during old age.

PARSIMONY. Adlerian psychotherapy clearly fits the definition of a parsimonious theory. Adler believed in providing education to the masses and he deliberately kept his theory connected to communities and based on common sense; therefore, Individual Psychology is exemplary in being very parsimonious, and it tends to be easily understood by clients and new professions who are becoming acquainted with psychotherapy.

EMPIRICAL VALIDITY. As Corey (2001) noted, although the writings and research of Adlerian theory have improved over the last twenty years, the articles published through the *Journal of Individual Psychology* tend to be descriptive, and not quantitative and experimental. Many of the conceptual areas of Adlerian therapy have not been subjected to scientific inquiry. What is needed for Adlerian theory are clear operational definitions of concepts and experimental and qualitative research methodologies that test out various aspects of the theory. Clearly, more empirical validity is needed to support the ideas of Adler's theory.

PRECISION AND TESTABILITY. One can argue that since empirical validity has been compromised with Adlerian therapy, that precision and testability are also compromised, and actually this is the case. Unfortunately, many of Adler's concepts are conceptually simple but difficult to research because he did not provide operational definitions or agreed upon tools for assessing the variety of concepts within the theory. Mainly, Adler did not precisely define nor measure his concepts objectively nor reliably. Finally, precision and testability have been extremely compromised.

HEURISTIC VALUE. Clearly, Individual Psychology has excellent heuristic value, especially due to the fact that it has influenced most of the theories presented in this text. Unfortunately, many theorists and researchers are unaware of Adler's impetus on birth-order research. In terms of heuristic value, Adler's influence is probably greater than Freud's, although Freud is widely known in literature, anthropology, sociology, political science, human relations, social work, education, and so on. In fact, this writer believes that Adler has had a stronger influence on the development of psychotherapy than did Freud. For example, Adler's influence can be seen in social work, education, marriage therapy, brief solution-oriented or focused therapies, family therapy, group therapy, and many other forms of psychotherapy. In contrast, mainly psychiatrists are the largest group influenced by the work of Freud.

Adler has influenced many theories and therapies. For example, the phenomenology movement, the person-centered movement, and the existential movement were all influenced by Adler. Person-centered psychotherapy borrowed the emphasis of the client-therapist relationship and the focus on phenomenology from Adler. Gestalt psychotherapy also borrowed phenomenology, conscious behavior, and action strategies from Adler. In addition, transactional analysis borrowed Adler's concept of life script and the importance of analyzing social transactions. The use of contracts and the use of collaborative relationships and didactic relationships are shared by many of the forms of psychotherapy covered within this text. And many of the problem-solving strategies within cognitive-behavioral therapies are based on Adler's therapy.

Albert Ellis, grandfather of cognitive-behavioral therapies, and the founder of rational emotive behavior therapy (REBT) credited Adler as the major influence on his theory (Ellis & Dryden, 1987). Both Adler and Ellis endorse a cognitive view of emotional problems—namely, we are not so much affected by events but by our views and interpretations about events.

Finally, reality therapy's uses of commitment, skillful questioning, contracts, and humanistic-existentialism can be clearly traced to Adler. Moreover, Aaron Beck's notions of cognitive distortions are very similar to Adler's concept of private logic. In closing, even the collaborative relationship emphasized by George Kelly's cognitive therapy, called personal constructs psychotherapy, was influenced by Adler.

APPLIED VALUE. As is apparent, Adlerian psychotherapy has excellent applied value. In fact, this writer believes that it has more applications than psychoanalysis. For example, Adler's therapy can be applied to minority groups and it emphasizes the nature of existence of many minority groups within the United States, which is social. In closing, Individual Psychology can be used for group counseling, and marriage and family psychotherapy.

SUMMARY

Adlerian psychotherapy is the precursor to cognitive-behavioral forms of psychotherapy and has influenced most of the forms of psychotherapy that will be presented in this text. Unlike Freud's determinism, Adler adopted a soft form of determinism, and unlike Freud's historically oriented theory, Adler presented a theory with a present and future orientation. Actually, Adler addressed the past, present, and future in that it is a holistic and not reductionistic manner like psychoanalysis.

Glossary of Key Terms

Basic mistakes. Faulty errors in reasoning characterized by extreme errors in logic and thinking.

Birth order. The perceived birth order in which a child tends to identify within a family.

Community feeling. A more accurate translation of the term social interests that includes social activities but also includes a sense of community with the world at large.

Compensation. Striving attempts to overcome feelings of inferiority.

Constructivism. A new philosophy and trend in cognitive-behavioral therapies in which clients are seen as the active creators of their reality.

Discouragement. The feelings that clients have that they lack a place within their social worlds and doubt their abilities to compensate and adapt with the difficulties of life.

Early recollections. Detailed descriptions of early childhood memories that explain how a client chose a certain lifestyle. Usually, the therapist wants recollections before the age of ten.

Encouragement. The process is the inverse of discouragement, and it helps a client gain courage to face the challenges of life and to establish obtainable goals.

Family constellation. The social environment within a family that includes perceived birth order, parental interactions, siblings' interactions, and the formation of alliances within the family.

Fictional final goal. The conviction with a lifestyle that is also called self-ideal.

Feelings of inferiority. A client's sense of not feeling actualized.

Idiographic. The individual case method to research.

Lifestyle. Also called the style of life and it involves the way a client thinks, feels, and conceptualizes his or her life.

Lifestyle assessment. The method developed by Dreikurs and others that is used to explore early childhood situations and early childhood recollections. The information is provided to the client for feedback.

Life tasks. The task or life that people must meet in order to function effectively such as social, love, occupation, sex, self, spiritual, parenting, and family.

Masculine protest. Attempts by both men and women to compensate for inferiority feelings by acting socially superior.

Nomothetic. A group method of conceptualizing research.

Organ inferiority. An inherited deficiency within an organ that requires compensation.

Phenomenology. A philosophical position in psychology that examines the internal perceptions and internal world from the client's viewpoint.

Trauma. Stress that a client feels during a new situation. First, there is a trigger and a subjective way of interpreting the traumatic experiences.

Sideshows. Detours or evasions away from inadequacies. Attention is focused on areas of unimportance.

Social interests. Community feelings or interest characterized by bonding and forming social interactions with others. The global sense of being part of a community and world.

The question. The assessment technique that uses the following question, "What would be different if you did not have your symptoms?" This is also a technique used by solution focused therapies.

Teleology. The concept that beliefs and goals are purposeful and they determine behavior.

Review Questions

1. Early recollections. Describe an early memory that occurred in your life before the age of ten. How does that memory tend to currently influence you? Describe your family atmosphere as you remember it while growing up. Were there alliances in terms of siblings or family members?
2. Rate several members within your family on the following dimensions:
   a. Social interest
   b. Maturity
   c. Creativity
   d. Rigidity
   e. Conscientiousness
   f. Expressiveness
   g. Restrictiveness
   h. Materialism
   i. Altruism

Case Example: Applying Techniques From Individual Psychology

The transcription that follows is based on a male client in his fifties who was diagnosed on the DSM-IV-TR, the *Diagnostic and Statistical Manual of Mental Disorders* (Fourth Edition Text Revision). Psychologists, psychiatrists, social workers, counselors, and psychotherapists use this manual to diagnose patients and clients in order to receive reimbursement from insurance companies. Finally, the DSM-IV-TR is used to make a multiaxial diagnosis, one using five axes (DSM-IV-TR, 2000, pp. 27–38).

Axis I is used for the presenting problem or the reason a client came in for therapy. Several diagnoses can be made on this axis such as the following:

Anxiety disorders—disorders marked by feelings of stress, tension, and worry.
Dissociative disorders—disorders within which one or more parts of mental processes become separated and dissociation of memory, identity, and perception is used to cope with stress.
Mood disorders—disorders involving disturbances in mood such as major depressive disorder, dysthymic disorder, bipolar disorders I and II, cyclothymic disorders, and others.

Eating disorders—disorders in relation to the consumption of food that include anorexia nervosa, bulimia and others.

Sleep disorders—sleep difficulties that occur before sleep such as insomnia or during sleep such as sleep apnea.

Sexual and identity disorders—physical and psychological disorders that affect coitus or the way a client views maleness or femaleness.

Delirium, dementia, and amnesia, and other cognitive disorders—delirium is a disturbance of consciousness and a change in cognition. Dementia is a disorder that presents as multiple cognitive deficits such as memory, and amnesia is an impairment in memory without other cognitive impairments.

Substance-related disorders—disorders related to drug and alcohol abuse.

Schizophrenia and other psychotic disorders—schizophrenia is a psychotic disorder associated with delusions, inappropriate behaviors, hallucinations, emotional flatness, lack of motivation, and disorganized speech. Psychotic disorders are a loss of contact with reality.

Axis II is employed for personality and mental retardation diagnoses. When a patient or client has an Axis I and Axis II diagnosis, and the principal diagnosis is on Axis II, it is common to qualify that Axis II has the principal diagnosis by employing the phase "principal diagnosis." Axis II disorders include mental retardation and the following personality disorders:

Paranoid—traits clients have that are associated with distrust of others. Clients tend to have eccentric paranoia.

Schizoid—a personality disorder characterized by a disinterest in others and an aloofness within interpersonal relations that is not the result of fear.

Antisocial—a personality disorder with pervasive patterns of disregard for the rights of others.

Borderline—a personality disorder that is characterized by instability in moods, relationships, and the self-image.

Histrionic—a personality disorder associated with overly emotional and attention seeking behaviors.

Narcissistic—is characterized by grandiosity, self-centeredness and a lack of empathy toward others.

Avoidant—is associated with fear in social situations, but unlike the schizoid personality, these clients want to enjoy interactions with others.

Dependent—is marked by traits of dependent and submissive behaviors, and these clients require enormous amounts of reassurance from others.

Obsessive-Compulsive—is characterized by a preoccupation with perfectionism, orderliness, and the rigid control of self and others, but unlike obsessive-compulsive disorder, there are not repetitive actions related to persistent thoughts.

Axis III is used for general medical conditions, diagnosed by a medical practitioner or physician, that are pertinent to the patient's mental disorder. Examples of some of these disorders are the following:

    Diseases of the digestive system
    Diseases of the circulatory system
    Diseases of the nervous system and sense organs
    Diseases of the skin and subcutaneous tissue
    Endocrinal, nutritional, and metabolic diseases, and immunity disorders
    Diseases of the respiratory system

Axis IV is employed for psychosocial and environmental concerns that may influence the diagnosis and prognosis of Axis I and Axis II diagnoses. These are negative life events that produce interpersonal stress. Some of these categories are the following:

    Problems with primary support group-divorce, death of family member, sexual abuse, physical abuse.
    Problems related to the social environment such as death of a friend, living alone, adjustment to retirement.
    Educational problems such as academic difficulties, negative school experiences. Occupational difficulties such as unemployment, or threat of losing one's job.

Axis V is employed to report the client's overall level of functioning, and it is referred to as the global assessment of functioning scale (GAF). The scale has values that range from 0, inadequate information; to 10, persistent danger to self and others; to 50, moderate symptoms; to 100, superior functioning in a variety of areas.

    The male client had the following DMS-IV-TR multiaxial diagnoses:
    Axis I 300.02 Generalized Anxiety Disorder
    Axis III None
    Axis II None
    Axis IV None
    Axis V GAF = 45

Below is a brief excerpt of the transaction with this client and the writer employs his interpretation of Individual Psychology. During this transcription, the writer employed Level I, Level II, and Level III counseling skills. Finally, this writer attempted to provide the client with information about his early childhood experiences and early recollections. In closing, this writer tried to analyze several of the client's basis mistakes. Note that client's statements are denoted by Cs and therapist statements are denoted by Ts.

T-1: Let us start with letting you summarize what you got out of the session last week.

C-1: Well, I discovered I held several mistaken beliefs such as the world is not a fair place; I will always be a loser, and unexpected things should not happen to me. And I discovered from my family constellation and early recollections that my family resented me and my mother formed an alliance with me as a means of distancing me from my father. Also, as the only child, I never really had a childhood in that my mother used me as an adult.

T-2: Can you tell me what would be different in your life if you did not have your current symptoms?

C-2: Without this anxiety, I would have more freedom to meet women and I could possibly find a special woman to date.

T-3: If you could wave a wand, and have any woman you want, describe her?

C-3: She would be awesome. I know I would not choose a woman like my mother or my ex-wife and I want a woman who would be able to connect to me on a very personal level.

T-4: You are seeking a relationship as a means of strengthening your community feelings or interest.

C-4: Yes, before therapy, I was believing that I was doomed and nothing could be done to change my situations in life. I thought that the cosmos had it in for me.

T-5: How were you able to conclude otherwise?

C-5: Well, you respectfully challenged some of my faulty philosophies of life and you allowed me to take ownership for my thoughts, feelings, and behaviors.

T-6: It seems clear to you that you have choices and your thoughts can influence your feelings and your feelings can influence the things that you do.

C-6: Yes, I can really see the connection when I think back to early childhood experiences.

T-7: You were able to see that you had many misperceptions about your early childhood experiences.

C-7: At first, I thought that all mothers were loving, but I can see that my mother was not a loving mother but a cold bitch.

T-8: You feel hurt because your mother was not able to show love toward you.

C-8: I had the fantasy that my mother was an angel, but in reality, my earlier childhood experiences were hell.

T-9: In terms of your early childhood experiences, is it written anywhere that they have to affect you for the rest of your life?

C-9: No, I am beginning to put things in perspective, and I am realizing that I have a great deal of power on how I think, feel, and act. And, now, I am focusing more on establishing strong social relationships and I feel ok receiving social support.

T-10: At one point in therapy, you were discouraged, but now have insight into your lifestyle and I think you are ready to move toward changing things.

C-10: You know, I feel that you have really listened to me and guided me into learning how to help myself. You do not give me answers, but you help me to find answers for myself and you offer tentative hypotheses of why certain events may have occurred and how these events may have shaped my perceptions. I think I have the insight and I am now ready to change things.

Websites and Other Information About Adlerian Psychotherapy

The North American Society of Adlerian Psychology is committed to providing training in Adlerian psychology. It is located at 50 Northeast Drive, Hershey, PA, 17033. The telephone number is (717) 579-8795, the fax number is (717) 533-8616, and the e-mail address is nasap@msn.com. Finally, the website is located at http://www.alfredadler.org/aboutUs.htm.

Adler School of Professional Psychology is dedicated to advancing the principles of Adler within a psychological context. This school has North Central Association Accreditation starting from 2002 to 2012. This school is located at 65 East Wacker Place, Suite 2100, Chicago, Illinois, 60601–7298. The telephone number is (312) 201–5900, and the fax number is (312) 201–5917. For information through e-mail, the address is information@adler.edu and the website is located at http://www.adler.edu/.

Chapter 4

BEHAVIOR THERAPY

CHAPTER OVERVIEW

Behavior therapy became a challenge to the dominant form of psychotherapy of the 1950s and 1960s—psychoanalysis (Siegel, 1983, 1984). For example, within the United States, Joseph Wolpe developed systematic desensitization and Arnold Lazarus, in South Africa, and Hans Eysenck, in the United Kingdom, were beginning to employ results from animal psychology to treat anxiety disorders with humans. During the 1970s, it was clear that behavior therapy was the dominant paradigm in both psychology and education. For example, new procedures called self-control procedures were being developed. Likewise, there was an explosion of cognitive-behavioral therapies and techniques. To the regret of some therapists and theorists, during the 1980s, behavior therapy became more diverse and moved beyond its earlier roots of learning theories (Day, 1983).

For example, more emphasis was being given to client-therapist relationship issues and working with clients' feelings. During the 1990s, theories started emphasizing the common elements that are found in both behavior therapy and humanistic therapies (Corey, 1991, 1995; Wilson, 1989). Moreover, also during the 1990s and into the 21st century, two new techniques have been incorporated into behavior therapies—Francine Shapiro's Eye Movement Desensitization and Reprocessing (EMDR), and a more general procedure called the Eye Movement Technique (EMT)—to treat anxiety disorders. In addition, these eye movement procedures have been also combined with psychological hypnosis.

Finally, during the 21st century, Theodore Barber (1999, 2000) presented evidence that may end a major debate within the area of psychological hypnosis. Traditionally, psychologists have debated if hypnosis was an altered state of consciousness or was due to cognitive abilities and social cues. Barber found that there were three types of hypnotizable clients: one type that fit the altered state of consciousness notion, but with three subtypes, and another type of client that fit the nonstate hypnosis camp. Interestingly, Barber also found a third type that did not fit the state nor nonstate position. In closing, during the 21st century, researchers have found that there are brain correlates of hypnotizability and behavior (Raz & Shapiro, 2002; Ray & Oathes, 2003).

APPROACHES TO BEHAVIOR THERAPY

Becker (1987) stated that there are at least five forms of behavior therapy and they are the following: applied behavior analysis, neobehaviorism, cognitive-behavioral therapy, social learning theory, and multimodal behavior therapy (Cormier & Cormier, 1991).

Applied Behavior Analysis

A popular American experimental psychologist, Skinner (1988) is associated with applied behavior analysis. Simply stated, applied behavior analysis studies the relationship between behavior and the environment. For example, how does behavior change as a result of environmental events. Applied suggests that events have social importance (Gambrill, 1994), while behaviors are the things that we do (Skinner, 1974, 1987, 1988a, 1988b).

Unlike some other behaviorists, Skinner endorsed a philosophy of science called **radical behaviorism,** which is an attempt to account for behavior using only natural contingencies having survival, reinforcement, and social evolutionary links. Moreover, radical behaviorism is a radical departure for **Watsonian behaviorism** and **methodological behaviorism.**

Watson endorsed the philosophy called **methodological behaviorism,** based on truth by agreement, which is logical positivism. Things are true only if a group of people can agree on them. Watson (1879–1958), during the 1900s, criticized Wundt's introspective psychology and stressed an objective form of psychology; therefore, he did not emphasize environmental events, and he did not accept covert internal events; in essence, all behavior could be explained by stimulus and response learning or classical conditioning. Methodological behaviorism is based on public or consensual validation and it is a **nomothetic approach,** traditional group experimentation, and statistical inference approach. Watson (1930) shocked the world when he stated: Give me a dozen healthy infants, well-formed, and my specified world to bring them up in and I will guarantee to take any one random and train him or her to become any type of specialist I might choose—doctor, lawyer, artist, merchant-chief, and yes, even beggar-man and thief, regardless of his or her talents, penchants, tendencies, abilities, vocations, and race of his or her ancestors. **I am going beyond my facts and I admit it, but so as have the advocates of the contrary, and they have been doing it for many thousands of years**

(p. 104). This section that is bold within the quote is often omitted from books, and this quote suggests that Watson knew he was going beyond his facts and wanted to popularize psychology.

In 1920, Watson was forced to leave the academic world because he had engaged in inappropriate sexual intercourse with his female research assistant. After this incident, Watson's wife sued him and divorced him and destroyed his data on sexuality. This scandal forced Watson to resign from Johns Hopkins University, and in 1921, after marrying his former research assistant, he entered advertising and worked until his retirement in 1945. In 1957, Watson received an award for influencing modern psychology. Because Watson was still angry for being forced out of academic psychology, he burned all of his writing so that nothing could be left to science. Unlike Skinner, Watson viewed feelings, thoughts, and other internal states of mind as nonexistent. In contrast, Skinner's radical behaviorism is based on the **idiographic approach** and it does not insist on truth by agreement, and it can consider private events, but without a causal inference. In addition, what is radical about Skinner's position is, he viewed feelings, thoughts, and private events as behaviors like other behaviors that have environmental, evolutionary, and biological origins.

According to Skinner, feelings are the products of one's experiences and they are the by-products of reinforcement, and Skinner emphasized this point by stating that we do not cry because we are sad, but because something has happened. Moreover, unlike Watson, Skinner did not embrace associationism, operationalism, positivism, or **environmental determinism,** the notion that the environment totally determines behavior. Finally, radical behaviorism is an attempt to account for behaviorism entirely in terms of natural contingencies—such as survival, reinforcement, and social evolution.

To summarize, Sapp (1997a) presented the following table to summarize the difference between Skinner's radical behaviorism and Watson's neobehaviorism, a form of behaviorism based on classical conditioning.

TABLE 4-1

Skinner's radical behaviorism	*Watson's behaviorism*
1. Idiographic—single subjects' research or case study methodology	1. Nomothetic—experimental group research
2. Nonassociationism, nonoperationism, and nonpositivism	2. Association, operationism, and positivism
3. Relationship between environmental events and behavior	3. Stimulus-response psychology
4. Operant conditioning	4. Classical conditioning
5. Nonmediational theory	5. Mediational theory
6. No insistence on truth by agreement	6. Insistence on truth by agreement
7. Inductive	7. Deductive
8. Atheoretical	8. Theoretical

The mediational notion of neobehaviorism states that within the stimulus-response model there are intervening variables, or internal processes that occur within the individual; and in actuality, neobehaviorism is a S-O-R model (stimulus, organism, response), where organism is an intervening variable, and the internal processes that occur within the individual (Hull, 1952).

Cognitive-Behavioral Therapy

Cognitive-behavioral therapy is an eclectic range of techniques that combines strategies or techniques from cognitive and behavioral psychology. Dr. Albert Ellis, the grandfather of cognitive-behavioral therapy, the president of the Albert Ellis institute, and the pioneer of cognitive-behavioral therapy within the area of clinical psychology, founded cognitive-behavioral therapy. In addition, a psychiatrist, Dr. Aaron T. Beck, is a prominent figure who followed Ellis with his emphasis on what he called "cognitive therapy" (Beck & Freeman, 1990; Ellis & Dryden, 1987). Another clinical psychologist, Dr. Donald Meichenbaum (1994), gained a great deal of attention in terms of stress inoculation training, a cognitive-behavioral method for reducing stress. Within the area of adolescence, Dr. Philip C. Kendall has used cognitive-behavioral strategies with youths (Kendall, 1992).

There is a relatively new form of cognitive-behavioral therapy called **dialectical behavior therapy (DBT).** Dialectics is defined as the synthesis of opposing opposites. It was developed by Dr. Marsha Linehan at the University of Washington (Linehan, Dimeff, & Reynolds, 2002; Linehan, 1993), and she and her colleagues have developed techniques for dealing with more riskier behaviors like suicide, self-mutilation, substance abuse, borderline personality disorder (BPD), and other disorders. Leahy (2003) pointed out that DBT places more of an emphasis on the behavioral dimension of cognitive-behavioral theory. For example, a greater emphasis is placed on teaching clients behavioral skills for regulating negative cognitions, behaviors, and emotions.

There are at least four aspects of cognitive-behavioral therapy, and they are the following: schemata theory, continuity assumption, Socratic method, and cognitive-behavioral attributions. **Schemata theory,** with schema being the singular of schemata, was originally described by two noted theorists, Piaget (1926) and later by Barlett (1932). Freeman (1990) stated that schemata are formed during childhood and constantly change, even though they remained relatively stable. Schemata are conceptual frameworks that describe how thought processes develop within children. For example, society and socialization help determine how schemata are formed. In addition, as schemata developed, they are both conscious and unconscious, or below the level of awareness (Garner, Rockett, Davis, Garner, & Olmstead, 1993).

In terms of structures, schemata are composed of four interrelated concepts or structures: cognitive structure, cognitive propositions, cognitive operations, and cognitive products (Granvold, 1994). **Cognitive structure** is the way information is stored, represented, and processed within the mind. **Cognitive propositions** are information processing mechanisms that are selected, stored, encoded, and retrieved. **Cognitive products** are the results of information processing and they exist within the mind as opinions, self-cognitions, beliefs, attitudes, conclusion, judgments, and so on (Granvold, 1994; Clark, 1989).

Schemata on an abstract level are philosophies that guide a client's life, and synonyms for this term are irrational beliefs (Ellis & Dryden, 1987), personal constructs (Kelly, 1955), deep structures (Guidano, 1987), and dysfunctional cognitions (Beck, 1976). In closing, schemata can be rigid, broad, and irrational and rational beliefs (Blackburn, Eunsun, & Bishop, 1986).

The **continuity assumption** simply states that the same rules that govern covert learning such as operant conditioning and classical conditioning also govern thoughts or cognitions. In essence, covert learning (cognitive learning) occurs through the same rules that govern observable behavior. Finally, the continuity assumption is assumed with all the cognitive-behavioral therapies.

Individuals familiar with **Socratic method,** which is taken from philosophy, realize that it is a method of skillful questioning. And the goal is to permit clients to discover solutions for themselves. Sapp (1997a) provided the following examples: "What makes this assumption so or true?" "Provide evidence to support your belief." "What is the proof that your belief is true?" "Is this notion totally true?"

Cognitive-behavioral attributions, also called **cognitive distortions** by Beck (1976), which are taken from the area of social psychology, state that clients make inferential causal explanations about their behaviors and the behaviors of others (Epstein, 1982). Actually, clients tend to make the **major attributional errors,** and they tend to blame others for situational events. This is more likely to occur for others and not oneself. In reality, clients tend to underestimate situational explanations of behavior when the situations involve others. This leads to blame, and as the reader will see, with therapies like Rational Emotive Behavior Therapy (REBT), blame is one of the core emotional disturbances—blaming others, blaming oneself, and blaming the world. Moreover, blame can be viewed as broad schemata. There are a variety of cognitive-behavioral attributions or cognitive distortions such as negative attributions, misattribution, personalization, dichotomous or polarized thinking, selective abstraction, arbitrary inference, which includes mind reading and negative predictions, and overgeneralization, which includes magnification and minimization.

Negative attribution is the attribution of blame toward others as core schemata. For example, "I could not help myself." "You made me do this." "You made me mad." "I cannot stand you." "You make my life hell."

In addition to the words cognitive distortions, Beck refers to personalization, dichotomous thinking, selective abstraction, arbitrary inference, and overgeneralizations as **misattributions.**

Personalization is where a client assumes responsibility for things that are outside of his or her control. And often the client is apologizing for things that are out of his or her control. For example, once when I was seeing a client during a thunderstorm and the lights went out, the client stated, "I am sorry." And I indicated to the client that the thunderstorm had made the lights go off. On a cognitive level, the client had assumed that she was the cause of object of the lights going out. This assumption was made through an implication that I, the subject, caused the lights to go out, and that I am the object of the negative events.

Dichotomous or **polarized thinking** is extreme or absolutistic or polarized thinking. Things are viewed in black or white terms or right and wrong, or good and evil. Some cognitive-behavioral therapies refer to this thinking as all-or-nothing thinking since the client does not leave any room for in-between or gray areas of seeing things. This form of thinking is a distortion and it tends to simplify life events. Sapp (1997a) provided the following examples: "I am a total fool." "I am always wrong." "I am the worst bitch." These statements suggest that the subject is nothing other than a fool, wrong, worst bitch, and so on. Usually as the result of such thinking, the clients experience negative effects such as depression, anger, misery, and so on.

Selective abstraction only focuses on the negative aspects of a situation, and this form of thinking ignores other salient features of a situation. Actually, a situation is viewed as totally bad or negative. For example, suppose you asked your boss for a 15 percent raise and your boss agrees to a 10 percent raise. As a result of this interaction, one could feel worthless and underpaid, but only after focusing on the exact outcome as opposed to the fact that you received a raise. If one focused on the process of obtaining a raise, it is difficult to have extreme negative emotions connected with the encounter.

Oftentimes clients reach a negative conclusion and this is called an arbitrary inference. If a client cannot provide data to support his or her inference, chances are it is an arbitrary one. **Mind reading** and **negative predictions** are two examples of this form of misattribution of cognitive distortion. **Mind reading** is when clients attempt to predict what someone is thinking based on random nonverbal cues or clues. For example, "I knew that our relationship would end, because I had bad feelings toward my husband, and I assumed that my feelings represented what he was thinking." It has to be pointed out to a client that it is not possible to determine another's thoughts based on arbitrary circumstantial evidence. When clients report that they have a feeling that something bad is going to happen without evidence or data to support the prediction, through a self-fulfilling prophesy, the client can nonconsciously bring about the desired negative prediction or outcome.

Overgeneralization is drawing conclusions from one or a few isolated pieces of data and applying the conclusion in a broad way. Clients can magnify or exaggerate the negative aspects of a situation or he or she can minimize the positive aspects of a situation. In summary, when clients tend to magnify negative aspects of a situation and minimize the positive aspects of the situation, the client is overgeneralizing.

Finally, cognitive-behavioral attributions or cognitive distortions are the results of processing information improperly and cognitive distortions are partly the result of individual differences and partly the results of socialization (Wilson, 1989; Blaine et al., 1989; Guidano & Liotti, 1983).

Social Learning Theories

There is a **family of social learning theories;** however, Bandura (1985) has contributed a great deal to this area. Unlike radical behaviorism, social theory, also a cognitive-behavioral or sociocognitive theory, gives explanatory roles to cognitions. As the reader may remember, radical behaviorism was a radical rejection of Watsonian behaviorism and it did not view cognitions or thoughts as an explanation of behavior. Simply stated, cognitions are by-products of behaviors and they do not initiate behaviors.

Bandura endorsed **reciprocal determinism,** or the notion that environmental, cognitive, and behavioral factors interacted simultaneously together to determine behavior. In essence, social learning theory is a blend of cognitive-behavioral therapies and social-psychological theories. In contrast to cognitive-behavioral therapies that place most of their emphasis on cognitions as determinants of behaviors, social learning theories are more comprehensive in that they place emphasis on the client, his or her environment, and cognitions as mutually interactive factors in determining behaviors.

The notion of **expectancies theory** was discussed earlier in Chapter 1, and the notion of expectancy is derived from social learning theories. Rotter (1966), another social learning theorist, defined expectancy as a client's subjective perceptions about an event, situation or person. It is a client's covert perception about reality. Readers may have heard about a common expectancy called **internal locus of control,** or the belief that one has the ability to produce certain outcomes. In addition, there is another expectancy that readers are familiar with that is called **self-efficacy** or the belief or conviction that one can produce a certain outcome. Moreover, Seligman (1975) defined another common expectancy within psychology that he referred to as

learned helpless, and this concept is the opposite of self-efficacy. This expectancy, learned helplessness, also corresponds to Rotter's notion of external locus of control expectancy or the belief that things are totally out of one's control. Therefore, outcomes are the results of outside events or pure luck. The concept of learned helplessness describes clients' expectations of being depressed, helpless, paralyzed, and ineffective.

Multimodal Behavioral Therapy

Lazarus (1980) refers to this as eclectic behaviorism, and he was the first theorist or therapist to coin the term behavior therapy. He uses the term **technical eclecticism** to refer to using procedures and techniques from various theories without subscribing to the individual theories. In addition, he noted that **theoretical eclecticism,** drawing from diverse theories and trying to integrate them, leads to confusion in that certain theories are epistemologically incompatible and cannot be logically integrated. Lazarus recommended analyzing and treating clients in terms of their behavior from seven interacting modalities: behavior, affect, sensation, imagery, cognition, interpersonal relationships, and drugs and physiology. Lazarus refers to his form of assessing and analyzing clients as the BASIC-ID, an acronym for a client's behavior, affect, sensations, imagery, cognitions, interpersonal relationships, and drugs and/or biology or physiology. An assessment is made in terms of a client's strengths and weaknesses with these seven modalities. Clearly, multimodal behavior therapy is the most comprehensive intraindividually-based behavior theory, and social learning theories are the comprehensive nonintraindividually-based theories (Lazarus, 1976, 1986, 1989c, 1992, 1995; Burnett & Pulvino, 1990).

COMMON CHARACTERISTICS OF BEHAVIOR THERAPIES

Even though there are not any unifying set of assumptions about behavior therapies that can incorporate all existing procedures and theories within the behavioral field, there are three shared common characteristics (Becker, 1987). All therapies view the client's concerns within behavioral terms, the changing of behavior. Second, all behavior therapies use principles of learning such as respondent (classical) and instrumental (operant) conditioning (Day, 1980). Third, all behavior therapies, implicitly or explicitly, employ the scientific method. The scientific method involves testing hypotheses and making adjustment to hypotheses based on data that is collected. In essence, the scientific method is an investigative or experimental approach. The next section discusses anxiety disorders which have been more thoroughly investigated and treated by behavioral therapies than any other group of therapies (Guidano, 1987).

ANXIETY DISORDERS

Anxiety disorders are affective or mood disorders in which a client experiences debilitating anxiety. Most of the research about anxiety disorder came from the area of test anxiety. Sapp (1999) defined test anxiety as a special case of a general anxiety disorder consisting of phenomenological, physiological, and behavioral responses related to the fear of failure. These feelings are the harsh feelings that have physiological and behavioral concomitants that clients experience in evaluative situations. Spielberger and Vagg (1995) theorized that test anxiety is composed of at least two factors or constructs—worry and emotionality, and this theory is a state-trait one, where worry is analogous to trait anxiety, and emotionality corresponds to state anxiety. This theory of anxiety states that the interaction of high worry and high emotionality produce test anxiety. In essence, worry is the cognitive concern about performance, while emotionality is the physiological arousal response to anxiety.

Recently, Spielberger and Vagg (1995) introduced a transactional process model of test anxiety. This comprehensive model of test anxiety specifies that interpersonal perceptions, cognitions, informational processing, and retrieval mechanisms mediate the effects of worry and emotionality on performance. Moreover, they identified other important correlates of test anxiety such as study skills or habits, test-taking skills, test-wiseness, and task-irrelevant cognitions. This, too, is an essentially trait-state theory of test anxiety which states that test anxiety is a trait that is evoked by states during evaluative situations.

Sarason (1984) extended Spielberger's model of test anxiety into four factors: first, worry and emotionality, but he conceptualized worry as existing of two distinct dimensions he called bodily arousal and tension. Finally, his fourth dimension was test-irrelevant cognitions. Sapp (1999) also found that test anxiety was composed of two constructs that correspond to Sarason's model. Sapp (1994, 1996a, 1996c) conceptualized test anxiety within a cognitive-behavioral theory, and he viewed worry as the cognitive component of test anxiety and emotionality as the behavioral response. He viewed the cognitions and affects that result from test anxiety as behaviors and logically cognitive-behavioral treatments would be the treatments of choice.

The *Diagnostic and Statistical Manual of Mental Disorders* (Fourth Edition [DSM-IV-TR]) describes nine anxiety disorders: panic disorder with agoraphobia, panic disorder without agoraphobia, agoraphobia with history of panic disorder, specific phobia, obsessive-compulsive disorder, posttraumatic stress disorder, acute stress disorder, generalized anxiety disorder, anxiety disorder due to . . . [Indicate the General Medical Condition]. Specify if diagnosis is: With Generalized Anxiety/With Panic Attacks/With Obsessive-Compulsive Symptoms, and anxiety disorder not otherwise specified. The reader can review the DSM-IV-TR (pp. 429–484) for a detailed discussion of each disorder; however, there are some general features of anxiety disorder that are important from a clinical standpoint. Panic attacks are common characteristics of anxiety, and these are sudden feelings that something horrible will happen. Often, clients will have feelings of a shortness of breath, heart palpitations, choking sensations, chest pains, a sense of going crazy and losing control. Actually, panic disorder parallels test anxiety in that there are somatic complaints and excessive worry.

Kendall and Hammen (1998) defined the following anxiety disorders: generalized anxiety disorder, specific phobia, agoraphobia, obsessive-compulsive disorder, posttraumatic stress disorder (PTSD), and acute stress disorder.

Generalized anxiety disorder (GAD) is excessive worry anxiety and emotionality anxiety that lasts for six months. **Specific phobias** are simple phobias, or the unrealistic fear of a certain situation or object. **Social phobia** is worry anxiety about social or performance situations. **Agoraphobia** is worry anxiety and emotionality anxiety in which escape from a situation is difficult, and this disorder can occur with or without panic attacks. **Obsessive compulsive disorder (OCD)** can be diagnosed if a client presents obsessions—recurrent cognitions or images, and compulsions—rituals or repetitive behaviors that a client is driven to perform. **Posttraumatic stress disorder (PTSD)** is an anxiety disorder that is the result of extreme psychological trauma. PTSD can include symptoms such as an exaggerated startle response, reliving the traumatic event, sleep difficulties, and cognitive distortions. When a client presents symptoms of PTSD that have occurred less than a year, the appropriate diagnosis is **acute stress disorder.**

Anxiety disorders can be treated by psychological or medical means. Cognitive-behavioral approaches view anxiety disorders as the results of error in information processing and irrationality philosophies about life. Medical therapies such as benzodiazepines or anxiolytics are antianxiety medications; these include such brand name drugs as Xanax, Valium, Ativan, and Dalmine. These medications reduce central nervous activity by lessening anxiety and by producing calming effects. Kendall and Hammen reported that antianxiety medications or minor tranquilizers work by increasing the activity of a neurotransmitter gamma-amino butyric acid **(GABA),** which is an inhibitory neurotransmitter. In summary, the theory states that benzodiazepines increase the effects of GABA. OCD is believed to be the result of high levels of the neurotransmitter serotonin, and antidepressant medications such as clomipramine or anafranil have been shown to be effective within dosage ranges of 75–300 milligrams. Clearly, some anxiety disorders run within families and there are biological aspects of these disorders.

As previously stated, there are many cognitive-behavioral techniques that can be used to treat anxiety disorders such as relaxation therapies, systematic desensitization, hypnosis, eye-movement techniques, exposure procedures, and so.

THERAPIES BASED ON PRINCIPLES OF CLASSICAL CONDITIONING

Van Den Hout and Merkelbach (1991) have challenged the notion that classical conditioning is just the temporal pairing of conditioned and unconditioned stimuli, and they have stated that clients' expectations lead to the reaction of one stimulus to another. Furthermore, they presented a **neo-Pavlovian model** of classical conditioning, which is the following: conditioned stimulus➡ cognitive representation of unconditioned stimulus➡ evaluation of unconditioned stimulus➡ conditioned stimulus. This model asserts that we are genetically prepared to respond to certain conditioned stimuli (Rescorla, 1988).

Systematic desensitization is a therapy based on the reciprocal inhibitions theory of counterconditioning. Wolpe (1958, 1973, 1997) stated that if an antagonistic response is made during the presence of an anxiety-producing stimulus, the feared response can be decreased. Wolpe labeled this process whereby two antagonistic responses could not occur simultaneously as **reciprocal inhibition.** For example, Wolpe theorized one could not experience bodily tension and relaxation at the same time. In essence, bodily relaxation cancels out bodily tension.

Systematic desensitization (SD) can be used not only to reduce stress, anxiety, and anger, but also sexual disorders and so on. Unlike the claims of Wolpe's theory of reciprocal inhibition, it appears that systematic desensitization works because of imaginal exposure and in vivo exposure. The interested reader who is interested in treatment scripts for systematic desensitization can consult Sapp (1993, 1999); however, there are several steps to this treatment. The first step is **muscular relaxation.** The client is taught to tense and relax muscle groups throughout the body, and eventually through the process of conditioning, the client is able to mentally relax the body without muscular tension.

The second step of SD is an anxiety or **stress hierarchy,** or the arrangement of feared or stressed items or situations from least to most stressful or anxiety evoking. The third step of SD is teaching clients the **Subjective Units** of Distress Scale or (SUDS), which is a method of teaching clients to rate the amount of stress or anxiety evoked during the stress or anxiety scenes. There are a variety of ways of presenting SUDS to clients, and some psychologists use a scale from 0 to 100, while others use a scale from 0 to 10. The idea is that the smaller the value, the smaller the degree of stress or anxiety.

The third stage of SD is **interposition,** or the pairing of relaxation with the anxiety or stress scenes using the clients' imaginations. The final phase of SD is **in vivo desensitization** or real-life exposure to the things that produce stress or anxiety. Sapp (1997a) reported that clients with agoraphobia or the fear of social situations respond better to in vivo desensitization than SD without in vivo exposure. In addition, Sapp reported that the entire process of SD is more effective than exposure or relaxation alone. The mechanisms that underlie SD are exposure and response expectancies. Clients have a belief in SD and it meets their expectations; coupled with exposure, it is a powerful treatment. Finally, expectations are factors that probably influence all psychological and medical treatments.

Suinn and Richardson (1971) and Suinn (2001) developed **anxiety management training (AMT)** due to the length of time needed for the development of hierarchies and the length of treatment with SD. Unlike SD, this process can take less than three hours, and it employs a variety of visual and fantasy techniques to elicit anxiety within clients. Suinn theorized that anxiety was a drive state and he stated that we can learn behaviors to eliminate that drive. In summary, first clients are taught to identify the internal signal of anxiety, and then to later learn to react to these signals with responses that are designed to remove them such as relaxation, self-monitoring, and so on. Finally, Suinn described how AMT can be conducted within five structured sessions (Heimberg, 1990).

Aversive counterconditioning is another technique or therapy based on classical conditioning principles. An **aversive stimulus** is an unpleasant or undesirable stimulus. For example, antabuse, a drug used to treat alcoholism, is an aversive drug since it produces nausea. Antabuse is given to a client each time he or she consumes alcohol. The drug works by being repeatedly paired with alcohol and eventually through conditioning produces nausea. In addition, apomorphine is another drug that produces nausea and has been used with smoking cessation. When the drug is repeatedly paired with smoking, the result is **counterconditioning,** and eventually smoking produces nausea. Moreover, stale cigarettes and electric shock have been used as part of aversive conditioning with smoking cessation. Finally, aversive conditioning has been used to treat childhood enuresis. In closing, special ethical considerations are needed with aversive techniques, but as the reader will see, covert sensitization is an alternative.

Joseph Cautela (1967) developed **covert sensitization** as an alternative to aversive conditioning. This technique uses imaginal aversive stimuli as opposed to actual aversive stimuli. For covert sensitization to be effective, a client must be capable of elaborate mental imagery and must be committed to mentally exposing oneself to mentally aversive stimuli.

Behavior therapy is also popular in the treatment of sexual disorders. For example, **sensate focus,** a technique based on classical conditioning, involves in vivo desensitization. This technique is common for couples with sexual disorders. First, couples are requested to abstain from sexual intercourse and to explore a series of graduated exercises such as touching, caressing, and holding. Once a couple is able to touch each other without feeling extreme anxiety, which is a relaxing response, they are instructed to gradually engage in sexual activity. In summary, sensate focus is used to reduce sexual performance anxiety by having couples learn to associate pleasurable sensations (relaxation) with what were once anxiety producing situations.

Assertion training is the last technique discussed within this section. Again, like all the techniques discussed within this section, it is based on classical conditioning. Wolpe (1973) viewed assertion training as the correct response for emotional expression in contrast to anxiety toward others. In essence, assertion training is used to reduce anxiety, and it differs from aggression in that the goal is expression without harming others. Clients are taught to express their feelings without interfering with the expression of feelings of others. Often, relaxation, behavioral rehearsal, in vivo, and modeling are combined with assertion training.

THERAPIES BASED ON EXTINCTION

While many therapies based on classical conditioning are based on gradual exposure to anxiety-eliciting stimuli, extinction is based on the **immediate** and **intense exposure** to anxiety-eliciting stimuli (Sapp, 1997a). Since these techniques are based on immediate exposure, clients are at an added risk of psychological harm, and should be carefully assessed to determine if they can tolerate immediate exposure. The techniques that are discussed within this section are flooding, implosive therapy, paradoxical intention, aversive conditioning, and covert sensitization.

Flooding is usually conducted in vivo, and it prevents a client from making an avoidance response. Similarly, flooding can be conducted through a client's imagination, but it is probably more effective when used in vivo. If a psychologist combined flooding with modeling, the client can learn effective coping and decrease the anxiety response.

T. F. Stampfl, a distinguished professor emeritus of the department of psychology at the University of Wisconsin–Milwaukee, developed **implosive therapy,** and it was popular mainly during the 1960s (Stampfl & Levis, 1967). Like flooding, implosive therapy is designed to implode or extinguish anxiety by repeatedly having a client via imagery expose oneself to the conditioned anxiety-eliciting stimulus. In contrast to flooding, implosive therapy is an **imaginally-based therapy only;** however, another difference between flooding and implosive therapy is that implosive therapy uses **psychoanalytically-oriented concepts** during the imagery process. In addition, one goal of implosive therapy is to elicit **unconscious conflicts.**

It was the existential psychiatrist, Viktor Frankl (1959), who developed the technique of **paradoxical intention** or prescribing the client's symptoms. With paradoxical intensions, clients are instructed to increase their symptoms where the goal is to show clients that they have voluntary control of their symptoms. Even though paradoxical techniques have been used to treat a variety of disorders such as anxiety disorders, insomnia and so on, it is contraindicated in the treatment of suicide, violence, and substance abuse (Dattilio, 1994; Huddleston & Engles, 1986).

Aversive techniques were described with the previous section under therapies based on classical conditioning; however, aversive conditioning results in behavioral responses that prevent the occurrence of aversive stimuli (Sapp, 1997a). Moreover, aversive conditioning uses aversive stimuli such as physical punishment and electrical shocks that can be useful in extinguishing maladaptive behaviors (Iverson, 1994).

Finally, aversive techniques, like covert sensitization, were also described under the section entitled therapies based on classical conditioning. In contrast to the use of actual aversive techniques, covert sensitization asks clients to imagine aversive stimuli and it is an alternative to aversive conditioning and in vivo aversive counterconditioning.

THERAPIES BASED ON INSTRUMENTAL OR OPERANT CONDITIONING

Even though Skinner considered himself atheoretical, he developed the theory of instrumental conditioning, following the work of experimental animal psychologist Edward Lee Thorndike (1874–1949). Skinner did not see the value in giving causal emphasis to cognitions, emotions, nor neuropsychology. He emphasized the primacy of behavior, or the connection between the environment and behavior, and he believed cognitions, emotions, and so on were the by-products of behavior or responses to things that had happened within the environment. In addition, Skinner accepted evolutionary theory and believed that many behaviors were part of the evolutionary process.

In order to apply instrumental conditioning, Cormier and Cormier (1998) recommended applying an ABC model for the relationship between behavior and environmental events. This model suggests that behavior (B) is influenced by things that precede it (A-antecedents) and by things that follow it (C-consequences). Clearly, Cs or consequences can strengthen or weaken behavior.

Next, the following instrumental conditioning techniques will be discussed: positive reinforcement, negative reinforcement, schedules of reinforcement, successive approximation, Premack principle, token economy, contracts, punishment, time out, overcorrection, response cost, reinforcing incompatible behaviors, and operant extinction.

Both **positive reinforcers** and **negative reinforcers** increase behavior. Positive reinforcement is the application of rewards or some pleasurable event following a certain behavior or set of behaviors that leads to an increase in responding. Now, the notion of pleasurable is a matter of interpretation or judgment. Some examples of positive reinforcement are praise for a child for following the completion of homework, encouragement, hugs, stars for good behavior, and so on. The goal of reinforcements is to increase the desired behavior.

Negative reinforcement is reinforcement that is connected with the **termination of an aversive stimulus.** In other words, it is the **removal of negative consequence** following a performance of a certain behavior. For example, taking cold medication to remove or lessen the symptoms of a cold is an example of a negative reinforcer. In addition, in some cars, a buzzer sounds to alert the driver to put on the seat belt. The sounding buzzer serves as a negative reinforcer, since each time the driver hears the sounding buzzer, he or she puts on his or her seat belt in order to stop the negative consequence – the sounding buzzer. Finally, if parents prevent their children from watching television before they complete their homework, preventing children from watching television is a negative consequence that is removed once homework is completed.

Reinforcers must be contingent on target behaviors and they are the most effective when immediately following certain performances. Continuous or excessive reinforcement leads to satiation and this is why primary reinforcers like food and water are more susceptible to satiation than secondary reinforcers like money, stocks, bonds, and so.

The **schedules of reinforcement** also determine the rate of satiation. By definition, continuous reinforcement is providing reinforcement after each response. When continuous reinforcement is reduced to a partial reinforcement schedule, the process is called **thinning.** In addition, variable reinforcement, providing reinforcement on a variable rate, results in the highest rate of responding and is extremely resistant to extinction. For example, gambling casinos and lotteries operate on a variable ratio schedule of reinforcement in that they provide intermittent or irregular reinforcement. Since a person who is gambling never knows when he or she will win, the person continues gambling even though he or she loses money because the expectation is that he or she will win eventually. In many casinos, initially people are permitted to win early on, but once hooked, people continue playing hoping to win or receive reinforcement.

Successive approximation is a method of teaching complex tasks—especially to children. For example, it has been used to teach speech to autistic and schizophrenic children and other complex behaviors. **Differential reinforcement** of successive approximations is reinforcing behaviors that are similar to the approximated ones, and differential reinforcement is not providing continuous reinforcement and it is used to shape behavior. Finally, this process involves the gradual withdrawal of reinforcement until the desired behavior is performed.

The **Premack principle** can be useful when it is difficult to come up with reinforcers for a client, and it is the reinforcement of low-frequency behaviors with high-frequency behaviors. This is the performance of low-frequency behaviors before high-frequency behaviors. For example, if you are required to exercise and usually you enjoy watching television, you could make yourself exercise before watching television. Here, you would be linking exercise, a low-frequency behavior, with watching television—a high-frequency behavior (Premack, 1959).

Token economy is very useful for structured environments like schools and institutional settings, and it is the establishment of an environment in which tokens are given for desired behaviors. After clients collect tokens, they can trade them in for pleasurable items or activities. Within institutions, token economy requires that everyone work together and this includes therapists, institutional workers, and others. Even though token economy loses its reinforcing power once clients leave structured settings, parents, family members, and friends can keep the process going.

Contracts or behavioral contracting is a self-management strategy in which a client enters into an agreement with one or more persons to perform specific predetermined behaviors or responses (James & Gilliland, 2003). Usually, the contract specifies consequences for not following the contracted behaviors. Clearly, for contracts to be effective, they must be explicit and monitoring and record keeping is important for feedback. The following is a general contract.

General Contract_____

I agree to agree to follow the terms of this contract, and if I do not meet the terms of this contract I forfeit the right to the following activity or rewards.
Signature_____

The next contract is one to prevent suicide.

Suicide Prevention Contract_____

I agree to not harm myself, and if I get to the point of not being able to comply with this contract, I will call 911 and seek immediate help.

Signature_____

In summary, contracts can be elaborate or simple, but the notion is that it allows the client and psychologist to agree on terms that can strengthen the therapeutic relationship, and often when clients do not believe in or are unwilling to comply with a contract, they will not sign.

In contrast to reinforcers, **punishment** is an operant or instrumental procedure designed to decrease behavior; however, very similar to negative reinforcement, it uses aversive stimuli, but the goal is to decrease behavior and not to increase it. What is often missed with punishment is the fact that it has to be **intense** and **immediate** to be effective. When punishment is intense, it can **suppress behavior.** Moreover, punishment must be **consistent** to be effective and when desirable behaviors are reinforced, it is even more effective. Finally, there are ethical concerns in using punishment, but with injurious behavior, sometimes it becomes the last resort.

Time out has been a common instrumental or operant procedure used by parents and teachers, and it is the removal of positive reinforcers. For example, children who fight or misbehave are often removed from the classroom or other reinforcing environments. In essence, time outs are given when children perform undesirable behaviors. In order for time out to work, it is necessary to see if the environment is reinforcing to the client.

Overcorrection uses corrective procedures following disruptive episodes. For example, when a child has a temper tantrum, it can be useful to have the child straighten out a destroyed room, put away chairs, and place items back in order. In summary, overcorrection uses a penalty after undesirable behavioral episodes, where is it hoped that overcorrection will reduce disruptive behaviors. **Response cost** is the removal of positive reinforcers following inappropriate behaviors. For example, if a child misbehaves, his or her allowance can be lowered as a result. Often, response cost is combined with token economy—especially if alternative behaviors can be positively reinforced.

Reinforcing incompatible behaviors is the reinforcing of all appropriate behaviors but not inappropriate behaviors, and it is another operant or instrumental procedure.

Operant extinction is the process of removing reinforcement, and extinction is more likely to occur if continuous versus partial reinforcement has been applied. Moreover, often before behavior is extinguished, it can increase before gradually decreasing. Finally, with extinction, there can be spontaneous recovery, or the temporary reoccurrence of a response or behavior without reinforcement.

SELF-CONTROL PROCEDURES

Self-control strategies are procedures that clients implement themselves. These techniques would include but are not limited to self-monitoring, self-reinforcement, self-punishment, self-instructional training, biofeedback, bibliotherapy, eye-movement desensitization and reprocessing (EMDR), eye-movement technique, and hypnosis.

Self-monitoring involves the client monitoring or recording behavior that is the focus of change. For example, students can monitor study behavior. In addition, if a client comes in for smoking cessation, the first step is the monitoring of behavior, since this can provide a baseline of when smoking peaks and so on. In addition, an integral part of weight reduction programs is the monitoring of weight and calories. Often, at least initially, monitoring has a reactive effect in that it tends to change the targeted behavior.

Self-reinforcement involves clients giving themselves reinforcement. This can be done in an overt way with rewards, gifts, and presents to oneself and cognitively by accepting oneself and by covertly giving oneself reinforcement.

Self-punishment is very similar to self-reinforcement, but, in contrast, it is where a client gives himself or herself punishment. Even though both self-reinforcement and self-punishment appear easy, clients have to be trained in these procedures.

Self-instructional training was developed by Donald Meichenbaum (1997), and it involves the **restructuring of cognitions** through cognitive-behavioral techniques. First, clients are taught to identify maladaptive cognitions and next they learn to explore the nature of these cognitions; finally, they learn adaptive cognitions that have to be practiced during the therapy session and outside of therapy.

Biofeedback involves attaching electrical devices to a client's body to measure things like heart rate, blood pressure, muscle tension, and body temperature. Through continuous feedback, a client learns to increase and decrease bodily functions like heart rate and blood pressure. Biofeedback has been used to treat a variety of disorders such as tension and migraine headaches, hypertension, and cardiovascular conditions. Some psychologists believe that biofeedback increases alpha brain waves—these are the brain waves connected with relaxation and pleasure; nevertheless, research has not consistently found this to be true.

Bibliotherapy is the therapeutic use of reading material for clients, where clients learn to apply techniques on themselves without the help of a psychologist. For example, there are books on depression (*Overcoming Depression* by Mark Gilson and Arthur Freedom, *Breaking the Patterns of Depression* by Michael D. Yapko; *The Complete Idiot's Guide to Beating the Blues* by Ellen McGrath; *Teen Depression: A Guide for Parents* by Miriam Kaufman);

Divorce (*The Good Divorce* by Constance Ahorns; *Coping with Divorce, Single Parenting and Remarriage* by Mavis Hetherington; *Forgive you Parents, Heal Yourself* by Barry Grosskopf; *Helping Children Cope with Divorce* by Edward Teyber; *What Can I Do? A Book for Children of Divorce* by Danielle Lowry);

Eating Disorders (*Good Enough* by Cynthia N. Bitter; *Bulimia/Anorexia* by Marlene Boskind-White and William White, Jr.; *Weight Watchers Stop Stuffing Yourself* by Weight Watchers);

Families and Stepfamilies (*Stepfamilies* by James H. Bray and John Kelly; *The Family Recovery Guide: A Map for Healthy Growth* by Stephanie Brown et al.; *Why Can't I Be the Parent I Want to Be?* by Charles Elliott and Laura Smith; *The Parent to Parent Handbook* by Betsy Santelli et al.; *7 Steps to Bonding with Your Stepchild* by Suzen J. Ziegahn; *Making the Best of Second Best: A Guide to Positive Stepparenting* by Kathleen Fox), Infants and Parenting (*Secrets of the Baby Whisperer* by Tracy Hogg and Melinda Blau; *Becoming Parents* by Pamela Jordan et al.; *What to Expect: The Toddler Years* by Arlene Eisenberg et al.);

Love and Intimacy (*Couples* by Barry Dym and Michael L. Glenn; *Relationship Rescue* by Phil McGraw; *Fear of Intimacy* by Robert Firestone and Joyce Catlett; *Making Intimate Connections* by David Arp et al.), Marriage (*Should We Stay Together?* By Jeffrey H. Larson; *Married for Better, Not Worse* by Gary and Joy Lundberg; *Loving Midlife Marriage* by Betty Polston and Susan Galant; *Love for a Lifetime* by James Dobson; *The Seven Principles for Making Marriage Work* by John Gottman), Men's Issues (*Four Pillars of a Man's Heart* by Stu Weber; *Ten Secrets for the Man in the Mirror* by Patrick Morley; *Men in Midlife Crises* by Jim Conway; *When a Man Turns Forty* by Curtis Pesmen, *FatherLoss* by Neil Chethik; *Masculinity Reconstructed* by Ronald Levant), Pregnancy (*The Girlfriend's Guide to Pregnancy* by Vicky Iovine; *The Expectant Father* by Armin A. Brott and Jennifer Ash; *Pregnancy for Dummies* by Joanne Stone et al.; *The Price of Motherhood* by Ann Crittenden; *Mothering the Mother* by Marshall Klaus et al.), Schizophrenia (*Getting Your Life Back Together When You Have Schizophrenia* by Roberta Temes; *Coping with Schizophrenia: A Guide for Families* by Kim T. Mueser and Susan Gingerich; *Schizophrenia Simplified* by John F. Thonton and Mary V. Seeman);

Self-Management and Self-Enhancement (*Success Is a Choice* by Rick Pintino and Bill Reynolds; *Ten Days to Self-Esteem* by David Burns; *Self-Directed Behavior* by David Watson and Ronald Tharp; *Stand Up for Your Life* by Cheryl Richardson), Sexuality (*Becoming Orgasmic* by Julia Heiman and Joseph Lo Piccolo; *For Women Only* by Jennifer Berman and Laura Berman; *The Sexual Male: Problems and Solutions* by Richard Milsten and Julia Slowinski; *The Complete Idiot's Guide to Amazing Sex* by Sari Locker; *The Good Girl's Guide to Bad Girl Sex* by Barbara Kessing; *Permanent Partners: Building Gay and Lesbian Relationships* by Betty Berzon), Spiritual and Existential Concerns (*Sacred Self* by Wayne W. Dyer; *Sacred Contracts* by Caroline Myss; *The Secret of the Soul* by Gary Zukav; *The American Paradox: Spiritual Hunger in an Age of Plenty* by David G. Myers; *The Power of Now: A Guide to Spiritual Enlightenment* by Eckhard Tolle et al.);

Stress Management and Relaxation (*The 10 Step Method of Stress Relief* by Albert Crum; *The Art of Doing Nothing* by Veronique Vienne and Erica Lennard; *Learn to Relax* by C. Eugene Walker);

Suicide (*Suicide Survivor's Handbook* by Trudy Carlson; *A Parent's Guide for Suicidal and Depressed Teens* by Kate Williams; *Living When a Young Friend Commits Suicide* by Earl A. Grollman), Teenagers and Parenting (*What Teenagers Want to Know About Sex* by Boston Children's Hospital; *Bringing Up Parents: The Teenager's Handbook* by Alex J. Packer; *Queen Bees and Wannabes* by Rosalind Wiseman; *Yes, Your Teen Is Crazy* by Michael Bradley and Carroll O'Connor; *The Inside Story on Teen Girls* by Karen Zager and Alice Rubenstein; *101 Ways to Help Your Daughter Love Her Body* by Brenda Richardson and Elane Rehr);

Trauma/PTSD (*The PTSD Workbook* by Mary Beth Williams and Soili Poijula, *Trauma and Recovery* by Judith Herman; *The Scared Child* by Barbara Brooks and Paula Siedel; *Post-Traumatic Stress Disorder Sourcebook* by Glenn Schiraldi);

Weight Management (*Lifetime Weight Control* by Patrick Fanning; *Get With the Program!* by Bob Grenne; *Body for Life* by Bill Philips);

Women's Issues (*The Mismeasure of Women* by Carol Tavris; *The Company of My Sister: Black Women and Self-Esteem* by Julia Boyd; *The Wisdom of Menopause* by Christiane Northrup; *The Seven Aspects of Sisterhood* by Debra Gawrych);

Violent Youth (*How to Protect Our Children in School: A Step by Step Guide* by Daphne Lichter; *Everything You Need to Know About School Violence* by Anna Kreimer; *High Risk: Children Without a Conscience* by Ken Magid and Carole McKelvey; *Your Defiant Child* by Russell Barkley and Christine Benton). Many of these books can be found at the amazon.com website.

Eye-movement desensitization and **reprocessing (EMDR)** was developed by Dr. Francine Shapiro (1989, 1991, 1994; Beere, 1992; Fish, 1992) as a treatment for posttraumatic stress disorder. Shapiro discovered EMDR while noticing, within herself, that disturbing memories disappear as she became relaxed from performing back and forth eye movements (Sapp, 1997a). James and Gilliland (2003) noted that the R was added to indicate the reprocessing of information that changed from negative cognitions to positive cognitions and the desensitization of the traumatic memory. Even through Shapiro claims that EMDR has roots in both psychodynamic and behavior theories, James and Gilliland and the current writer believe it more closely fits within the cognitive-behavioral umbrella. According to Sapp (1997) and James Gilliland (2003), EMDR treats negative memories by working on one or more of the following concepts that the client hold within conscious awareness:

1. The image of the memory.
2. Negative self-statements.
3. Assessment of the trauma.
4. Anxiety response.

Shapiro believes that it is best when all four concepts are held by the client at the same time, but she believes that either one can be used for desensitization.

The process of EMDR is similar to many other desensitization procedures. First, the client is taught to assess anxiety using Wolpe's 1982 subjective units of distress scale (SUDS). Next, an assessment of the cognitive view of the traumatic event is done using Shapiro's **validity of cognition scale (VOC),** where value of 1 means the cognition is completely untrue, while 7 means the cognition is completely true. Now, the client is asked to focus on the traumatic event and to think about the most traumatic aspect of the memory. This process is similar to other mental imagery exposure procedures described within this chapter. Essentially, the client is exposed repeatedly to the traumatic event and asked to rate SUDS levels and VOC levels. During this juncture of therapy, the client is asked to report exactly what is happening cognitively. Specifically, the client is asked to report when mental pictures or images change and when they do not change. Moreover, clients are asked to let happen whatever happens and just report it. At this point of therapy, the client is instructed to continue visualizing the traumatic image or picture and to rehearse negative statements, to concentrate on emotional sensations, and to visually track the therapist's finger. The therapist moves his or her index finger rhythmically back and forth, from left to right, across the client's visual field. Between 12–24 movements is called a set or saccade.

During this process, the client is asked to think about the traumatic event and to let emotions surface and to assess them with SUDS levels. After about two sets, the client is asked if the image has changed or if anything new has happened. After each set, the client is asked to blank out the image and take a deep breath and relax. Throughout this process, the therapist is looking for insights in terms of how to proceed during therapy and which images to explore again. Shapiro noted that when the client experiences a mismatch among the images, cognitions, and emotions, the SUDS levels may not decrease; therefore, it is important for all three to be congruent for therapy to be successful. Eventually the client will report a positive cognition, and he or she is asked to focus on that image, and finally the client is asked to return to the earlier traumatic image only when constructive insights no longer surface. Shapiro reported that after 3–15 sets, clients usually report SUDS of 0 to 1, and if the VOC increases or the client reports new images or memories, the desensitization process is repeated.

Even though EMDR appears to be a single technique, Shapiro has pointed out that it is an eight-phase process. The EMDR website http://www.seinstitute.com/EMDR.html claims that this approach brings together many elements of a variety of psychological approaches, including psychodynamic, cognitive-behavioral, person-centered, gestalt, and bio-energetic. In addition to being a treatment for trauma, it is claimed that EMDR can treat anxiety, depression, guilt, and anger. The theory of EMDR is that stress, anxiety, and trauma are processed differently by the brain than nonstressful emotions. It is believed that during acute stress, the amygdala, the part of the brain that regulates emotions, shuts down the hippocampus, a part of the brain that processes memory; hence, stressful events are trapped outside of the normal brain processing centers, and EMDR helps a client access the experiences and transform them into declarative memory using the hippocampus. It is believed that with EMDR, the hippocampus is not shut down by evoked stressful emotions and that clients can tolerate doing the processing by distracting their attention by bilateral stimulation; however, how bilateral stimulation works is not understood.

There are eight phases of EMDR (Shapiro, 2001). During phase one, a client's history is gathered and over several sessions a treatment plan is developed. With phase two, the therapist works at establishing a relationship with the client and if the two decide to use EMDR, the steps in the process of the therapy are described. In addition, clients are taught soothing techniques such as mentally going to a safe place and relaxation and breathing techniques that tend to be soothing. Finally, the therapist and client decide which type of bilateral stimulation is preferred by the client. Phase three is the assessment phase, and the client is asked which target incident produced the trauma. Moreover, the client is asked which picture captures the worst part of the traumatic incident, and the client connects words that best describe the negative cognitions, or negative beliefs. Next, the client determines what he or she would like to believe in contrast to the negative thoughts, or what are referred to as positive cognitions. The validity of the positive cognitions are assessed on a seven-point scale, and the client describes the bodily feelings.

During phase four, desensitization starts with the client holding a focused picture of the negative self-perceptions and bodily feelings associated with the traumatic event. The therapist employs the bilateral stimulation procedure that was agreed upon during phase two, and usually this is the eye-movement desensitization procedure. In addition, the bilateral stimulation could consist of moving lights in the client's visual field, alternating tones to the ears, or alternating taps on the hands. The bilateral stimulus can last for a few moments to several minutes, depending on the client's responses. Next, the client is asked to clear his or her mind and to allow which ever thoughts surface to rise within the client's mind. Once the client describes what has surfaced to conscious awareness, he or she is given another set of bilateral stimulation. After each set of bilateral stimulations, the client is guided through the process of letting whatever surfaces to conscious awareness to surface.

Phase five is the installation of positive cognitions. Once the processing of traumatic memory is complete, positive cognitions are revisited along with additional bilateral stimulations until the positive cognitions are expressed as being totally valid as compared to the original traumatic event.

Phase six is the body scan and the client is asked to mentally scan his or her total body and if negative sensations or a lack of sensations are reported, additional bilateral stimulations are applied until positive sensations are reported.

Phase seven is called the closure phase, and the client continues to process the mental material obtained through the therapeutic process which may take weeks. At this juncture of therapy, the client can become retraumatized and needs to be monitored closely by the therapist for potential relapses (Sweet, 1995; Puk, 1994; Rosen, 1992).

Phase eight is the reevaluation and the client reviews the week and discusses any new experiences or sensations from his or her log. Essentially, the disturbances of previous sessions are assessed to determine the course of treatment.

In summary, Shapiro provided a number of precautions when using EMDR therapy. For example, she stated that unresolved memories can surface through EMDR, and some clients experience high levels of emotional and physical sensations. In addition, she claimed that memories of past events may be altered. Finally, she recommended that therapists be formally trained in EMDR so that the risk to clients is minimized. Readers interested in a dialogue with Dr. Francine Shapiro can read about her explanations of the process at the following website: http://www.behavior.net/cgi-bin/nph-display.cgi?MessageID=4&Top=-1&config=emdr.

For an interesting debate about EMDR, *Behavior Therapist* (2001, October; Volume 24[9]) provides a detailed critique of EMDR. In addition, Davidson and Parker (2001) stressed that EMDR is not any more effective than other exposure techniques and the most important technique from the process is imaginal exposure. *The American Journal of Clinical Hypnosis* (2001, Volume 43[3–4]) described many applications of combining EMDR with hypnosis. Finally, Dr. Shapiro has a website at: http://www.emdr, and she has an institute located at Pacific Grove, California, 93950-6010, USA; telephone number (831) 382-3900; fax: (831) 647-9881. In closing, clearly EMDR is in need of complex meta-analytic studies and research that focuses on confidence intervals on a variety of treatments for PTSD and traumatic disorders.

EYE-MOVEMENT TECHNIQUE

Dr. Larry Smyth has developed another protocol for the treatment of PTSD and trauma (Smyth, 1999). Unlike Shapiro, Smyth's protocol is based on traditional cognitive-behavioral strategies for PTSD. He starts by showing clients the eye-technique that is similar to the strategy discussed under the EMDR portion of this chapter, but unlike Shapiro, he gradually turns the eye-movement technique into a self-control procedure where the client learns to do it without the direction of the therapist. In addition, Smyth points that there is nothing spectacular about the eye-movement technique except its novelty and placebo effects. He emphasizes, like many cognitive-behavioral therapists, that imagery exposure and in vivo exposure is the best treatment for PTSD and traumas. In summary, Smyth has a protocol that will appeal to cognitive-behavioral therapists, and uses the eye-movement technique, relaxation response, cognitive-restructuring, and imaginal exposure to treat PTSD. Dr. Smyth has a website at: http://qualityfilmvideo.com/smyth/seven.html, and Dr. Fred Friedberg has a do-it-yourself eye-movement technique book that teaches the reader how to self-administer a variety of eye-movement techniques.

APPLICATIONS OF PROGRESSIVE RELAXATION TECHNIQUES

Within this section, there are two treatment transcripts, one employing traditional muscle tension relaxation exercises and the other employing guided imagery. A therapist needs to assess which transcript is appropriate for a client, and if a client has good imagery capacity, there is the possibility of combining both transcripts. Finally, each transcript can be read to a client in a slow soft voice in about thirty minutes. It is important to instruct to the client that he or she should tense muscles for about five to ten seconds to allow tension to build up and not to tense muscle to the point of building up pain. For additional transcripts and similar procedures the reader can consult Sapp (1997a; 1999, Jacobson 1938).

Transcript

Can you get into a relaxed position? Please close your eyes. I want you to first take a few deep breaths. I want you to inhale—hold it and relax. Once again—inhale and exhale and just focus on your breathing. Notice as you inhale and exhale that you become more and more relaxed. Focus on your breathing. Inhale. One . . . two . . . three . . . now you can exhale. Let us do this again. Inhale . . . one . . . two . . . three . . . now exhale and slowly relax. I want you to bring attention to your arms. That is it. I want you to tense both arms. This includes the biceps, hands, and so on. Bring tension into your arms. Now, let the tension go, and I want you to notice the difference between tension and relaxation. Let us do this again. Bring tension into both arms. Allow the tension to slowly build, and let it go. Let both arms feel very relaxed.

Now we will move to the muscles in both legs. This includes the feet, calves, and so on. Tense both legs by allowing the tension to slowly build up. Now, let the tension go. Let us repeat this process. Allow tension to build up in both legs. Slowly allow the tension to increase. Now, slowly let the tension go. Yes, feel the difference in your legs and arms. Notice how different they feel in comparison to other parts of your body.

Now, let us move to the stomach muscles. I want you to draw in your stomach as though someone punched at your stomach. Tightly draw in your stomach muscles. Hold the tension for a few seconds. Let it go and relax and focus on the rhythm of your breathing. Notice as you inhale and exhale that you become more and more relaxed. Notice how relaxed your stomach, legs, and arms are. Allow the relaxation to spread throughout your body.

Let us tense the neck muscles. Make your neck really tight. Allow the tension to build. Now, relax these muscles. Let us do it again. Tense the neck muscles, and now you can relax. Notice the relaxation spreading throughout the relaxed parts of your body.

I want you to now make your shoulders very tense. Tense your shoulder muscles. Try to bring your shoulder muscles up to your ears. Notice the tension and relax. Let us do this again. Try to bring your shoulders up to your ears. Steady the tension and relax. Notice the difference in the relaxed parts of your body.

Let us relax the facial muscles. Tense the muscles of your forehead by raising the eyebrows of your forehead. Steady the tension and relax and let it go. Now, I want you to wrinkle your face. Make a very wrinkled face by holding the tension and now slowly relax and let the tension go. Now, let us move to the lips. I want you to pucker your lips as though you were kissing someone. Really pucker your lips. Hold the tension and now you can relax. Let us move to the eyes. Tightly close your eyes. That is it. And now relax and let the tension go.

I want you to notice your breathing and by noticing it you can become even more and more relaxed, and if there is tension in any part of your body, just relax and let it go. Now, we have relaxed the muscles of your arms, legs, stomach, neck, and face. Again, if there is any tension in your body, just relax and let it go by breathing or retensing muscles and relaxing.

It is now time to start ending this exercise, and I will count from one to three as a way to terminate this process. One . . . two . . . three. Whenever you sleep, you will find that you will get a restful and wonderful sleep. Now, it is up to you at your own rate and pace.

Debriefing

It is important to process this experience with the client. You can do this by asking, "How was the exercise?" Allow the client to express any concerns or areas of the body that were difficult to relax, and use this information to adapt the transcript to the client. Finally, it is important to stress to clients that relaxation is a conditioning process that involves practice.

GUIDED IMAGERY TRANSCRIPT

Close your eyes and I will describe a very relaxing beach scene. I want you to picture this scene as clearly as possible. Let us begin. I want you to think about the time that you saw a beach. This could be an actual beach or through a movie or from television, but it does not matter because your imagination can create a scene just from an image. We can start with creating the image of a sun in your mind. If you want, there is the sun within your mind's eye. It is in the sky and you can notice that its imaginary warmth relaxes your hands, arms, face, neck, chest, stomach, back, and legs. Use your imagination to create relaxation moving throughout your entire body.

I want you to now imagine walking near a lake and beach on a warm sunny day. As you are walking, be aware of your surroundings. Notice what is around you, and if you want, you can give your attention to things within your environment. It could be the sound of the waves or the birds. Maybe it is the sounds of people playing volleyball or the sounds of people relaxing and enjoying the lake and the beach. What you choose is completely up to you. If you want, you can include some friends within your scene. Think about this scene and relax very deeply. Notice how free you feel being at the beach and near the lake. You are getting energy and you feel very free. If you need some additional energy or added amounts of self-esteem, imagine yourself taking it from the sun. Take in as much energy as you need to feel strong, alert, and relaxed. Allow yourself to experience this scene as though it were real. Let your mind expand throughout the entire beach scene by being aware and relaxing and letting go. Let your mind and body experience infinite relaxation, peace, and wisdom. Take in as much energy and relaxation as you need. And if there are any parts of your body that need more relaxation, just let the imaginary sun relax those parts. If you want, you can take off your shoes and walk on this imaginary beach. Let your mind feel the sand that is beneath your feet, and if you want, just stretch out and relax by erasing any tension, worries, or discomfort from your mind. Take a few moments to enjoy this scene and knowing that whenever you want, you can return to this place and relax and enjoy yourself again.

It is now time to start ending this experience. I will count from one to three as a means of ending this experience. When I am counting, you will feel yourself becoming more relaxed. Once this experience is over, it will seem as though you have had a wonderful nap, and when you go to sleep you will get a very pleasant rest. Now, one . . . two . . . three. It is up to you at your own rate and pace.

Debriefing

Like the progressive muscle relaxation exercise, it is important to process this experience with the client. For example, ask the client, "How were the imagery scenes?" If the client mentions scenes that were unpleasant or difficult to imagine, you can modify the scene during the next session. Finally, like the muscle-tension exercises, mental imagery relaxation requires practice.

PSYCHOLOGICAL HYPNOSIS

Sapp (2000) defines hypnosis as a situation or set of procedures when one person (term therapist) offers suggestions to another person (termed client) that can produce psycho-physiological changes and responses (Golden, Dowd, & Friedberg, 1987). This is one approach that clearly emphasizes the connection between the mind and body, and the applications for hypnosis tend to be underutilized by the medical community (Libet, 1985). For example, hypnosis is useful for pain control, burn patients, the control of bleeding, the control of hypertension, cardiovascular disease, and many other medically related problems (Wester, 1987). What the medical community tends to forget is the fact that almost any medical condition has psychological aspects and that it makes sense to treat a client medically as well as psychologically (Kroger, 1977; Kroger & Fezler, 1976; Sapp, Ioannidis, & Farrell, 1995; Hensel, Sapp, Farrell, & Hitchcock, 2001). In addition, hypnosis is useful for a wide range of psychological disorders such as dissociative disorders, anxiety disorders, eating disorders, sexual disorders, and others (Bowers, 1992; Sapp, 2002b). In addition, hypnosis is one of the techniques that has multicultural applications; for example, after over 40 years, Sapp and Hitchcock (2001; 2003a) have provided data about hypnosis and African Americans (Hensel, Sapp, Farrell, & Hitchcock, 2001). In addition, hypnosis data exists for several populations such as Canadians, Australians, the United Kingdom, European Americans, Germans, Finnish, Italians, and Spanish. In reality, is it possible to look at hypnosis across several cultures and the multicultural applications appear to be infinite (Crasilneck & Hall, 1985).

Sapp (2002b) reported that current thinking within hypnosis research is that hypnosis is a multidimensional construct (Wagstaff, 1981, 1991). For example, recently, Dr. Theodore X. Barber (1999, 2000) has proposed a multidimensional paradigm or theory of hypnosis. However, during the 1950s, Dr. Theodore Sarbin was one of the first theorists to reject the altered state of consciousness notion of hypnosis, and he viewed hypnosis as a social psychological construct. Sarbin theoretically viewed hypnosis as a dramaturgical metaphor and he used role theory to explain hypnosis. From Sarbin's point of view, clients enact the role of how a hypnotized client is supposed to behave (Sarbin & Coe, 1972). Clearly, Sarbin did not suggest that hypnosis was a sham, but he did not view it as a conscious altering state, because he found that many psychological variables affected hypnotic responsiveness such as increasing clients' expectations and motivations. Sarbin and Barber explained hypnosis without proposing an altered state of consciousness paradigm, and they viewed contextual variables like defining a situation as hypnotic and goal-directed behavior as the theoretical basis for hypnosis. Theodore X. Barber (1969) was the second major theorist to reject the altered-state notion of hypnosis, and he found that hypnosis could be elicited without hypnotic inductions, and that motivation and expectations influenced hypnotizability.

Currently, Barber argued that the reason that researchers disagree if hypnosis is an altered state of consciousness or not is due to the fact that they tend to see one or two of the three hypnotic types that he has referred to as fantasy-prone (with three subgroups: sex-fantasizers, escape-fantasizers, and encouraged fantasizers), amnesic-prone, and positively-set. Barber referred to the fantasy-prone as very good hypnotic subjects with excellent fantasy capacity and the amnesic-prone as also good hypnotic subjects but with amnesia for hypnosis and general proneness to forgetting (Wilson & Barber, 1983). Recently, Barber (2000) has further broken down the fantasy-prone into the following three subtypes: the sex fantasizers—these individuals engage in romantic and sexual fantasies; escape fantasizers—use fantasies to escape from isolation, loneliness, and unstable living conditions; encouraged fantasizers—these individuals were encouraged to fantasize as children. Finally, about 75 percent of the fantasy-prone individuals are sex fantasizers. The positively-set are not hypnotic virtuosos like the fantasy-prone and amnesic-prone, but they have a positive attitude toward hypnosis and tend to respond to the social psychological aspects of hypnosis. Several researchers have described this type of subject (Spanos, 1991; Kirsch, 1991; Wagstaff, 1991; Sarbin, 1998; 1999; Coe & Sarbin, 1991; Lynn & Rhue, 1991). Interestingly, the positively-set clients tend not to report that hypnosis is an altered state of consciousness like the amnesic-prone clients (Connery, 1982).

Kirsch and Lynn (1999) have proposed a response set theory of hypnosis that has become popular within the area of the nonstate view of hypnosis. As this writer alluded to in Chapter 1, Kirsch and Lynn have a new sociocognitive therapy of hypnotic automaticity. Response set theory states at the moment of activation all behavior is automatic and that automaticity is the result of a client's response expectancies. One assumption of this theory is that clients prevent hypnosis from occurring as voluntary acts, as a result clients experience hypnosis as automatic (Kirsch, Burgess, & Braffman, 1999; Kirsch & Council, 1992; Kirsch & Lynn, 1995; Kirsch, Montgomery, & Sapirstein, 1995).

However, hypnosis is far more complex than Kirsch and Lynn's position (Sheehan & McConkey, 1982). In fact, one would not expect clients with inattention disorders to be very responsive to hypnosis; nevertheless, Barabasz and Barabasz (1996) and James Kirsch and Sapp (2000) found that clients with attention deficit hyperactivity disorder were extremely hypnotizable. Apparently attentional resources may be needed for some hypnotically suggested effect but not for others, and Bartis and Zamansky (1990) found that clients could respond to hypnotic suggestions when they visualized conflicting scenes (Pekala, Kumar, & Marcano, 1995). This would indicate that Kirsch and Lynn are incorrect with their theory that clients always use imagery or visualizations to produce hypnosis. Moreover, the evidence suggests that clients can experience hypnosis with and without mental imagery. Apparently, there are aspects of hypnosis that do not depend on just cognitive abilities and expectations (Shor, 1959). In addition, Barber (1999, 2000) provided evidence that supports the state or trance view of hypnosis for the amnesic-prone, and the nonstate or sociocognitive theories he believes describe hypnosis for the positively-set clients. In conclusion, Barber believes that the tension that exists between the state and nonstate theories is due to the fact that neither group has seen the amnesic-prone clients and positively-set clients simultaneously, and neither group has seen the fantasy-prone clients (Rhue, Lynn, & Kirsch, 1993; King & Council, 1998; Hammond, 1992; Hilgard, 1973, 1994).

What is absent from Barber's new paradigm is the connection between hypnosis and the brain. Barabasz et al. (1999) found that participants with high hypnotic abilities showed greater cortical hallucinations—suggestions to experience competing stimuli instead of the presented ones. Nevertheless, low hypnotizable individuals did not show amplitudes in cortical event-related potential when experiencing negative hallucinations. These researchers concluded that now it is possible to distinguish hypnotic conditions from normal waking states of consciousness using physiological markers (Ray & Oathes, 2003). Other researchers have presented an explicit relationship between hypnosis and the brain (Balthazard & Woody, 1989; Woody & Bowers, 1994). In addition, Woody and Bowers found that rountinized hypnotic responding is correlated with response expectancies, but difficult hypnotic responding has little to do with response expectancies. Clearly, there is an overlap in brain functioning and hypnosis, and many new brain imaging techniques will show more specific connection between the brain and hypnosis (Barabasz, Barabasz, Jensen, Calvin, Trevisan, & Warner, 1999; Raz & Shapiro, 2002; Laurence & Perry, 1983).

Finally, hypnosis has features that include, but are not limited to, automaticity, dissociation, absorption, suggestibility, fantasy-proneness, amnesic-proneness, response expectancies, and alterations in consciousness (Tellegen & Atkinson, 1974). In conclusion, hypnosis is a complex phenomenon that will take the complex synthesis of several areas to continue to shed more light on this elusive construct (Crasilneck & Hall, 1985; Woody & Farvolden, 1998).

HYPNOSIS AS ADAPTIVE REGRESSION

Edwards and Sapp (2002) and Nash (1987) presented evidence that hypnosis can be viewed as a form of adaptive regression. The notion of adaptive regression stems from the psychoanalytic theory that held that hypnosis elicits a regressive shift from secondary to primary process thinking. This process is produced by relaxation of ego control and a shift toward unconscious thinking. This theory of viewing hypnosis, which is called topographical regression, is based on a reversal or change in thinking from reality based to nonreality based. Adaptive regression is using hypnotic regression as a healing process for psychological disorders (Shor 1959). Edwards and Sapp used a nonrandomized, two-group, pretest post-test design to see if a regression hypnotic transcript would produce greater reduction in conflict responses than a relaxation transcript, and they found that hypnotic regression produced greater changes in conflict responses than hypnotic relaxation (Edmonston, 1981).

These researchers believed that this was the first study to show that hypnosis can produce adaptive regression (Orne, 1959, 1979). This study showed that one form of hypnosis is psychological regression; however, this notion is similar to dissociation theories of hypnosis in that participants produce changes in conscious experiences. In addition, relaxation is another process that can produce hypnosis and a change and shift from conscious to unconscious experiencing. In essence, there are many forms of hypnosis, and this study suggests that there are many features of hypnosis such as regression, relaxation, dissociation, and so on (Zeig, 1980). Moreover, this study offers support for Barber's new multidimensional theory in that it found that there is a variety of forms of hypnosis. Finally, this study suggested that hypnosis is a multivariate construct that has many features (Erickson, 1944, 1958, 1967; Erickson & Rossi, 1979; Erickson, 1980; Crawford, Kendel, & Vendemia, 1998).

COGNITIVE-BEHAVIORAL HYPNOSIS (CBH)

Cognitive-behavioral hypnosis (CBH) is a term for combining hypnosis with cognitive-behavioral strategies. One assumption of this approach is that psychological problems are the result of negative self-hypnosis (Arazoz, 1985; Spanos, 1986; Spanos & Chaves, 1989). This is similar to the principles emphasized by Ellis (1993), who stated that emotional disturbances are the result of irrational thinking. The CBH approach is a nonstate theoretical approach (Sapp, Farrell, Johnson, Kirby, & Pumphrey, 1997; Coe & Sarbin, 1991). The transcript that follows is a CBH one.

CBH TRANSCRIPT

Get into a relaxed position, close your eyes, and I will show you how to elicit cognitive-behavioral hypnosis within yourself. First, I would just like you to relax. You can relax by just thinking about relaxation. Use your thoughts to relax your mind, which in turn will relax your body. Learning to use cognitive-behavioral hypnosis involves controlling your thinking and attention. Thoughts are the things we say to ourselves. Thinking or using your mind is the first step toward change.

We can talk more about thinking. Many of our thoughts are based on the way we think about social situations. Often, social situations such as public speaking and so on do not produce anxiety, but it is the way we look or think about social situations that produces anxiety and fear. For example, some students who have difficulty in school will tell themselves that negative things are going to happen, that they are not good, and the result is negative emotions. If you can get rid of self-defeating thoughts, all the musts, and other derivatives, you will be better off. You will be even better off if you can replace self-defeating thoughts with realistic ones.

Now let's proceed with cognitive-behavioral hypnosis. If the phone rings or if someone comes to the door, I will take care of it. The important thing for you is just relaxing. If you think about relaxation, your body will feel relaxed. And to help you, I will count from ten to one. As the numbers are going down, your level of relaxation will increase. 10 . . . 9 . . . 8 . . . 7 . . . 6 . . . 5 . . . 4 . . . 3 . . . 2 . . . 1.

Cognitive-behavioral hypnosis involves cognitively imagining a scene. In your mind's eye, imagine a very relaxing scene. You can choose a scene that is indoors or outdoors. Take your time and visualize every aspect of that scene.

See it as clearly as possible. Notice the time of day or night. Yes, cognitive-behavioral hypnosis uses your imagination to produce changes in your inner experiences. Really let your imagination get you into this scene. When I say the word "now," you will count to yourself from one to ten. When you say the number ten, you will come out of cognitive-behavioral hypnosis feeling relaxed, refreshed, and confident in your ability to use cognitive-behavioral hypnosis.

Debriefing

Have the client describe his or her experience and make adjustments in the script based on the client's comments.

THERAPEUTIC PROCESS

Therapeutic Goals

One goal of behavioral therapy is for the client to learn new ways of behaving. Interpersonal concerns are conceptualized in behaviorally terms such as antecedents, contingencies, consequences, reinforcement, and so. Essentially, the therapeutic process parallels the scientific method. Once a client's concerns are put into behavioral terms and a case history has been obtained, the client and therapist select treatments and determine ways of monitoring progress. Throughout the therapeutic process, modifications are made due to individual differences within a client, and finally, the therapist discusses with the client ways of continuing to implement treatment using self-control procedures.

Role of Therapist

Even though behavior therapists use Levels I and II counseling skills to establish a counseling relationship, after a relationship is established, mainly Level III counseling skills are used. In addition, the therapist uses himself or herself as a model, and he or she models adaptive responses for the client. One important point that is sometimes misunderstood by professionals with a superficial understanding of behavior therapy is that the client determines which behavior to change and the therapist shows the client how to change the behavior. The relationship between client and therapist is collaborative. Finally, even though there is structure within behavior therapy, it does not have to be employed in a robotic fashion and the therapist-client relationship is important.

Therapeutic Relationship

Most behavioral therapists admit that the therapeutic relationship is important—except for Albert Ellis. Unlike the theorization of psychodynamic theorists, clients tend not to develop symptom substitution (Kazdin & Wilson, 1978; Sloane, Staples, Cristol, Yorkston, & Whippler, 1975). Moreover, as opposed to seeing behavioral therapy as treating symptoms, behavioral therapists see themselves as changing maladaptive behavioral, and, as mentioned earlier, concepts are used to negotiate behavioral changes and to strengthen the therapeutic relationship.

Multicultural Applications and Limitations

Unlike psychoanalysis that requires insight, behavioral therapies focus on behavioral changes and have applications to many cultural groups who may want changes in maladaptive behavior and not deep insight. For cultural groups wanting deep emotional and psychological understanding, they may find behavioral therapies limiting in that they can be viewed as simple in that they deal with overt behavior and do not address the historical roots of maladaptive behavior. In addition, due to the fact that behavior therapies have large effect sizes, the potential for harm increases with the large effect sizes; however, understanding the potential for early therapy termination, multiculturally skillful therapists can make adjustment to minimize the potential of harm.

Critique

COMPREHENSIVENESS. In comparison to psychoanalysis and psychodynamic therapies, behavior therapies are not comprehensive. Moreover, paradigms of behavior therapy do not address nonconscious factors that underlie behavior. Possibly, only social learning theories approximate comprehensive theories of behaviorism. Finally, behavior therapies are not comprehensive systems of psychotherapy.

PARSIMONY. Modern behavior theories are not parsimonious because there are hundreds of techniques. Moreover, some of the modern behavioral theories are far more complex than the early stimulus and response theories of the 1950s and 1960s. For example, the automaticity theories are quite complex and they offer some links of behavior with the brain.

EMPIRICAL VALIDITY. In terms of the treatment of anxiety, depression, weight reduction, sexual dysfunction and many other disorders, behavior therapy has very high empirical validity. Unlike some psychoanalytic, Adlerian, and humanistic therapists, behavioral therapists encourage research and the testing of hypotheses.

PRECISION AND TESTABILITY. Since empirical validity is extremely good with behavior therapy, precision and testability are also good. In addition, with EMDR and EMT, behavior therapy has two new techniques for the treatment of PTSD and traumas and this research has strengthened the forces of behavior therapy within psychology (Parrot & Howes, 1991). In addition, cognitive-behavioral therapies are the strongest paradigms within counseling and clinical psychology.

APPLIED VALUE. Behavior therapy has applications that have not actually been realized. For example, it has applications within medicine for pain reduction, the control of bleeding, the treatment of burns, and the prevention of cardiovascular disease which are relatively unexplored areas. Moreover, in terms of general public health, behavior therapy is a good approach to use for educating the public about mental and physical health. Finally, behavior therapy has been used to treat groups, families, and couples (Abram, 1983; Bauer, Sapp, & Johnson, 2000; Farrell, Sapp, Johnson, & Pollard, 1994; Sapp & Hitchcock, 2003b).

SUMMARY

Unlike the naive notion of some therapists and theorists, behavioral therapies are collections of techniques and are not a unitary approach. In addition, techniques like relaxation therapy, guided imagery, hypnosis, reinforcement, covert sensitization, EMDR, and EMT are all behavioral techniques. Behavioral therapy is the strongest paradigm within psychology. And during the 1950s, behavioral therapy developed into a systematic assessment and treatment for psychological disorders. The Association for the Advancement of Behavior Therapy (AABT), the largest behavioral therapy organization, continues to spearhead changes within behavior theory and practice. As previously stated, behavior therapy has large effect sizes and AABT tends to encourage research. Finally, this writer believes that behavioral therapy will continue to be the leader for empirical treatment strategies (Sapp, 1997a, 1997b, 1997c, 1997d; Sapp, Durand, & Farrell, 1995; Sapp, Farrell, & Durand, 1995a, 1995b; Sapp & Evanow, 1998; Sapp, Hitchcock, & Johnson, 1999; Sapp,

Ioannidis, & Farrell, 1995; Sapp, Farrell, Johnson, & Ioannidis, 1997; Sapp, 1990; 1991, 1992a, 1992b, 1993, 1994, 1995; Sapp, 2000a, 2000b; Smith, Sapp, Farrell, & Johnson, 1998; Piccone, Hilgard, & Zimbardo, 1989; Farrell, Sapp, Johnson, & Pollard, 1994; Fairburn, Jones, Peveler, Hope, & Doll, 1991; Munuchin, 1974).

Glossary of Key Terms

Adaptive regression. A theory of hypnosis that states hypnosis is the result of adaptive regression. This is a psychoanalytic theory of regression.

Applied behavioral analysis. An instrumental conditioning theory that emphasizes the relationship between behavior and the environment and that behavior can be controlled by the environment.

Assertion training. A set of procedures that teaches clients appropriate social skills that involve behavioral rehearsal and coping skills.

Automaticity. A theory that states at the point of initiation all behavior is automatic.

BASIC-ID. Arnold Lazarus' theory of multimodal therapy that assesses personality through seven interacting modalities: behavior, affect, sensations, images, cognitions, interpersonal relationships, and drugs/physiological bases of behavior.

Behavioral rehearsal. A technique where clients role play new behavior during therapy. It is hoped that this will help with generalizing the new behaviors in actual situations.

Biofeedback. The use of technology and other means to provide clients with feedback of physiological processes.

Classical conditioning. A learning theory based on how reflexes are an integral part of learning and popularized by the work of Pavlov.

Cognitive-behavioral therapy. A theory that blends cognitive psychology and behavioral psychology. The goal is to show clients how thoughts affect behavior.

Counterconditioning. The opposite of learning in which a learned stimulus loses its capacity to bring about a learned response.

Covert desensitization. An imagery based theory that using aversive stimuli.

Extinction. The presentation of a stimulus without a response which can be viewed as a form of satiation.

Eye movement desensitization-reprocessing (EMDR). A desensitization technique created by psychologist Francine Shapiro to treat traumas. Part of this therapy involves clients visually tracking the fingers of therapists.

Eye movement technique (EMT). An alternative to EMDR that was developed by psychologist Larry Smyth based on traditional cognitive-behavioral strategies and self-control.

Fading. The slow withdrawal of behavioral prompts during the learning process.

Flooding. An imagery based technique that is used to extinguish undesirable behavior.

Guided imagery. The process of presenting imagery scenes to clients during therapy.

Hypnosis. A process where suggestions are given to a client where the results are psycho-physiological changes.

Implosive therapy. An imagination technique that is similar to flooding but uses psychodynamic based imagery.

Modeling. A process of demonstrating new behaviors to clients so they learn parts of the behaviors through observing.

Negative reinforcement. The removal of a negative consequence after performing a certain behavior. Like all forms of reinforcement, behavior increases and not decreases in contrast to punishment that suppresses behavior.

Operant conditioning. Instrument learning or learning through operating on the environment.

Positive reinforcement. The applications of positive stimuli followed by a behavioral response such as money, candy, tokens and so on.

Premack principle. Connecting low-frequency behaviors with high-frequency behaviors to increase low-frequency behaviors.

Progressive relaxation. Edmund Jacobson developed this muscle tension process that is often used with systematic desensitization. In addition, imagery based techniques can also produce relaxation.

Prompting. The use of prompts or cues to modify behavior.

Punishment. The application of aversive stimuli following behavior. The goal is to decrease or suppress behavior.

Radical behaviorism. A radical departure from neobehaviorism and popularized by Skinner who believed that behaviorism was just simply the relationship between behavior and environmental events and evolution. Skinner did not believe in giving primacy to cognitions, affect, brain science, or social psychological factors.

Reciprocal inhibitions. This is Wolpe's theory of why systematic desensitization works, and it states that two incompatible responses such as relaxation and tension, cannot happen at the same time.

Response cost. A form of punishment where there are penalties following undesirable behaviors.

Self-control. These are techniques that a client can implement himself or herself.

Self-monitoring. A form of self-control where the client charts or monitors his or her behavior.

Sensate focus. A strategy for reducing the anxiety connected with sexual intimacy.

Shaping. The use of prompts or cues to teach new behavior. Eventually the prompts are slowly faded through the method of successive approximation.

Social learning theory. A group of social-cognitive-behavioral theories that state the client, situation, and social context all interact together to influence behavior.

Stress inoculation training. Donald Meichenbaum developed this cognitive-behavioral technique to reduce stress through a process of cognitive inoculation.

Subjective units of distress scale (SUDS). A scale used by clients to rate their levels of anxiety and is used in other therapies such as EMDR, EMT, and systematic desensitization.

Systematic desensitization. Joseph Wolpe developed this technique to treat anxiety related and other disorders. Essentially, it is the pairing of relaxation with anxiety-evoking imagery.

Thinning. The movement from continuous reinforcement to variable or intermittent reinforcement.

Token economy. A structured environment in which tokens are used as positive reinforcers, and the tokens are traded for secondary reinforcers such as toys, food, and so on.

Review Questions

1. Describe five forms of behavior therapy.
2. Describe Barber's multi-dimensional theory of hypnosis.
3. Compare and contrast Watson's and Skinner's theories of behaviorism.
4. What is the mediational notion of neobehaviorism?
5. What is dialectical behavior therapy?
6. What is the importance of viewing hypnosis as adaptive regression?

Behavior Associations

American Association for the Advancement of Behavior Therapy
This is the largest behavior therapy association and it publishes a newsletter called *The Behavior Therapist* and has two journals, *Behavior Therapy* and *Cognitive and Behavioral Practice*.

The website is as follows: http://www.aabt.org/
The address, telephone number and fax number are the following:
305 Seventh Avenue, 16th Floor, New York, NY, 10001-60008
Telephone: 212–647–1890
Fax: 212–647–1865

Association for Behavioral Analysis
The website is the following: http://www.abainternational.org/
The address, telephone number and fax number are the following:
1219 South Park Street, Kalamazoo, MI 49001
Telephone: 269–492–9310
Fax: 269–492–9316.
Email: mail@abainternational.org.

Chapter 5

FAMILY OF SOCIAL LEARNING THEORIES

CHAPTER OVERVIEW

As stated in Chapters 1 and 4, social learning theories are sociocognitive or social-cognitive-behavioral approaches to psychotherapy. And as stated in previous chapters, these approaches influenced the work of Kirsch and Lynn and how they developed their notions of hypnosis and automaticity of responding. It can be said that social learning theories integrate cognitive-behavioral theories and social psychological theories, and the client is seen as an actor who is influenced by the interaction of interpersonal, behavioral, cognitive, environmental, and social determinants. Unlike the simplistic notions of many undergraduate psychology and personality theories presentations, these approaches involve more than just observation; rather they involve the complex interaction of the client, his or her social environment, the social context, and the client's cognitions and behaviors along with any environmental and social determinants.

MILLER AND DOLLARD'S SOCIAL LEARNING THEORY

Neal Miller (1909–2002) and John Dollard (1900–1980) were the first theorists to use the term social learning theory (Miller & Dollard, 1941). Neal Miller was born in Milwaukee, Wisconsin, and after obtaining his Ph.D. from Yale in 1935, he completed a social science research fellowship at the Institute of Psychoanalysis in Vienna, but he abandoned Freud's notions and concentrated on brain and behavior research. In addition, Miller pioneered work on biofeedback and psychological methods for treating medical problems. During World War II, he showed how through conditioning experiments, rats could control heart rate, blood pressure, and brain waves. Until that time, it was assumed that functions like heart rate and blood pressure were under the control of the automatic nervous system and could not be controlled through conscious means. Finally, Miller was regarded as a leading expert for over forty years on animal learning abilities.

Dollard and Miller broadened Clark Hull's learning theory by adding a social learning and social cognitive perspective. Hull believed that learning was the result of four events: drive, cue, response, and reinforcement. Readers may remember from introductory psychology that there are two types of drives—primary and secondary. Primary drives are biological drives like food, water, and so on. In contrast, secondary drives are associated with primary drives. In addition, cues are the stimuli that dictate when, where, and how clients respond to drives. Social models help determine how cues are interpreted. For example, at a formal dinner, one may not know which spoon or knife to use, but by observing others at the table, it is possible to interpret the social cues and choose the appropriate eating utensils (Miller & Dollard, 1941).

Dollard and Miller assumed that social learning occurred through trial-and-error and, according to Liebert and Spiegler (1990), stated that this is the major weakness of their theory because Liebert and Spiegler believed that humans could learn by one trial by simply observing others, provided that the humans have the repertoire of skills necessary to perform the behavior modeled. Finally, Dollard and Miller believed that reinforcement involved drive reduction, and their notion of drive reduction has the same meaning that Freud used. This was their attempt to combine psychoanalytic theory with behavioral theory. In closing, even though there are few studies based on Dollard and Miller's theory, it has served as the basis for other social theories such as those of Rotter (1954) and Bandura (1982).

ROTTER'S SOCIAL LEARNING THEORY

Julian B. Rotter (1916–   ), following World War II, spent several years at Ohio State University where George Kelly was the director of the clinical psychology program (Schultz & Schultz, 2001). Rotter believed that people learned through social experiments, and he is credited as the second person to use the term social learning theory in his book *Social Learning and Clinical Psychology*. Rotter was in disagreement with Skinner's idiographic approach and Skinner's lack of emphasis on social learning experiences. In addition, unlike Skinner, Rotter addressed cognitive influences of behavior. Rotter tried to integrate reinforcement theory and cognitive theory, and his theory has more of a cognitive emphasis than Bandura's social learning theory. Through

Rotter's perspective, personality is the interaction of a client and his or her environment, and as previously stated, he influenced the view of Kirsch and Lynn. In summary, unlike Dollard and Miller and more so than Bandura, Rotter emphasized cognitive constructs within his theory.

Rotter has four basic components or constructs within his theory and they are the following: behavior potential, reinforcements value, expectancy, and psychological situation.

Behavior potential is the chance or probability that, due to reinforcement, behaviors will occur in a set of situations. Clearly, cognitive variables such as interpretations will determine responding. **Reinforcement value** is a client's subjective preference for one reinforcer over another, while **expectancy** is the client's belief that certain behaviors will result in certain reinforcers (Rotter, 1954, 1966, 1967, 1980, 1982, 1990, 1993). There are two kinds of expectancies: specific and generalized. **Specific expectancies** are a client's expectations in a certain situation; in contrast, **generalized expectancies** are a client's expectations in a variety of situations with general expectancies, responses made in one situation will also occur in similar situations. **Psychological situation** is the combination of internal and external factors that influence clients' perceptions and responses to stimuli (Schultz & Schultz, 2001). In essence, psychological situation has to be defined within the perspective of the client, and the reinforcement value assigned to a situation depends on a client's expectation about that situation. To summarize, behavioral potential is a function of clients' expectancies and reinforcements value, and the way clients respond depends to the social context.

LOCUS OF CONTROL

Locus of control is a generalized expectancy and is probably Rotter's most important concept; it is how a client generally perceives the sources of his or her outcomes. In other words, what is a client belief about the source of his or her reinforcement, and locus of control is very similar to Bandura's concept of self-efficiency and Seligman's notion of learned helpless. When a client believes that reinforcements and punishments are the result of his or her abilities, he or she has an **internal locus of control** orientation; in contrast, external locus of control, which has two subtypes, means a client's reinforcements and punishments are believed to be the consequence of outside influences. **Congruent external locus of control** individuals fit the stereotypical model of individuals who believe that their outcomes are not under their control. Defensive external control individuals are not consistent with their beliefs. For example, these individuals take credit for positive aspects of their lives and they blame the others and the world when negative things occurred within their lives.

There are multicultural differences in terms of locus of control. For example, there are racial and socioeconomical differences in locus of control. Heckhausen and Schulz (1995) found that more college students had internal rather than external orientations. Okeke, Draguns, Skebu, and Allen (1999) found individuals from lower socioeconomic classes and minority groups had greater amounts of external locus of control. Moreover, African American and Black African children tend to score higher on external locus of control than European American children. In addition, Hispanic American and Native American teenagers tend to be more externally controlled than European American teenagers (Maqsud & Rouhani, 1991). Uba (1994) found that Asians tend to be more externally focused than Americans, which is due to Asians' cultural beliefs. In contrast to American culture that is based on individualism and self-reliance, Asians tend to come from communities that are based on interdependence and are collectively focused. Interestingly, the more contact Asians tend to have with Americans, the more internally focused they tend to become.

Marshall (1991) reported a connection between physical health and locus of control. Internal-oriented people tend to pay more attention to their health and they tend to be healthier than people with an external locus of control orientation. When people with an internal locus of control orientation get ill, they tend to have a belief that they can overcome and cope with their illness and they tend to cooperate with health professionals more than people with an external locus of control orientation.

Rotter (1966, 1971, 1982) developed a self-report questionnaire called the Internal (**I**)–External (**E**) locus of control scale. The I–E Scale contains twenty-nine forced-choice items, and twenty-three of these items measure locus of control and six items are used to obscure the nature of the scale.

INTERPERSONAL TRUST

Interpersonal trust is possibly Rotter's second most important concept, and it, like locus of control, is a generalized expectancy, and it is the degree to which the world, promise, or statement of another individual can be relied upon. More specifically, Rotter defined interpersonal trust as a generalized expectation held by an individual or group that the word, promise, verbal or written statement of another individual or group can be trusted or relied upon (Rotter, 1967, 1971), and he developed a forty-item self-report inventory to measure interpersonal trust; twenty-five of the items measure interpersonal trust and fifteen are filler or distracter items.

Individuals with religious affiliations tend to show more interpersonal trust than do individuals without religious affiliation. Higher socioeconomic status is correlated with interpersonal trust, and individuals with higher levels of interpersonal trust are more likely to be trustful and treat others fairly. Within families, children tend to adapt the interpersonal orientation of their parents and Rotter explained this through the fact that parents tend to model their style of interpersonal orientation. Finally, individuals high in interpersonal trust tend to be more popular and happier than individuals low in interpersonal trust. In closing, individuals high in levels of interpersonal trust tend not to be gullible and they mistrust information when situations dictate it.

BANDURA'S SOCIAL LEARNING THEORY

Albert Bandura started his career as a traditional behaviorist, and he developed his theory approximately a decade after Rotter's theory. Bandura quickly learned that classical and operant conditioned theories could not explain human learning within its complex forms, and he found that when someone possessed the required skills for certain behaviors, he or she could learn to extend a repertoire of skills by observing a model performing those behaviors. During the 1960s and 1970s, Bandura showed through several studies that humans can learn through modeling (Sapp, 1997a; Bandura, 1982, 1983, 1984, 1985, 1986, 2000).

It was not until the 1970s that Bandura extended his theory into a sociocognitive one, and he theorized about a process called **reciprocal determinism,** which is behavior determined by the complex interaction of personal, behavioral, and situational or contextual factors; this is also called triadic reciprocality, meaning that behavior, cognitive processes, and environmental variables interact. Another aspect of Bandura's theory is the concept of self-efficacy or a client's perception that he or she can successfully perform certain behaviors to produce desired outcomes (Sapp, 1999). Zimmerman (1995) found a significant positive relationship between self-efficacy and academic performance. Teachers with high degrees of self-efficacy tend to promote higher self-efficacy within students. Students with higher levels of self-efficacy tend to be less anxious, have higher degrees of motivation than students with low degrees of self-efficacy, and tend to be persistent during classroom situations. Hackett (1995) found gender differences in self-efficacy and career choice, and the research found that men perceived themselves higher in self-efficacy for both traditional male and traditional female career choices, but women perceived themselves higher in self-efficacy for only female careers but lower in self-efficacy for traditional male careers. Finally, increasingly vocational psychologists are employing self-efficacy as an important concept that is related to performance and career choice.

In terms of observational learning, for it to be useful in psychotherapy, three phases are necessary: exposure, acquisition, and acceptance.

Exposure is exposing a client to a model who models certain behaviors. For exposure to be effective, the client must pay attention to the model and recall the model's behavior, which is called **acquisition.** Finally, **acceptance** is where a client uses those behaviors that were modeled. As Sapp (1997a) stated, if one views observational learning as imitation, phases one and two are necessary—but not sufficient—to bring about imitation, because for imitation to occur, the client must accept the therapist or model as a model. In closing, Bandura found that children model many behaviors such as violence from television.

THERAPEUTIC PROCESS

Therapeutic Goals

The goals of special learning theories are to create new learning experience for clients. For example, a therapist can teach certain behaviors to clients. In addition, social learning theorists believe that many specific phobias and fears are due to social influences and not due to the direct exposure to negative events. The process of modeling is a social-cognitive vicarious form of learning that is not based on the traditional behavioral notion of trial-and-error learning. Moreover, the therapist can teach clients a variety of social skills such as assertion training, appropriate social interactions, appropriate communication styles, and ways of coping with stress. Finally, like other behavioral theories, social learning theorists assess and treat simultaneously and the client and therapist must agree on the goals of psychotherapy.

Role of Therapist

Social learning psychotherapists function as role models and they portray self-enhancing and prosocial behaviors, and even though Levels I and II counseling skills are employed, these therapists tend to use Level III or action strategies.

Therapeutic Relationship

Generally, the relationship between client and therapist is collaborative, but unlike some humanistic therapists such as person-centered, social learning psychotherapies use psycho-educational strategies and employ behavioral interventions. In closing, unlike nondirective therapists, social learning therapists are active and directive and they model a variety of behaviors for their clients.

Multicultural Applications and Limitations

For socially oriented minority groups like American Indians, Asians, Hispanics, and African Americans, social learning theories have many applications. The difficulties of using social learning theories with minority groups are skills levels. Because each cultural group is different, an understanding of a specific minority group is important and also knowing when to employ a strategy can also be complicated. Another difficulty with social learning theories is loosing the individual clients within the social context, and from a social context it becomes easy to blame social forces—systems, media, and others than to take personal responsibility for things that can be changed. Even though this writer values social learning theories, these theories have to be tempered by stressing the importance of hard work and personal responsibility with cultural groups.

Critique

COMPREHENSIVENESS. Social learning theories can help explain complex human learning and they have applications to the treatment of anxiety disorders, sexual disorders, and so on. Rotter's and Bandura's theories are more comprehensive than the theory of Dollard and Miller. In addition, possibly Bandura's theory is the most compressive since it describes the developmental process of modeling. Finally, as a whole, social learning theories are probably the most comprehensive behavioral theories.

PARSIMONY. Because the family of social learning theories is based on a relatively small number of concepts, they are parsimonious, but Dollard and Miller's theory is the most parsimonious. Due to the nature of these theories, researchers can conduct investigations of the impact of sociocognitive influences on behavior.

EMPIRICAL VALIDITY. Both Bandura and Rotter have theories with excellent empirical validity. For example, many clinical studies have shown the importance and influence of models on behavior. In addition, there is an abundance of research on locus of control, interpersonal trust, and several other concepts from Rotter's theory. Bandura's theory has had a strong impact within the area of vocational psychology and issues of self-efficacy and career choice. In summary, both Rotter's and Bandura's theories have excellent empirical validity.

PRECISION AND TESTABILITY. The concepts of both Rotter and Bandura have been operationally defined and researched in detail. For example, self-efficacy, locus of control, interpersonal trust, and response expectancies have been defined and tested.

HEURISTIC VALUE. Social learning theories have excellent heuristic value and have stimulated research in vocational psychology, counseling psychology, personality theory and research, sociology, social work, developmental psychology, and social psychology.

APPLIED VALUE. Bandura's and Rotter's theories have excellent applied value. Bandura's work has implications for the government and policy makers. In addition, Rotter's work has demonstrated that therapies that are consistent with a client's personality orientation—internal or external control—are more beneficial than therapies that are incongruent or inconsistent with a client's response expectancies.

SUMMARY

Social learning theories are possibly the most comprehensive theories and they combine aspects from cognitive psychology, behavioral psychology, applied behavioral analysis, social psychology, and neobehaviorism.

Glossary of Key Terms

Behavioral potential. The possibility that a certain behavior will occur in a given situation.

Expectancy. A client's response expectancies that the probability of behavior will result in certain behaviors.

Generalized expectancies. Response expectancies that have applications across various situations.

Interpersonal trust. A generalized response expectancy in which the word of another can be trusted or relied on.

Locus of control. A generalized response expectancy in which a client perceives the sources of his or her outcomes.

Observational learning. The process of counseling in which a client changes by observing a therapist model certain behaviors.

Reciprocal determinism. A reciprocal triad theory, which states that behavioral, personal, and situational factors interact simultaneously.

Reinforcement value. A client's desire for one reinforcer over another.

Self-efficacy. A client's belief that he or she can perform certain behaviors and produce desired outcomes.

Review Questions

1. From a counseling psychology vantage point, what is the importance of self-efficacy, locus of control, and interpersonal trust?
2. The media often portrays the roles of minority groups and women in certain ways, but these images from the media may not reflect reality. What are the social implications of misrepresenting women and minorities within the media?
3. Describe the process of modeling?
4. Describe how the media tends to moderate violence and stereotyping of minorities. Provide several examples of such stereotypes.

Chapter 6

RATIONAL-EMOTIVE BEHAVIOR THERAPY

CHAPTER OVERVIEW

Rational Emotive Behavior Therapy (REBT) is an emotion, cognitive, and behavioral form of psychotherapy. It is humanistic-existential and cognitive-behavioral, and like other Level III theories, it is active and direct; however, unlike some Level III therapies, its goal is to change clients' irrational philosophies about life. Finally, Albert Ellis, the founder of REBT, was one of the pioneers of cognitive-behavioral therapies (Ellis, 1962, 1973, 1977, 1985, 1989, 1992a, 1992b, 1993, 1994a, 1994b, 1995, 2003).

HISTORICAL DEVELOPMENTS OF REBT

Albert Ellis founded REBT in 1955 when he was working as a clinical psychologist in New York. In New York, Ellis gained a reputation as an expert on sex therapy and marital therapy. Like many clinical psychologists of his era, Ellis was trained as a psychoanalyst and found that psychoanalysis was not effective and efficient and he started experimenting with a variety of forms of psychoanalysis and eclectic-analytic therapies.

During the 1950s, Ellis started studying philosophy in a search for a more effective and efficient form of psychotherapy, and he was influenced by the Greek and Roman stoic philosophers, Epicurus, Epictetus, and Marcus Aurelius. These philosophers emphasized the **primary view of psychological disturbances.** This view deemphasized the role of the past, and it stated that people were not so much disturbed by events as they were about their beliefs about events (Ellis & Dryden, 1997; Ellis & Dryden, 1990; Ellis & Velten, 1992).

Ellis learned from the stoic philosophers that humans have and develop hypotheses about events. For example, humans have and develop hypotheses about good, evil, fairness, injustice, and so on. Even though Ellis is accused of being antireligious, his beliefs are not at variance with religion, but he teaches self-acceptance and he is against any form of human rating (Dryden, 1987; Ellis, 1985; Ellis & Dryden, 1991; DiGiuseppe, 1990; Dryden & DiGiuseppe, 1990). In reality, Ellis is an **ethical humanist** and he opposes the deification and devilification of humans. Finally, Ellis was also influenced by the semanticist Korzyski, who emphasized the impact that language has on thinking and emotions (Ellis & Dryden, 1991; Ellis & Grieger, 1986; Ellis & Bernard, 1985; Frankl, 1983; May, 1983; Yalom, 1980).

MAJOR PSYCHOLOGICAL INFLUENCES

Ellis received his training as an analyst through the Karen Horney School, and Horney's concept of the "tyranny of the shoulds" influenced his emphasis on the importance of dogmatic and absolutistic thinking on the creation and maintenance of psychological problems (Ellis & Dryden, 1997).

Adler also influenced Ellis by emphasizing inferiority feelings, goals, purposes, values, and meanings that clients give to experiences. Ellis found that inferiority feelings lead to self-rating and ego-anxiety. Moreover, REBT is similar to Individual Psychology in that it is active directive and psychoeducational. In addition, another similarity of Adler and Ellis is the emphasis on social interests, the use of holistic and humanistic philosophies, and the use of cognitive-behavioral strategies (Ellis, Abrams, & Dengelegi, 1992).

Originally, REBT was called Rational Psychotherapy, and later Ellis called his approach Rational Emotive Therapy. Currently he calls his approach Rational Emotive Behavior Therapy (Ellis, 1994a, 1994b). Ellis points out that REBT has always endorsed behavioral, cognitive, and emotive methods. Actually, Maxie C. Maultsby, Jr. (1990, 1984) developed a form of REBT that he called **Rational Behavior Therapy** and used the term behavior before Ellis incorporated it into the name change.

KEY CONCEPTS

Rational emotive behavior therapy is based on six theoretical concepts: irrationality, rationality, hedonism, enlightened self-interest, humanism, and two biologically determined tendencies. **Irrationality** is beliefs that lead to self-defeating emotions and behaviors.

Ellis described the following thirteen irrational beliefs:

Ellis's Thirteen Irrational Beliefs

In his earlier writings, Ellis (1962) formulated thirteen irrational beliefs that lead to self-defeating emotions and behaviors.

1. **It is necessary to be loved and approved by significant others.** This is irrational because love and approval are not necessary for survival. They are desirable, but the ultimate thing is to accept oneself.
2. **It is necessary to be competent, adequate, and achieving 100 percent of the time in order to be worthwhile.** This belief suggests humans are perfect. Ellis suggests that no one is perfect. Also, the lack of perfectionism is not connected with human worth. Humans are worthwhile because they exist.
3. **When individuals act obnoxiously (bad, wicked, and villainous), we should blame them for their wrongdoing.** The idea that there is universal fairness or objectivity is irrational. Ellis separates an individual's behavior from his or her personhood. For example, if someone is behaving obnoxiously, it is the behavior that Ellis concentrates on—not the person.
4. **It is catastrophic and awful when things do not go the way I would like.** This is irrational because frustration is part of life, and it is not written that things have to go our way. Holding this illogical assumption can result in aggression and frustration.
5. **Unhappiness is the result of external events that are beyond my control.** Ellis believes in rectifying external events when one can; but if one cannot, it is either necessary to accept the external event or to psychologically stay distracted so there is minimal focus on the event.
6. **If certain things are dangerous and fearsome, the individual should constantly be preoccupied with them.** If something is truly dangerous, try to alleviate it; or accept that it exists, but do not exaggerate its meaning.
7. **It is easier to avoid facing difficult life situations than to face them.** If a difficulty exists, it is better to deal with it than to avoid it. Avoidant behavior does not change the situation; only action can change a difficult situation.
8. **Individuals should be dependent on others, and individuals need others—especially someone who is stronger to rely on.** This concept is irrational because it can lead to over reliance on others and a lack of independence.

9. **The past is the sole determinant of present behavior.** Assuming that the past totally determines present behavior prevents individuals from solving their problems.
10. **Individuals should worry, be upset, and be concerned about other people's concerns.** If an individual concentrates on another's concerns, he or she will not solve his or her concerns. Also, one person's concerns often have little to do with others' concerns.
11. **A correct or perfect solution exists for every problem, and it is terrible if such a solution is not found.** A problem often has several solutions. Searching for the perfect solution leads to anxiety and can result in poor solutions.
12. **The notion that human happiness can be achieved by inertia.** Humans are happiest when they are actively engaged in creative pursuits.
13. **One can have no control over emotions.** If one says rational sentences to oneself, it is possible to have enormous control over one's emotions.

Ellis and Grieger (1977) reduced these thirteen irrational beliefs to three major themes—condemnation of the self, condemnation of others, condemnation of the world.

Rationality has two goals—one to stay alive, and two to be happy. Unlike popular beliefs, rationality does not mean unemotional. Rational beliefs, behaviors, and emotions aid clients in achieving their goals and purposes. There is no absolute gold standard of rationality and therapists must assess it in their terms of clients' goals and purposes.

Hedonism is emphasized with REBT in that clients seek to stay alive and to achieve a certain amount of happiness; however, REBT encourages long-term hedonism, which is the pursuit of humanistically and personally meaningful goals and not goals based on the pleasures of the flesh, **short-term hedonism.**

Enlightened self-interest differs from selfishness in that selfishness is the pursuit of one's goals while disregarding the goals of others. In contrast, enlightened self-interest is a rational alternative to selfishness. And enlightened self-interest is putting oneself first the majority of the time while putting important others a close second. Long-term hedonism and enlightened self-interest are both based on Adler's concept of social interest. This notion emphasizes the complexity of determining whose needs to put first, and the decision depends on the social context (Dryden, 1987).

Humanism means REBT is neither totally objective nor scientific, and it subscribes to a humanistic-existential approach to human problems. Although REBT is very scientific and rational, it only uses rationality and the scientific method as aids for clients to live and to seek happiness.

REBT assumes that all humans have worth because they exist—even ones who perform antisocial acts. Like Bandura's concept of reciprocal determinism, REBT emphasizes the interaction of social structures, biological forces, free will, and choice. REBT tries to maximize human freedom and stresses; like Adler, insight gained through psychotherapy must get translated by the client into action in order for clients to get the maximum results from psychotherapy.

REBT hypothesizes that humans have two biologically-based tendencies. **First,** clients tend to think irrationally. **Second,** clients tend to work on changing irrational thinking, so there is a tendency for clients to think rationally and irrationally. To summarize, Ellis hypothesized that clients have a biological tendency to think both rationally and irrationally, he contended that clients can transcend, however not completely, irrationality.

TWO BASIC HUMAN DISTURBANCES

Ego disturbance and discomfort disturbance are two fundamental disturbances. **Ego disturbance** is when a client makes demands on the self, others, and the world. **Discomfort disturbance,** like ego disturbance, again is when the client makes absolutistic demands on the self, significant others, and the world, but these commands are connected to unrealistic demands that comfortable living conditions have to exist. When the client does not receive what he or she wants, he or she becomes disturbed (Hajzler & Bernard, 1991).

PSYCHOLOGICAL INTERACTIONISM

As previously stated, REBT is a cognitive, emotive, and behavioral approach to psychotherapy. REBT contends that clients' cognitions, emotions, and behaviors all interact simultaneously and they are overlapping processes. This process of simultaneous interaction is called **psychological interactionism.** Even though REBT subscribes to psychological interactionism, it tries to change clients' cognitions as a means of changing feelings and behaviors. Theoretically, changing behaviors should lead to a change in thoughts and feelings.

Three Psychological Insights

INSIGHT NO. 1: *Psychological problems are primarily caused and maintained by absolutistic irrational beliefs that people cling to concerning negative life events.* REBT hypothesizes that clients maintain their psychological problems by clinging to naïve theories concerning the nature of their problems, and they tend to have several distorted cognitive attributions. REBT teaches clients to change their irrational beliefs and to realize that negative situations only play a minor role in how one feels.

INSIGHT NO. 2: *Through constant reindoctrination with irrational beliefs, individuals maintain their disturbances in the present by seeking historical causes of their irrational beliefs.* Foolishly clients assume if they can find the causes of their problems by focusing on the past that they will get better; however, REBT contends that clients need to challenge and confront their irrational beliefs from a present orientation and not seek historical causes for their irrational beliefs, since philosophically there can be an infinite number of causes for a belief.

INSIGHT NO. 3: *It takes constant work and practice in the present and future toward changing irrational beliefs.* REBT does not contend that this form of psychotherapy is an easy cure, but clients must continue to work hard at changing their thoughts, behaviors, and feelings in order to be *minimally disturbed*.

EXPANDED ABCs OF REBT

Originally, Ellis conceptualized a simple ABC method to describe clients' concerns, and in his earlier schema theory, Ellis defined **A** as an **activating event, B** the **clients' belief systems** (rational and irrational) about **A,** and **C** clients' emotional and behavioral reactions or **consequences** for holding a given **B. Cs** can be both positive and negative emotional consequences.

Currently, Ellis defines **A** as events that block a client from attaining goals. **As** can be embedded memories or triggers from a client's past and they can be conscious and nonconscious, and **As** seldom exist in their pure states but tend to interact with **Bs** and **Cs**. This point underscores the REBT notion of psychological interactionism. Ellis stated that **Cs,** which can be cognitive, emotional, and behavioral consequences, are the result of **A** interacting with **B**. Mathematically, $C = A \times B$. In essence, **C** is the two-way interaction of **A** and **B**. Ellis makes the point that even though **C** is partially influenced by **A,** the major influence is due to **B**. Finally, the expanded **ABCs** of REBT is an interactionistic theory that states all three factors interact and one factor cannot exist without the other factors.

THE NATURE OF EMOTIONS

REBT teaches clients to define emotions as precisely as possible and it distinguishes between rational and irrational emotions. The following emotions are discussed within this section: **anxiety, shame, embarrassment, depression, guilt, anger, hurt, and irrational jealousy.**

Anxiety is the feeling that a client has that something threatening will occur and can present as ego anxiety and discomfort anxiety. When a client experiences anxiety, he or she may signal or tell himself or herself that something terrible "should not be happening to me, and terrible things should never happen to me, and finally, I cannot bear anxiety-producing events." A pattern of obsessive and compulsive avoidance can be part of anxiety. Avoidance tends to strengthen the anxiety response through learning and obsessive thoughts tend to lead clients to seek assurance that something anxious or threatening will not occur.

Concern is the rational alternative to anxiety. With concern, a client assumes that something threatening can occur, but he or she holds the following rational belief: "I do not like it when threatening things occur, but I can handle them." The client verbalizes and comes to believe that he or she can cope with unfortunate events, and unlike a client with anxiety, the concerned client tends to be assertive and tends not to withdraw.

Shame is the fear that someone will discover a personal flaw or weakness, and **embarrassment** results from inferences that clients draw from shame. The feelings tend not to be as severe as shame. The core underlying belief surrounding shame and embarrassment is that "Because I have a low opinion of myself and see myself as a piece of shit, others will have the same view."

Regret is the rational alternative to shame and embarrassment, and it involves the following lines: "I have revealed personal weaknesses and others may draw negative evaluations about my personal weaknesses, but I can accept myself as a person with personal weaknesses and there are no rules written that I should not have weaknesses. And I can accept myself as a person who can behave foolishly and can make mistakes."

Depression occurs when a client infers that he or she has experienced a major loss to his or her personhood such as contracting a chronic disease, death of loved ones, loss of relationships, loss of limbs, and so on. Depressed clients often withdraw and conclude their situations are hopeless, meaningless and they engage in self-destructive and defeating behaviors. Very similar to anxiety depression, there can be ego depression or the loss of self-worth and discomfort depression or the loss of personal comfort (Ellis & Dryden, 1997).

Sadness is the rational alternative to depression, and even though the client acknowledges that loss has occurred, he or she thinks along the following rational lines: "Even though I have experienced a loss, there is not any reason why this loss should not have happened. I feel sad about this loss, but I am not devastated and I will eventually not feel as sad."

Guilt happens when clients' personal codes or moral values are broken. The following irrational beliefs tend to underlie guilt: "I should not have done what I did. I should be punished and I am damnable and should be damned for being the terrible person that I am."

Remorse is the rational alternative to guilt, and it is more in line with sorrow and the client acknowledges the violation of his or her personal codes, but he or she believes the following rational beliefs: "I violated my personal code of ethics, and I do not like what I have done but I am a fallible human who has done a wrong thing; however, this does not make me damnable."

There are two kinds of **anger—damning** and **nondamning.** Damning anger occurs when a frustrating event blocks a client from reaching his or her goals. Damning anger can be directed toward the self, others, and the world. In addition, damning anger can happen when others transgress against one's personal rules or codes. Moreover, damning anger can be a form of self-defense when one's self-esteem is threatened. The irrational belief underlying anger is the following: "If anyone violates my rules, he or she must be damned." Often, clients will respond with damning behavioral responses by becoming physically aggressive or through verbal aggression. Also, withdrawal, another behavioral response, can be a response to damning anger, such as leaving quickly from a room during a verbal altercation.

Annoyance is the rational alternative to damning anger, and the rational beliefs underlying annoyance may be as follows: "You have violated my ethical and moral codes, but there are not any reasons why you should have not done so, and you acted badly since you are an imperfect human being."

HURT

When significant others treat clients unfairly often there is a feeling of **hurt.** The irrational cognition underlying this belief is that it is totally wrong to be treated unfairly by significant others.

Disappointment is the rational alternative to hurt. With disappointment, the client infers that he or she has been treated unfairly, but holds the following rational beliefs: "I would prefer to be treated fairly, but there is not any reason why I must get what I want." When a client endorses the rational alternative—disappointment—he or she becomes emotionally free to adopt a range of emotions such as remorse, annoyance, feelings of assertion, and so on.

IRRATIONAL JEALOUSY

Dryden (1987) stated that **irrational jealousy** is composed of four major inferences. First, I lost my partner and will never get another. Second, I do not have the exclusive love of another, and it is only possible to love one person at a time. Third, at a 100 percent level, I am not the most important person in my lover's life. Fourth, any lover only belongs to me, and if I cannot have him or her 100 percent of the time, I am worthless.

Rational jealousy is the rational alternative to irrational jealousy. Rational jealousy may be as follows: "I wish my lover was only in love with me, but it is not terrible that he or she loves someone else also. I do not like what my partner is doing, but he or she is only a fallible human who can love more than one person at a time." Like disappointment, rational jealousy allows a client to become more assertive, makes it possible to place limits on outside activity and it helps a client not to take a partner for granted.

DISRUPTING CLIENTS' IRRATIONAL BELIEFS

REBT focuses on **D** or disputing irrational beliefs. The elaborate methods of disputing clients' irrational beliefs is one way REBT differs from other cognitive-behavioral approaches, and Beal, Kopec, and DiGiuseppe (1996) suggested that **D** may take up to 90 percent of the therapeutic hour.

Four disputational strategies are helpful for weakening clients' endorsement of irrational beliefs (IB), and these strategies are the following: logical disputes, empirical disputes, functional disputes, and rational alternative disputes.

Logical disputes weaken clients' endorsement of IBs by pointing out the error in logic of IBs. For example, "Is it logical that you are an ass? Does it logically follow that you are a dog? Does it seem consistent to you that because you made a mistake that now your are totally worthless? Does feeling depressed make logical sense?"

A point that professionals fail to realize when attempting to employ REBT is that at point B, clients have both rational and irrational beliefs, so it is often helpful to point out the rational belief first and then to proceed to point out the irrational belief. For example, "Now in keeping with your preference to be loved by Jim, does it logically follow that he has to love you?"

Empirical disputes weaken clients' IBs by showing how they are inconsistent with empirical reality or evidence. REBT is based partly on the scientific method that states that hypotheses must be tested against empirical evidence, so clients are encouraged to provide empirical evidence to support their beliefs. For example, "Where is the evidence that you must be successful and worthwhile as person? Where is the evidence that you will never be happy? Prove to me that you are a worthless son of a bitch. Where is the evidence that you are a rotten bastard? Do the laws of the universe dictate that once you fail at love once or twice that you will always fail?" In summary, with empirical disputes clients' are forced to come up with empirical evidence for their disputes.

Functional disputes attempt to weaken clients' acceptance of IBs by focusing on the pragmatic consequences of accepting IBs. The role of the therapist is to point out to the client that if he or she accepts IBs, this acceptance will lead to negative emotional and behavioral consequences. For example, "Does holding onto the belief that you are a piece of shit help you? Which behaviors are you likely to experience by accepting the IB that all women will always reject you, or that you will never find a date? Does holding the belief that you are cursed help you to realize your goal of happiness?" Finally, functional disputes examine the emotional and behavioral consequences of clinging to a particular IB.

Rational alternative disputes involve the therapist providing the client with a rational alternative belief that provides the same or better results and positive consequences. According to Beal, Kopec, and DiGiuseppe (1996), the key to rational alternative disputes is to identify clients' IBs and to take out the demanding and self-downing and to leave the client with his or her desires. For example, "I want Jane to love me; there is no reason why she has to love me. It would be disappointing if I get rejected when approaching women for dates, but it is not awful and I can cope with disappointment and learn from the experiences."

Each of the four disputational strategies can be presented in four styles: didactic, Socratic, metaphorical, and humorous. The **didactic style** is the common style used in REBT and it is teaching the client the distinctions between rational and irrational beliefs; however, didactic styles can have clients agreeing with the therapist without thinking through the ideas, so like Adlerian therapists, REBT therapists tend to have clients summarize the main points throughout therapy to ensure that clients actually understand what is being taught.

Socratic style is just asking questions about the nature of the clients' irrational beliefs. For example, "How does it follow that you are going to be in the same situation you are in forever?"

The **metaphorical style** is taking the clients' IBs and applying them to a domain that the client knows well such as sports, cooking, parenting, and so on and demonstrating the maladaptive nature of the IBs. For example, "Suppose women would have assumed during the 1960s that they should not have to work so hard against sexism, where would that have gotten them?" "Let us assume that African Americans had not fought to eliminate segregation laws, where would they be now?"

The **humorous style** is disputing clients' IBs by carefully using humor. If the therapist can get the client to laugh at the foolishness of his or her beliefs, chances are the IBs will be weakened. Dr. Albert has a garland of humorous rational songs that this writer has found useful for helping clients laugh at their irrational beliefs.

THERAPEUTIC PROCESS

Therapeutic Goals

One goal of REBT is to teach clients rational philosophies of life. Another goal is to teach them to stop blaming themselves, others, and the world when things go wrong. Yet another goal is to teach clients the ABCs. In addition, REBT teaches clients to examine their values and to explore how certain values can lead to psychological disturbance. For example, things like enlightened self-interest, high frustration, tolerance, flexible thinking, acceptance of uncertainty, commitment to creative pursuits, applying the scientific method to thoughts, self-acceptance, risk-taking, long-term hedonism, and acceptance of personal responsibility for one's psychological disturbances tend to promote good psychological health (Dryden & Hill, 1993).

Role of Therapist

REBT therapists are active and directive and employ a host of Level III counseling skills such as logical disputes, empirical disputes, functional disputes, and rational disputes along with the four styles of disputing **Bs:** didactic, humorous, Socratic, and metaphysical (Mylott, 1994).

In addition, REBT therapists tend to use a variety of cognitive, emotive, and behavioral techniques. Cognitive techniques are used to dispute irrational beliefs through detecting, debating, and discriminating irrational beliefs. Clients are taught to be aware of using "shoulds, oughts, musts, have tos, and so" when speaking and thinking. Moreover, clients learn flexible ways of thinking and expressing their preferences, desires, values, and nonabsolustic goals. Clients are taught **unconditional acceptance** by learning to distinguish between behaviors and self-worth as a human. REBT therapists teach clients that humans are fallible.

Humor is used to get clients to emote without being too serious and rigid. In addition, Ellis uses stories, poems, aphorisms, role playing, and rational humorous songs to teach clients rational philosophies. Moreover, Ellis employs **shame-attacking exercises** where clients are instructed to perform a shameful or embarrassing act that is not illegal in public and to learn self-acceptance.

Ellis claimed that since its inception in 1955, REBT has always employed behavioral techniques such as systematic desensitization, flooding, imagery, reinforcement, the Premack principle, hypnosis, and response cost (Weinrach, 1995).

Maultbsy (1984) employed rational-emotive imagery as an emotive technique, and Maultsby used imagery to show clients how they could change self-defeating emotions into self-enhancing emotions (Sapp, 1999; Corey, 1991). For example, first clients are asked to imagine the worst things that could happen and then they are instructed through their imaginations to change inappropriate feelings into appropriate feelings. For example, "Imagine that your husband left you for a young attractive bombshell. Feel the feelings. Tolerate those feelings of being betrayed, rejected, and let down. Notice how worthless you feel and feel that pain as strongly as you can. Now, change your inappropriate feelings into rational alternatives like regret, disappointment and change self-downing feelings into self-accepting feelings."

Unlike some REBT therapists, Ellis uses force and vigor to get clients to move from intellectual understanding to emotional insight. He instructs clients in how to use strong dialogues with themselves to challenge and confront irrational beliefs, and it is common for Ellis to use reverse role playing, where he role plays clients' irrational philosophies and has clients challenge and confront his irrational philosophies; and finally, Ellis uses force and vigor with shame-attacking exercises (Gerbode & Moore, 1994; Warren & McLellan, 1987).

Therapeutic Relationship

Unlike other humanistic-existential forms of psychotherapy, REBT does not place a premium on the client-therapist relationship; however, like person-centered psychotherapy, REBT teaches clients unconditional positive regard or **full tolerance or acceptance;** that is, teaching clients how to minimize self-downing and self-rating. In contrast, clients are taught to rate their behaviors and not themselves. REBT therapists point out to clients that certain behaviors are self-defeating while not rating clients' personhood (Livneh & Wright, 1995). Ellis does not believe that the client and therapist relationship is necessary and sufficient to bring about therapeutic change for clients, but some REBT therapists emphasize building collaborative relationships with clients (Sapp, 1997a). Unlike interpersonal therapists, and psychoanalytic and psychodynamic therapists, REBT therapists tend not to give attention to free association, transference phenomena, and dream analysis, and even though REBT is an emotive form of psychotherapy, it does not allow an endless expression and exploration of clients' feelings like person-centered and Gestalt therapists. Finally, like other cognitive-behavioral approaches to psychotherapy, REBT is present-centered, active, directive, and psychoeducational (Dryden & DiGuiseppe, 1990).

Multicultural Applications and Limitations

Sapp and Farrell (1994) and Vernon (1989) described REBT applications for academically at-risk and special education students. Moreover, Sapp (1994) showed that REBT was effective in improving the academic self-concept and achievement of academically at-risk African American students at the middle-school level (Sapp, 1996b). In addition, Sapp, McNeely, and Torres (1997) described how REBT could be used to help aging African Americans and Latinos deal with the process of death and dying (Sharf, 2004).

Even though REBT has multicultural applications, the active-directive orientation puts some cultural groups at risk for early termination from psychotherapy, and some psychotherapists may use their directive and action orientation to get minority clients to acquiesce due to intimidation. Finally, REBT has demonstrated that it has benefits to various cultural groups, but therapists must use caution when dealing with clients who have a minority orientation.

COMPREHENSIVENESS. In comparison to psychodynamic therapies, REBT is not extremely comprehensive. Weinrach (1995) claimed that there are many misconceptions about REBT that are due to Ellis's 1965 demonstration with Gloria in a film called *The Three Approaches to Psychotherapy* (Shostrom, 1965). Ellis did not use Levels I and II counseling skills and he quickly proceeded with therapy, and he did not demonstrate the various aspects of his theory.

Weinrach (1995) claimed that Ellis's interview with Gloria, who by the way died in 1980, did not accurately represent the comprehensive nature of REBT, and he believed that the profession of counseling and psychotherapy has been reluctant to accept REBT because of Ellis's demonstration with Gloria. Moreover, Weinrach argued that even though REBT is a system of parts, it is philosophically and psychologically complex, and that it is more difficult to analyze and dispute clients' thoughts, beliefs, and philosophies of life than to reflect their feelings. Clearly, REBT is currently more comprehensive than it was during the 1950s, 1960s, 1970s, 1980s, and 1990s, and it is a straightforward and logical system. However, Weinrach believed that counseling professionals often select a theory that feels good and is easy and enjoyable to use, rather than one that is effective with clients.

Another reason that REBT has been criticized as lacking comprehension is that Ellis is known to use expletives and some professions react to these with offense rather than realizing that this is just the style of Ellis and it does not represent REBT as a whole. Moreover, Ellis enjoys being outspoken, humorous, and forceful (Kopec, Beal, & DiGuiseppe, 1994).

Finally, REBT has been criticized for not being spiritual and as being antireligious, but it is Ellis who is an atheist, though he does not oppose religion, only religiosity—which he defines as a fixed or rigid belief within a theological religion, such as Catholic, Baptist, Methodist, and so on, or secular religions such as communism and fascism (Weinrach, 1995).

In conclusion, REBT does not address developmental psychology or attachment theory or nonconscious processes; however, this writer believes that it is more comprehensive than many cognitive-behavioral theories—especially cognitive therapy and cognitive-behavior modification.

PARSIMONY. As alluded to throughout this chapter, REBT is parsimonious and it uses few constructs, but on another level, it is complex and can be difficult to employ with clients. Finally, REBT is a parsimonious, eclectic, cognitive, emotive, humanistic, and a behavioral form of therapy.

EMPIRICAL VALIDITY. Lyons and Woods (1991) performed a meta-analysis on seventy REBT outcome studies and concluded that REBT was an empirically validated form of psychotherapy. As stated previously, REBT is based on the scientific method, and researchers have supported empirically concepts of this theory. In conclusion, REBT has good empirical validity (Walen, DiGuiseppe, & Wessler, 1980; Silverman, McCarthy, & McGovern, 1992).

PRECISION AND TESTABILITY. REBT has good precision and testability and REBT researchers have defined operationally concepts and tested them experimentally. Finally, Ellis has encouraged over the years the experimental evaluation of REBT.

HEURISTIC VALUE. REBT has excellent heuristic value and it has stimulated a great deal of research in cognitive-behavioral therapies. Ellis's work has influenced most theorists in the cognitive and cognitive-behavioral areas. Finally, without a doubt, Ellis has been the most prolific theorist within the cognitive-behavioral area.

APPLIED VALUE. REBT has excellent applied value, and it has been applied with academically at-risk African American students, aged African Americans and Latinos, issues of women, and so forth. Moreover, REBT has been combined with hypnosis and used to treat reactive depression, anxiety, and test anxiety. In conclusion, REBT rates very high in applied value.

Case Example: Applying REBT with an African American Adult Male

The transcription that follows was from an 18-year old African American adult male who had several irrational beliefs, and he had the following multiaxial diagnosis from the *Diagnostic and Statistical Manual of Mental Disorders-Text Revision* (DSM-IV-TR): Axis I, 300.02, Generalized Anxiety Disorder; Axis II, 301.81, Narcissistic Personality Disorder, 301.7, Antisocial Personality

Disorder; Axis III, None; Axis IV, Problems with Primary Support Group; Axis V, GAF 60 (current).

T-1: What would you like to work on?

C-1: My friends are getting on my nerves. I am having trouble with my family and I cannot see how I can make it. Life is a bitch and I do not stand a damn chance.

T-2: It sounds like your life is tough, but let me ask you something. What are you telling yourself to make things worse?

C-2: Man, what in the fuck are you talking about? Didn't you hear what I just fucking told you?

T-3: Yes, I heard, but I was wondering how you were making things worse.

C-3: Life is a fucking bitch and I can't get anywhere because of crackers, niggers, and my family.

T-4: Clearly your life appears to be tough, but what are you doing to change things?

C-4: Not a damn thing except worrying and getting fucked up.

T-5: So, within your mind you make things worse by telling yourself that things will be like they are forever.

C-5: Man, I do not tell myself shit. You think that people talk to themselves?

T-6: Yes, and I believe that you are telling yourself things that are not helping your situation. Let me be frank, I think that the things we do and feel are affected by our thoughts. Now, if you follow my line of reasoning, you may find that if you change your thinking and the things you do, you will feel differently and happier.

C-6: You mean that the things I say to myself or rehearse in my mind have a strong impact on what I feel and how I react?

T-7: Yes, and if you can learn to detect your self-defeating thoughts, I think that you will see how to change those irrational thoughts into ones that allow you to achieve your goals and to be happier.

SUMMARY

REBT is a comprehensive form of psychotherapy, and it emphasizes that cognitions, emotions, and behaviors interact and are overlapping constructs.

The goal of REBT is to change clients' irrational philosophies of life and not individual distorted cognitions.

Glossary of Key Terms

ABCs (activating events, belief systems, and emotional consequences). Ellis argued that C (emotional consequences) is interactively caused by (A X B), even though more emphasis is generally put on the client's B.

Acceptance. The acceptance that humans are error prone and that life is uncertain.

Cognitive restructuring. Philosophically helping a client restructure or change irrational philosophies.

Debating. Challenging clients to change and challenge their irrational beliefs.

Detecting. Teaching clients to detect and notice irrational beliefs.

Discomfort anxiety. The disturbed feeling that clients have when they do not get what they want.

Discrimination. Teaching clients the distinction between rational and irrational beliefs.

Ego anxiety. Anxiety that occurs when one's demands on the self, others, and the world are not successful.

Enlightened self-interest. Pursuing one's goals and purposes without disregarding the rights of others. This is the rational alternative to selfishness.

Ethical humanism. A philosophical position that opposes viewing people as inherently good or bad, but as humans who can perform good or bad acts.

Hedonism. A philosophical stance that encourages the pursuit of long-term and meaningful goals and purposes.

Humanistic. A philosophical view of seeing human existence within existential terms.

Insight No. 1. Absolutistic beliefs are at the core of psychological disturbances.

Insight No. 2. The realization that searching for historical causes for events helps maintain psychological disturbances.

Insight No. 3. The concept that irrational thoughts are common and that it takes work and practice to change irrational beliefs.

Internal dialogue. The internal signal, thoughts, pictures, and images that occur in the minds of clients.

Irrational. Thoughts, behaviors, and feelings that do not aid clients in achieving their goals.

Musturbation. A term coined by Ellis which refers to rigid internal dialogues that often have rigid statements such as must, should, ought, and other absolustic statements.

Primary view of psychological disturbances. A philosophical position that states that clients are not so much disturbed by events but by their beliefs about thoughts.

Psychological interactionism. The notion that feelings, thoughts, and behaviors interact and changing one changes the others.

Rational. Thoughts, feelings, and behaviors that help one to achieve goals and purposes.

Rational-emotive behavior therapy (REBT). A cognitive, emotive, and behavioral form of psychotherapy developed by Albert Ellis. The goal is to teach clients how to change their irrational beliefs.

Shame-attacking exercises. An anxiety reducing strategy that REBT employs where clients are taught to feel unashamed by doing things that would normally cause embarrassment, shame, and anxiety.

Stoic philosophers. Philosophers who stressed testing thoughts against reality as opposed to assuming that thoughts are reality.

Two biologically based tendencies. The tendencies to think both rationally and irrationally.

Chapter 7

MULTIMODAL BEHAVIOR THERAPY

CHAPTER OVERVIEW

Arnold Lazarus endorsed a philosophy called **technical eclecticism,** which suggests using procedures and techniques from many theories without subscribing to the individual theories. Lazarus suggested that it is possible to be eclectic within a broad theoretical framework without haphazardly attempting to integrate vastly opposing theories. Lazarus also noted that theoretical eclecticism, drawing from diverse theories, can lead to confusion for students and professionals because many theories are epistemologically incompatible. Very similar to other behavioral theories, multimodal behavior therapy (MMBT) is a Level III theory and it is a comprehensive assessment and multifaceted treatment that is individually tailored to assess clients' functioning in seven modalities (Keat, 1979, 1990).

KEY CONCEPTS

MMBT is the comprehensive intraindividually based form of behavior therapy, and it addresses what Paul (1967) proposed concerning psychotherapy: which treatments and by whom under which conditions are effective for which kinds of clients with which kinds of specific concerns or disorders. In addition, MMBT is a broad spectrum behavior therapy and it is an eclectic system that goes beyond the narrow stimulus-response forms of behaviorism (Lazarus, 1976, 1989a, 1989b, 1990a, 1990b, 1990c, 1995; Lazarus & Beutler, 1993; Lazarus, Beutler, & Norcross, 1992).

Lazarus, a clinical psychologist, in 1958 introduced the terms behavior therapy and behavior therapist into the psychology literature. As previously stated, MMBT endorses technical eclecticism and not theoretical eclecticism and Lazarus believes that technical eclecticism leads to hypotheses that can be tested and that theoretical eclecticism can lead to confusion (Martin-Causey & Hinkle, 1995).

Because MMBT is technically eclectic, it is based on several other behavioral approaches such as social learning theories, the work of Joseph Wolpe, rational-emotive behavior therapy, and cognitive-behavior therapy. In addition, MMBT is based on group psychotherapy and communications theory (Gerler, Drew, & Mohr, 1990).

MMBT describes and assesses seven modalities in acronym form called the **BASIC-ID** or **IB,** and this acronym refers to the following modalities: behavior, affect, sensation, imagery, cognition, interpersonal relationships, and drugs/biology. The **D** refers not only to drugs/biology but all physiological information such as medication, nutrition, and exercise.

Behaviors are things that people do and these are observable actions. Clients are asked which behaviors they would like to increase or decrease.

Affects are feelings such as anxiety, depression, and so on. Clients are asked if there are emotions that should be increased or decreased.

Sensations are tactile sensations like bodily tension and abdominal pains. Clients are asked if there are sensations that need to be increased or decreased.

Imagery are the images that clients have such as self-concept, self-image, and the visual sense of self. Clients are asked for areas of strengths and deficits within the imagery modality.

Cognitions include all cognitive functioning such as thoughts both rational and irrational and cognitive distortions.

Interpersonal relationships include all relationships such as family, siblings, spouses, and other interpersonal relationships.

Biology/drugs requires an evaluation by a physician or other medical professional, and again, clients are asked if there are areas that need to be increased or decreased.

STRUCTURAL PROFILES

Structural profiles is a graphical representation of the assessment of the BASIC-ID and can be used to obtain responses to the following seven questions proposed by Lazarus (1995):

> **Behaviors:** Are you an active person? If so, to what degree on a 10-point scale, where 10 is the most active.
> **Affects:** On a 10-point scale, to what degree are you emotional?
> **Sensations:** To what degree do you focus on your bodily sensations, on a 10-point scale.

Imagery: On a 10-point scale, to what degree do you think using images, pictures, and other mental signals?
Cognitions: Using a 10-point scale, how much do you like to analyze and think about things?
Interpersonal Relationships: On a 10-point scale, how social are you?
Drugs/Biology: On a 10-point scale, how physically healthy are you?

To summarize, structural profiles assess clients' strengths and weaknesses across the BASIC-ID. When a client favors one modality over another, Lazarus refers to this as a **reactor.** For example, **behavior reactors** respond to situations by actions or doing things. In addition, clients who respond to situations primarily through mental imagery or images are called **imagery reactors** or **sensory** or **cognitive reactors.**

COPING IMAGERY

Coping imagery is a form of guided imagery that can be appropriate with imagery reactors, and it involves having a client imagine a stressful situation and to imagine himself or herself coping and remaining in control and relaxing by applying relaxing imagery. This technique is similar to Meichenbaum's (1977) self-instructional training and the guided imagery, hypnosis and related techniques described in the behavior therapy chapter.

COGNITIONS SCALE

Like REBT and other cognitive-behavioral therapies, MMBT assesses irrational cognitions. Lazarus and Lazarus (1991) have a Multimodal Life History Inventory that helps with the BASIC-ID assessment, and the following items are similar to the ones used to assess irrational cognitions.

	Strongly Disagree 1	*Disagree* 2	*Strongly Agree* 3

1. Mistakes are terrible.
2. I should be perfect.
3. There are perfect solutions to problems.
4. My life is controlled by the stars.

5. Things are either totally right or wrong.
6. I should always play it safe.
7. Others are happier than I am.
8. People are either totally good or totally bad.
9. I must be happy.
10. Life should be easy for me.

This instrument provides a quantitative measure of clients' irrational beliefs or distorted cognitions. The range for this scale is from 10 to 30. If the reader collects data on several clients or participants, consult Sapp (2002b) for methods for analysis Likert-scaled instruments. For example, reliability indices can be found and descriptive statistics for such data.

Previously it was stated that MMBT is related to other therapies such as social learning, REBT and other cognitive-behavioral therapies; however, Lazarus pointed out MMBT differs from other forms of psychotherapies in the following six ways:

1. MMBT employs the entire BASIC-ID.
2. MMBT uses second-order BASIC-ID assessments.
3. MMBT uses modality profiles.
4. MMBT employs structural profiles.
5. MMBT uses bridging procedures.
6. MMBT tracks the modality firing order.

BRIDGING

Bridging is where a therapist deliberately tunes into the client's preferred modality and then gently moves the client into other modalities. For example, if a client presents information from his or her cognitive modality, the therapist first works with that modality and then smoothly moves into other modalities such as affects, behavior, and so on.

TRACKING

Tracking is the exploration of firing order of various modalities. For example, panic attacks begin with unpleasant bodily sensations (S) followed by negative or irrational cognitions (C), which results in panic attacks. Lazarus believes that most clients report a stable firing order with BASIC-ID, and a therapist can use tracking to give clients insights into how their BASIC-IDs operate and how to intervene. This insight allows the client and therapist to select the most useful therapeutic techniques.

Lazarus uses the term **nonconscious** to describe clients' various levels of self-awareness and self-comprehension that affect cognitions, affects, and behaviors, but unlike psychoanalytic theorists, Lazarus does not reify this concept nor does he accept the psychodynamic interpretation of the unconscious. Likewise, Lazarus uses the term **defensive reactions** to denote defenses that clients use to control anxiety, but again this concept is not connected with psychodynamic theories.

When impasses are reached in therapy, a second-order BASIC-ID can be used. This is just subjecting an item from a client's modality profile into a detail inquiry in terms of another BASIC-ID. For example, if a client reported depression, the therapist could use the BASIC-ID to assess that affect.

Sapp (1997a) provided the following applications of the BASIC-ID as an assessment exercise:

Instructions: Assume a client has a broadly defined problem and it cannot be easily assessed. Complete the BASIC-ID by answering the following questions:
Behaviors. Behaviors are observable acts that are overt and measurable. Are there any behaviors that you would like to increase or decrease?
Responses: _____
_____

Affects. Affects are feelings, moods, and other strong feelings. Are there any feelings that you find problematic? If so, describe them.
Responses: _____
_____

Sensations. Do you experience unpleasant sensations from any of the five basic senses such as touch, taste, sight, smell, and hearing? Do you experience unpleasant physical states such as abdominal pain, tingling, numbness, dizziness, tension, nausea, excessive perspiration, dry mouth, hearing things, back pain, tremors, fainting spells, or panic attacks?
Responses: _____
_____

Imagery. Imagery refers to the ability to visualize events. Do you have images of failure? How do you picture yourself? Do you often vividly daydream or become lost in fantasy?
Responses: _____
_____

Cognitions. Cognitions are thoughts, attitudes, beliefs, philosophies, and values that we hold. Do you have many thoughts that are based on absolutistic thinking and underlying musts, shoulds, have-tos, and so on? Also, the client can complete the cognitions scale presented earlier within this chapter.

Responses: _____

Interpersonal Relationships. How are your interactions with others? How are your relationships with your family? Are they negative or positive? Do you have supportive relationships? Are you a gregarious person?
Responses: _____

Drugs/Biology. Drugs/biology is one's overall physical health and medications or drugs that one is taking. Do you exercise? Are you physically active? Do you have medical concerns? Have you had any surgeries? Do you have any physical disabilities? Do you take vitamins? Do you use marijuana or hallucinogens such as LSD? Do you smoke? Do you wake early during mornings? Do you experience constipation? Do you overeat? Do you take painkillers, narcotics, stimulants, or use alcohol? Do you eat junk foods?
Responses: _____

Once you complete the BASIC-ID, which modalities interact? Now take a problem from the BASIC-ID from the above exercise and perform a second-order BASIC-ID.

THERAPEUTIC PROCESS

Therapeutic Goals

MMBT clients' function within seven modalities and this assessment allows the therapist and client to determine which modalities to increase and decrease.

Role of Therapist

Unlike Ellis, Lazarus believes that a good client-therapist relationship is important for therapy to proceed, and he would endorse the use of Levels I and II skills. However, very similar to REBT, but not as forceful and as vigorous, MMBT is very active and direct and it uses Level III counseling skills.

Therapeutic Relationship

As previously stated, MMBT is a Level III counseling theory, and Lazarus stressed the importance of a good therapeutic relationship for therapy to be effective, but Lazarus stressed that the exact nature of such a relationship depends on the client. Lazarus tends to be a chameleon and he changes depending on the client with whom he is working with and the client's BASIC-ID.

Also, as previously stated, MMBT is a technically an eclectic form of psychotherapy and it draws from behavioral therapy, REBT, and cognitive-behavioral therapies. Because MMBT is technically eclectic theory, it draws techniques from various theoretical approaches without subscribing to those approaches. All MMBT therapists are eclectic, but not all eclectic therapists are multimodal (MM).

MMBT, like many cognitive-behavioral forms of psychotherapy, is short-term, lasting between fifteen to twenty sessions and seldom lasting beyond fifty sessions.

MMBT is a flexible form of psychotherapy, and it is a holistic problem-solving approach where a therapist must be flexible enough to assess a client within seven modalities, and then tailor therapy based on those modalities.

MMBT endorses theoretical parsimony and not theoretical rigidity or dogma, and two techniques are primarily used: bridging and tracking. With bridging the therapist tunes into the client's dominant modalities before exploring other modalities, and tracking explores the firing order of clients' BASIC-IDs.

To summarize, MMBT uses the BASIC-ID to explore a problem and once problems are identified, secondary or second-order BASIC-IDs are used to gather additional information. Finally, the BASIC-ID can be depicted graphically using structural profiles.

Multicultural Applications and Limitations

MMBT is very valuable to multicultural groups, and since it focuses on behavioral changes, this is the preference of some minority groups such as African Americans. In addition, MMBT can assess a client's difficulties within a multicultural context, and it can take into account the social and political forces than can affect minority clients such as racism, sexism, anti-Semitism, social class discrimination, and other environmental factors that can affect minorities. Like other cognitive-behavioral therapies, minority clients are taught how to cope with a hostile environment and, unlike some other approaches to psychotherapy, minority clients are not blamed for external forces that are out of their control. In closing, possibly one limitation of MMBT is the rigidity of some therapists who fail to assess minority clients holistically and MMBT can be applied in an inflexible manner (Nieves, 1978a, 1978b).

Critique

COMPREHENSIVENESS. MMBT is the comprehensive intraindividually-focused cognitive-behavioral approach, and it thoroughly assesses a client's functioning in seven modalities. The BASIC-ID is an operational manner to determine what works best for certain clients and under which conditions.

PARSIMONY. MMBT is a parsimonious and straightforward approach and it does not endorse dogma or rigidity.

EMPIRICAL VALIDITY. According to Lazarus, empirical validity is good for MMBT, and because it is based on the scientific method, like other behavioral therapies, empirical validity appears to be strong.

PRECISION AND TESTABILITY. Due to the fact that MMBT is parsimonious, both precision and testability are specious and MMBT concepts have been defined operationally and tested experimentally.

HEURISTIC VALUE. MMBT has stimulated research in the area of behavior therapy and has expanded the practice of behavior therapy and has had an influence on other cognitive-behavioral theorists such as Ellis, Beck, and Meichenbaum.

APPLIED VALUE. MMBT has excellent applied value and has applications to many areas of counseling, psychology, and psychotherapy, particularly anxiety disorders, children, youths, at-risk students, and so on (Burnett & Pulvino, 1990).

SUMMARY

MMBT is similar to other cognitive-behavioral theories and it uses Level III techniques. In addition, it has depth and breadth and it uses specific techniques to treat specific issues obtained from the BASIC-ID. MMBT is also similar to social learning theories and it can be viewed as a practical form of behaviorism.

Glossary of Terms

BASIC-ID. Developed by Arnold Lazarus, a comprehensive therapeutic systematic method of intraindividually assessing a client's behavior, affect, sensation, imagery, cognition, interpersonal relationships, and drugs/biology.

Bridging. Engaging a client in his or her preferred modalities, before moving into other modalities.

Broad-Spectrum Behavior Therapy. A form of behavior therapy that has depth and breadth, which goes beyond the restrictive nature of stimulus-response behaviorism.

Coping Imagery. The pairing of self-control imagery with anxiety-producing situations. Progressive relaxation is often part of this process.

Imagery Reactor. A client who is referred to as a sensory reactor because auditory and visual systems are the means of responding to situations.

Modality Profile. The assessment made with a client's BASIC-ID.

Nonconscious. Lazarus' term for a client's lack of awareness.

Second-order BASIC-ID. A second BASIC-ID performed after the first, to provide additional information about a particular aspect of the first-order BASIC-ID.

Structural Profiles. A graphical analysis of the BASIC-ID.

Tracking. Examining the firing order of the BASIC-ID.

Review Questions

1. Compare and contrast MMBT with REBT and Adlerian psychotherapy.
2. Which issues of technical eclecticism are highlighted by MMBT?
3. MMBT assesses cognitions. Which are techniques that could be borrowed from REBT to assess cognitions more thoroughly and which techniques from REBT could be used to change irrational cognitions?
4. MMBT assesses drugs and biological. What is the importance of assessing this modality within a multicultural society?

Chapter 8

COGNITIVE THERAPY

CHAPTER OVERVIEW

Even though cognitive therapy has a great deal in common with other cognitive-behavioral approaches, it is a mistake to not see how it differs from other cognitive-behavioral approaches, too.

Aaron Temkin (Tim) Beck, M.D. is the founder of cognitive therapy, and unlike REBT and MMBT, cognitive therapy is based on an informational-processing theory. More will be said about this informational-processing theory later within this chapter.

Beck, like psychiatrists of the 1950s, and even today, was trained in psychoanalysis, but unlike many psychiatrists, he was influenced by the review of George Kelly's book of 1955 in contemporary psychology; however, Beck abandoned Kelly's use of the word constructs for schemas—which he referred to for cognitive structures, since he did not accept Kelly's notions of bipolar constructs, but rather viewed schemas as categorical. In addition, Beck was influenced, like Ellis, by Karen Horney and indirectly by Alfred Adler, and temporarily Beck identified himself as a neo-analyst of the Adler, Horney, and Harry Stack Sullivan tradition.

Gradually during the 1960s, Beck developed his cognitive therapy theory and in 1961 he published the Beck Depression Inventory—a twenty-one-item inventory that assesses the severity of depression (Weishaar, 1993). In 1963, after reading an article that Beck published, Ellis and Beck started communicating, and Ellis lectured many times at Beck's Depression Research Unit at Philadelphia General Hospital. This is one reason why the two men have similar but different theories of cognitive-behavioral therapies. Beck learned from Ellis that clients' beliefs are readily accessible and Ellis credits Beck as being an extremely clear and noncontroversial thinker.

In 1967, Beck became an associate professor and through his research with the help of research-oriented psychologists published *Depression: Clinical, Experimental and Theoretical Aspects and Depression: Causes and Treatment.*

It was not until 1970 that the journal *Behavior Therapy* published an article by Beck that investigated the relationship between cognitive therapy and behavior therapy. Michael Mahoney believed that this was a landmark article and lead to the shift from pure behavior therapy to the cognitive revolution (Mahoney, 1974, 1991; Rychlak, 1990).

It was not until 1971 that Beck became a full professor of psychiatry. During the 1970s, Beck teamed with psychiatrist A. John Rush and they performed ground breaking randomized control trials in which depressed outpatient clients received either antidepressant medication or cognitive therapy. This was the first manualized treatment study of cognitive therapy, and the original treatment manual grew from 12 pages until it was published as a book in 1979 to 200 pages. The book was entitled *Cognitive Therapy of Depression* (Beck et al., 1979). It was found that cognitive therapy was effective in reducing the symptoms of unipolar depression.

Beck's work was not widely known in psychology until he was introduced to behavior therapists in 1973 at the annual meeting of the Association for Advancement of Behavior Therapy (AABT). During this era, several psychologists influenced the cognitive movement such as Ellis, Meichenbaum, Mahoney, Marvin Goldfried, Gerald Davison, and Arnold Lazarus (Weishaar, 1993).

Mahoney (1974) published the seminal work, *Cognition and Behavior Modification,* and provided a strong rationale for cognitive therapy. Mahoney (1988) listed seventeen cognitive therapies and noted they differ in their view of reality, theories of knowing, and theories of causation. In 1977, Beck helped found the journal of *Cognitive Therapy* and nominated Mahoney as the first editor.

One of the strongest opponents of the cognitive movement was the developer of systematic desensitization, Joseph Wolpe. He criticized his former student Lazarus, and Ellis, Meichenbaum, Mahoney, and others. Wolpe, like Skinner, viewed cognitions as a subclass of behaviors that follow the same rules of acquisition and extinction.

The American Psychiatric Association awarded Beck the Foundation Fund Prize for Research in psychiatry for his work on depression, suicide, and cognitive therapy, in 1979. Also in 1979, the National Institute of Mental Health (NIMH) designed a multisite outcome study of the effects of interpersonal psychotherapy, cognitive therapy, and imipramine (drug treatment) in the treatment of unipolar depression. Readers should be aware that interpersonal psychotherapy was developed by Gerald Klerman and Myrna Weissman at Yale University from psychodynamic models—but it is short-term.

This NIMH study of 250 depressed outpatient clients found no significant differences in recovery rates among clients receiving imipramine, interpersonal psychotherapy, or cognitive therapy. Beck and Brian Shaw have critcized this study because the therapist performing cognitive therapy did not have extensive training in the model, and Beck and his daughter, Judith Beck, have found that it takes at least a year to develop skills as a cognitive therapist (Beck, 1995).

In 1982, Beck received an honorary doctoral degree from Brown University and was named as one of the ten most influential psychotherapists in the *American Psychologist*. Beck published *Anxiety Disorders and Phobias: A Cognitive Perspective* in 1985. Within this book, he presented a cognitive model of anxiety disorders that was based on evolutionary theory and practical cognitive techniques to treat a variety of anxiety disorders. In 1987, Beck published *Love Is Never Enough* and outlined cognitive therapy for couples. Finally, in 1990, Beck published *Cognitive Therapy of Personality Disorders* with Freeman and associates.

Currently, Beck is integrating Darwinian theory, ethnology, and other evolutionary theories with cognitive therapy, and he has extended cognitive therapy in the treatment of substance abuse. Moreover, Padesky and Beck (2003) claimed that cognitions, emotions, behaviors, physical responses, and life events are interactively linked to each other, but still they believe that cognitions mediate all change efforts.

KEY CONCEPTS

Beck and Emery (1985; Beck, 1995) listed the following ten principles that underlie cognitive therapy:

1. It is a cognitive model that describes mental disorders.
2. It is a short-term form of therapy.
3. Unlike Ellis, Beck and Emery viewed the therapeutic relationship as necessary for cognitive therapy, and Levels I and II counseling skills are emphasized as prerequisites.
4. It uses collaborative empiricism.
5. Socratic questioning is skillfully implemented.
6. It is structured, directive, and active.
7. It is a problem-solving form of therapy.
8. It is psychoeducational.
9. It uses inductive reasoning.
10. Homework is used throughout therapy.

Depression

As previously stated, Beck was influenced by Adler, Horney, and Kelly. Early within his career, Beck attempted to validate Freud's notion that depression was retroflective anger or anger turned inward or onto the self. On the contrary, Beck found that depression was due to errors in informational processing, and this lead to Beck developing his cognitive model of depression. Also, as previously stated, Beck's research led to the development of several assessments and the most notable was the Beck Depression Inventory (BDI) (Beck, Ward, Mendelson, Mock, & Erbaugh, 1961; Beck & Weishaar, 1995). The BDI is a Likert-type scale used to assess depression. Scores on the BDI above 19 are considered to be clinical depression; scores above 24 suggest the need for treatment, and possibly the use of antidepressant medication such as Imipramine (Tofranil, daily average range of 75–300 mg), desipramine (Pertrofrane; Norpramin, daily average of 75–300 mg), Amitriptyline (Elavil, average daily range of 75–300 mg), Nortriptyline (Aventyl; Pamelor, average daily range of 50–150 mg), Protriptyline (Vivactil, average daily range of 10–60 mg), Doxepin (Sinequan, average daily range of 75–300 mg), Trimipramine (Surmontil, average daily range of 75–300 mg), and Clomipramine (Anafranil, 75–300 mg).

The reader should note that tricyclics and monoamine oxidase inhibitors (MAO) are two major subclasses of antidepressants. Imipramine, desipramine, Amitriptyline, Nortriptyline, Protriptyline, Doxepin, Trimipramine, and Clomipramine are tricyclic antidepressants. Phenelzine (Nardil, average daily range of 15–90 mg), Isocarboxazid (Marplan, average daily range of 10–50 mg), and Tranylcypromine (Parnate, average daily range of 10–50 mg) are all antidepressant medications.

Sapp (1996) stated that tricyclic antidepressants and MAO inhibitors prevent the reuptake of the neurotransmitter; thus more of the substance is available within the body. MAO inhibitors are agonists and they mimic the effects of neurotransmitters and bind to receptors sites that are normally activated by neurotransmitters such as dopamine, norepinephrine, epinephrine, and serotonin. By the way, neurotransmitters are brain and body chemicals that affect both depression and anxiety.

MAO inhibitors such as Nardil and Parnate can cause many negative side effects such as liver damage, hypertension, intracranial bleeding, and cardiovascular collapse. Combining MAO inhibitors with foods containing biogenic amines, chemicals similar to the neurotransmitters dopamine, norepinephrine, and epinephrine in terms of central nervous system effects, can produce heightened sympathetic reactions such as hypertension, the secretion of adrenaline, increased heart rate, and hyperglycemia.

There are many foods that contain biogenic amines such as aged cheese, yogurt, wine, yeast, breads, chocolates, and nuts. Normally, MAO inhibitors deactivate amines, but since this effect is prevented because of drug interactions, amines build up in the blood and tissues and the sympathetic nervous system is aroused. Specifically, MAO inhibitors are dangerous when combined with foods containing tyramine, an amino acid, such as aged cheeses, chianti wines, smoked fish, and many other foods. Needless to say, many foods contain tyramine and when MAO inhibitors are combined with barbiturates, amphetamines, and histamines, the result can be death.

Prozac (average daily range of 10–80 mg), Luvox (average daily range of 110–300 mg), Paxil (average daily range of 20–50 mg), and Zoloft (50–200 mg) are a new generation of antidepressants called serotonin reuptake inhibitors (SSRI). These drugs increase the amount of the neurotransmitter serotonin within the brain and body. The SSRIs relieve depression in about 70 percent of clients and they have few negative side effects. In contrast, tricyclic antidepressants can affect the heart muscles, produce dry mouth, and can cause urine retention. Prozac is not without negative side effects and it can cause nausea, weight loss or weight gain, anxiety, insomnia, headaches, and excessive perspiration.

The exact mechanisms of depression are not known and there are a variety of types of depression. Some studies support the dopamine hypothesis and others do not. Theoretically it is believed that depression is the result of the lack of activity at the monoaminergic receptor sites, and the insufficient amounts of norepinephrine and/or dopamine result in some forms of depression. Researchers are beginning to view depression as the interactions of biological vulnerability and stress (stress-diathesis hypothesis).

Also as previously stated, Beck has made major contributions to the area of suicide, and his major finding from longitudinal studies of inpatient and outpatient clients who had a score of nine or higher on the Beck Hopelessness Scale showed that this score was indicative of eventual suicide (Beck, Brown, Berchick, Stewart, & Steer, 1990; Beck, Steer, Kovacs, & Garrison, 1985). Hopelessness is a theoretical construct that has been found to predict eventual suicide (Beck, Kovacs, & Weissman, 1979; Beck, Rush, Shaw, & Emery, 1979a, 1979b; Beck, Schuyler, & Herman, 1974; Beck & Weishaar, 1995; Weishaar, 1993; Sapp, 2002a).

Unlike REBT, cognitive therapy is based on an informational processing theory of how clients process, code, store, and manipulate information from the environment. Cognitive therapy uses collaborative empiricism, or the use of the client-therapist relationship as a means to teach clients how to change dysfunctional thoughts. Like the process of Kelly, clients are taught to function as scientists and to be aware in the errors of processing information.

But unlike Ellis, Beck gets the client to tell his or her story of how his or her disorder developed and to be aware of the themes that run through cognitive distortions. This process is called **guided discovery.**

The specific way in that cognitive therapy differs from REBT is that cognitive therapy theorizes that each disorder has separate profiles or programs. To illustrate, with anxiety disorders, there is an arousal program and clients overreact to threats. Beck believes that anxiety disorders and depressive disorders are the result of a cognitive shift in informational processing (Beck & Emery, 1985; Beck & Weishaar, 1995). Beck also believes that when a client's normal programs for selecting and interpreting information malfunction, maladaptive programs like depression and anxiety are activated. Cognitive therapy tries to deactivate maladaptive programs and to shift clients' programs to neutral positions.

In contrast to REBT, cognitive therapy does not view cognitions as irrational but when cognitions are dysfunctional, clients have maladaptive cognitions in various informational processing programs and styles (Woody, Luborsky, McClellan, O'Brien, Beck, Blaine et al., 1983).

COGNITIVE THERAPY AND OTHER THERAPIES

Even though cognitive therapy is similar to psychoanalysis in that it examines clients' emotional reactions, cognitive therapy also explores clients' narratives. Moreover, cognitive therapy assumes that clients are affected by automatic thoughts and beliefs to which they are unaware, but unlike psychoanalysis, cognitive therapy does not equate cognitions with the unconscious. Even though automatic thoughts and core beliefs may be nonconscious, repressed and dissociated experiences and other reified constructs are not part of cognitive therapy.

Another way cognitive therapy differs from psychoanalysis is that cognitive therapy is short-term, lasting between twelve and sixteen sessions, and psychoanalysis is long-term, lasting for years. Moreover, generally psychoanalysts are passive and cognitive therapists are active and directive and they structure counseling along with Level III counseling skills (Freeman, 1990).

Cognitive therapy is similar and different from REBT. REBT attempts to change clients' irrational philosophies, while cognitive therapy tries to change the way clients process information. Cognitive therapy does not contend that clients have irrational beliefs, but dysfunctional thoughts, and REBT tends to be more deductive as a cognitive-behavioral model, pointing out clients irrational beliefs. In contrast, cognitive therapy tends to be more inductive – helping clients translate their beliefs and to explore the constructive nature of their beliefs (Gerbode & Moore, 1994).

As previously stated, a substantive difference between cognitive therapy and REBT is that cognitive therapy assumes that each disorder has its own cognitive profile, and that disorders like anxiety and depression have separate profiles and require different approaches.

Also as alluded to earlier, cognitive therapy is similar to multimodal behavior therapy (MMBT) in that both approaches fall under behavior therapy and both approaches are based on the scientific method; yet, cognitive therapy differs from MMBT in that the focus is on cognition and not the full coverage of behavior, affect, sensation, imagery, cognitions, interpersonal relationships, and drugs/biology. Clearly, MMBT stresses the assessment of several modalities, but cognitive therapy primarily stresses cognition-one modality (Freeman, Simon, Beutler, & Arkowitz, 1989; Beck, Brown, Berchick, Stewart, & Steer, 1990; Beck, Schuyler, & Herman, 1974; Beck, Steer, Kovacs, & Garrison, 1985).

PERSONALITY THEORY

Cognitive therapy takes an evolutionary approach to personality development and views it as the interaction of environment and innate predispositions (Beck & Weishaar, 1995; Freeman, Simon, Beutler, & Arkowitz, 1989). Beck believes that clients have idiosyncratic vulnerability to certain psychological distresses (Beck, Rush et al., 1979a, 1979b). Beck's view of how personality factors impact disorders is closely related to the diathesis-stress model which states that psychological factors and biological factors interact together to produce psychopathology (Abram, 1983; Agras, Rossiter, Arnow, Schneider, Telch, Raeburn et al., 1992).

LEARNED HELPLESSNESS AND DEPRESSION

The reader should be aware that depression is a mood disorder. According to the DSM-IV-TR, there are a variety of forms of depression, and there are two broad categories of depression—unipolar and bipolar. Unipolar depression has three subtypes—major depressive disorder, dysthmic disorder, and depression not otherwise specified. Bipolar disorder has three subtypes—bipolar I disorder, bipolar II disorder, and cyclothymia (Kendall & Hammen, 1998). To fit the diagnosis of unipolar depression, a client could have not had a manic or bipolar phase of depression. According to the DSM-IV-TR, to meet the diagnosis of major depression, the client for at least two weeks must have experienced at least five of the following symptoms almost daily: depressed mood, loss of pleasure from enjoyable activities, loss of weight, change in appetite, insomnia, too much sleep, loss of energy, fatigue, psychomotor agitation or retardation, feelings of worthlessness and doom, excessive guilt, inability to think clearly, inability to concentrate, inability to make decisions, and recurrent thoughts of suicide (Antonuccio, 1981).

Major depression can manifest itself as psychotic depression, where the client experiences a departure from reality such as hallucinations or delusions.

Seasonal affective disorder (SAD) is a subcategory of major depression that refers to the period of time in which clients experience depression. Common patterns for SAD is fall and winter periods when clients are less exposed to direct rays of the sun.

Dysthymic disorder is a prolonged phase of depression. Often this disorder has existed with a client for at least two years and the client must experience at least three of the following symptoms: low self-esteem, pessimism, hopelessness, general loss of daily enjoyment or pleasure, social withdrawal, constant tiredness, guilt, ruminating over the past, psychomotor retardation, inability to concentrate, problems with memory, and inability to make decisions.

The exact mechanisms that cause depression are not known, but there are biological theories. One such theory—the monoamines (norepinephrine, dopamine, and serotonin) stated that antidepressant medication works by increasing the availability of these neurotransmitters by blocking them from being reabsorbed into the presynaptic neurons. Kendall and Hammen (1998) argued that the monoamine hypothesis is too simple, and they believe that the hypothalamic-pituitary-adrenal (HPA) axis plays an important role in depression. This HPA theory of depression is a dysregulation theory of neurotransmitters and states that depression is the result of a maladaptive stress response that could be mediated by early traumatic experiences that alter brain activity. This HPA axis is believed to work when a client has a perception of stress. A synthesis of hormones is secreted by the hypothalamus and transported by the pituitary gland. The adrenal gland is stimulated and produces cortisol, which is a hormone that prepares clients for stress; however, cortisol blocks the hormones produced by the hypothalamus and pituitary gland, so that the body returns to a normal state when stress ends.

Kendall and Hammen (1998) reported that consistently elevated levels of cortisol are found among acutely depressed clients when compared to people without depression. In summary, researchers are beginning to theorize that the HPA axis plays an important role in depression.

Many readers assume that Beck's model is the only psychological one of depression. In fact, Martin Seligman (1975) and his colleagues also have a cognitive vulnerability of depression called learned helplessness. Seligman argued that some clients become depressed because they believe that they are helpless to change negative situations; however, this is an erroneous expectancy that one cannot change or control outcomes, therefore no actions are taken. In essence, some depressed clients assume that they are helpless and give up and the result is continued depression. Moreover, interpretations that the client has about situations are also part of this model. According to this theory, clients have errors in attributions and a sense of helplessness. Abramson, Metalsky (1988), and Alloy (1989) proposed a revised theory of hopelessness of depression, and this theory adds additional cognitive and environmental factors and the fact that depressed clients have a negative explanatory style and they interpret events in a self-defeating fashion.

Personality, according to Beck, is shaped by schemas (Beck & Emery, 1985), and he believes that certain personality structures are related to various personality disorders. To illustrate, borderline personality disorder is characterized by stormy and abusive relationships, intense emotions of love and hate, sporadic changes in emotions, and impulsivity and has been found to be related to the following three beliefs: (1) the world is a harmful place; (2) I have to control my environment, because I lack control over myself; (3) I am a worthless, useless, and meaningless person (Freeman et al., 1989; Beck & Weishaar, 1995).

Beck postulated that these core beliefs and distortions in information processing and cognitive distortions lead to emotional and behavioral instability with clients experiencing borderline personality disorder. In summary, in contrast to psychoanalytic theories which take an intrapsychic or object relations view of borderline personality, Beck views the instability in self-image, mood changes, stormy interpersonal relationships, and the instability of sexual orientation and career choices as the result of distorted schemas and core beliefs.

Correctly so, Beck points out that clients hold **conditional assumptions,** and these assumptions start with an **if.** For example, "If I were more pretty, I could find the perfect man." "If people do not like me, that means I cannot be loved." "If I did not come from a fucked up environment, I would not have problems for the rest of my life." "If I had not been abused as a child, I would not be crazy now." "If I become close to people, I will get hurt." Beck and his daughter, Judith Beck, point out that conditional assumptions are hard to change, since they become part of clients' core beliefs, and when clients hold conditional assumptions and experience psychological defeat and rejection, they are more likely to experience psychopathology.

Beck described two personality dimensions. The **sociotropic** or social dependent personality dimension is described as a client wanting nurturance, closeness, and dependence, and in contrast, the **autonomous personality dimension** is related to the desire for self-determinism and independence. Beck believes that clients are a combination of both personality dimensions (Beck, Weissman, Lester, & Texler, 1974; Beck & Weishaar, 1995).

In summary, in contrast to psychoanalysis, cognitive therapy views personality development as dynamic and as the result of cognitive structures, evolution, biology, social influences, and conditioning. In closing, from a cognitive therapy perspective, personality is neither the result of a single cause, nor a linear cause, but the complex interaction of environmental, biological, social interpersonal and intrapersonal factors interacting simultaneously.

COGNITIVE DISTORTIONS

Cognitive distortions are also called **cognitive-behavioral** attributions. This is where clients make attributional errors in thinking and, generally speaking, clients are more likely to blame someone else for a situation provided that the person is someone else. There is a tendency to underestimate situational explanations of behavior, provided that the situation involves others. Blaming someone for a situational event is called the major **attributional error** within social psychology.

Beck's notion of cognitive distortions and automatic thoughts ties into the automaticity theory that was discussed in Chapter 1, and the notion of automatic thoughts suggest that these cognitions are outside of the client's awareness and they do not require attentional resources or mental effort.

Beck (1976) described the following cognition distortions: personalization, dichotomous thinking, selective abstraction, arbitrary inference, and overgeneralization. **Personalization** is when a client assumes responsibility for events outside of his or her control. **Dichotomous thinking** is polarizing or thinking in absolutistic terms. For example, things are totally good or totally bad. **Selective abstraction** is when a client focuses on negative aspects of a situation while ignoring positive or neutral aspects, and **arbitrary inference** is when a client arbitrarily reaches a negative conclusion. Mind reading and negative predictions are two variations of this cognitive distortion.

Mind reading is when a client attempts to predict what someone is thinking based on subtle and nonverbal cues, and **negative prediction** is when a client assumes the worst will occur without supporting evidence. **Overgeneralization** is when a client draws conclusions from one or more isolated events and then applies these conclusions to a variety of situations. Magnification and minimization are variants of this concept. Essentially, a client **magnifies** the negative aspects of a situation and **minimizes** the positive aspects.

In summary, cognitive distortions are automatic thoughts that result in faulty informational processing. These cognitive attributions are intercorrelated and develop partly through socialization.

COGNITIVE MODEL OF DEPRESSION

As previously stated, Freud viewed depression as retroflective anger and Beck proposed a **cognitive triad** to explain depression; hence, depression is the result of a client having a negative view of the self, the world, and the future. As the reader is aware, Beck's model is not the only one of depression.

Seligman has a model, as well as Lewinsohn, Clarke, Hops, and Andrews (1990) who also have cognitive models of depression.

Beck found that feelings of hopelessness and a pessimistic view of the future are associated with depression (Beck, Rush et al., 1979a, 1979b; Beck et al., 1985). Since depressed clients lack coping skills, they tend to be paralyzed when they face unfortunate situations, and depressed clients tend to magnify the difficulties of everyday life. Depressed clients need structured activities and their cognitive attributions must be confronted. Problem solving-training can help depressed clients solve problems and develop hope. Finally, the Depression Checklist, developed by John Preston, Psy.D., is a clinical instrument to assess depression. The researchers who are using this instrument can see how it correlates with the Beck Depression Scale because reliable data are needed. The reader may recall in Chapter 1 that the SPSS control lines for finding confidence intervals for reliability indices were provided.

DEPRESSION CHECKLIST

Patient's Name: _____ Date: _____

Biological Functioning

A. Sleep Problems
1. No sleep problems ❑ 0
2. Occasional sleep problems ❑ 1
3. Frequent awakenings during the night or early morning awakening
    a. 1–3 nights during last week ❑ 2
    b. 4+ nights during last week ❑ 3

B. Appetite Problems
1. No changes in appetite ❑ 0
2. Some appetite change (up or down) but no weight gain or loss ❑ 1
3. Significant appetite change (up or down) with weight gain or loss (5 lbs. + or − during past month) ❑ 3

C. Fatigue
1. Little or no noticeable daytime fatigue ❑ 0
2. Fatigued or exhausted during the day
    a. Occasionally ❑ 1
    b. 1–3 days during the last week ❑ 2
    c. 4+ days during the last week ❑ 3

Cognitive Therapy

D. Sex Drive
1. No change in sex drive ☐ 0
2. Decrease in sex drive
   a. Slight ☐ 1
   b. Moderate ☐ 2
   c. No sex drive ☐ 3

E. Anhedonia (decreased capacity to experience joy)
1. Despite time of sadness, I am able to have times of enjoyment or pleasure ☐ 0
2. Decreased ability to enjoy life
   a. Slight ☐ 1
   b. Moderate ☐ 2
   c. Absolutely no joy in life ☐ 3

Total Score, Biological Functioning _____

Note: Scores of 2 or 3 on any of the above items suggest that biological functioning has likely been affected by the depression, and antidepressant medication treatment may be indicated (especially if any scores of 3 are present). If all scores are 0 or 1, antidepressant medications probably are not indicated.

Emotional/Psychological Symptoms

A. Sadness and Despair
1. No pronounced sadness ☐ 0
2. Occasional sadness ☐ 1
3. Times of intense sadness ☐ 2
4. Intense sadness almost every day ☐ 3

B. Self-esteem
1. I feel confident and good about myself ☐ 0
2. I sometimes doubt myself ☐ 1
3. I often feel inadequate, inferior, or lacking in self-confidence ☐ 2
4. I feel completely worthless most of the time ☐ 3

C. Apathy and Motivation
1. It is easy to feel motivated and enthusiastic about things ☐ 0
2. I occasionally find it hard to "get started" on projects, work, etc. ☐ 1
3. I often feel unmotivated or apathetic ☐ 2
4. It is almost impossible to "get started" with projects, work, etc. ☐ 3

D. Negative Thinking/Pessimism
1. I think in relatively positive ways about my life and my future ☐ 0
2. I occasionally feel pessimistic ☐ 1

3. I often feel pessimistic ❏ 2
   4. The world seems extremely negative to me and the future looks hopeless ❏ 3
E. **Emotional Control**
   1. When I feel unpleasant feelings, such emotions may hurt, but I do not feel totally overwhelmed ❏ 0
   2. I occasionally feel overwhelmed by inner emotions ❏ 1
   3. I often feel extremely overwhelmed by inner feelings *or* I feel absolutely no inner feelings ❏ 2
F. **Irritability and Frustration**
   1. I do not experience undue irritability and frustration ❏ 0
   2. I occasionally feel quite irritable and frustrated ❏ 1
   3. I often feel quite irritable and become easily frustrated
      a. 1–3 days during the last week ❏ 2
      b. 4+ days during the last week ❏ 3

Total Score, Emotional/Psychological Symptoms _____

Total Score: Biological _____ + **Emotional** _____ = _____

Developed by John Preston, Psy.D.

THERAPEUTIC PROCESS

Therapeutic Goals

The goal of cognitive therapy is to change clients' faulty styles of processing information. Very similar to other cognitive-behavioral approaches, cognitive therapy questions clients' dysfunctional cognitions and encourages applying the scientific method to thinking. During the initial phase of therapy, Levels I and II counseling skills are employed and toward the intermediate and later phases of therapy, Level III challenging skills are used. Moreover, cognitive therapy is a problem-centered therapy and one goal is symptom relief.

Another goal is to teach clients how to modify biased ways of processing information. During therapy, the client and therapist engage in experiments and they test the validity of beliefs. The client decides whether to accept or reject beliefs based on scientifically exploring beliefs. In contrast to popular misunderstandings, cognitive therapy is not positive thinking—substituting negative beliefs with positive ones; rather, it is based on the scientific principles of testing reality.

Treatment

Cognitive therapy uses cognitive and behavioral techniques. For example, decatastrophizing, reattribution, redefining, and decentering fall under the cognitive domain.

DECATASTROPHIZING is a "what if" technique that prepares the client for the worst possible consequences, and the client is taught coping strategies. For example, "Suppose your mother died, how would you cope with that?" The goal of decatastrophisizing is to decrease avoidance behavior and to enhance coping skills.

REATTRIBUTION tests automatic thoughts and it teaches clients to reinterpret their symptoms. For example, clients are encouraged to explore several possible causes of an event and not to just mentally lock into one interpretation. In summary, reattribution is a process of reexamining and reinterpreting events.

REDEFINING is a cognitive strategy to redefine a problem employing an activity that the client can perform concretely, and to show the client that personal control does exist. For example, if a woman says, "I cannot meet available men," the problem can be redefined as, "I need to introduce myself to more men and go through the large numbers so I can find ones that appeal to me."

DECENTERING is a cognitive technique to get the client to decenter from oneself and to perform behavioral experiments that show that he or she is not the center of attention, but has made an attributional error. Decentering is a method to help clients alleviate anxiety around embarrassment and shyness.

Six common behavior techniques from cognitive therapy are the following: homework, hypothesis testing, exposure therapy, behavioral rehearsal, diversion, activity scheduling, and graded-task assignment.

HOMEWORK is used to get clients to apply cognitive therapy techniques outside of therapy sessions. For example, clients can be given homework assignments to record daily thoughts and emotions and to hypothesize how thoughts influenced emotions.

HYPOTHESIS TESTING is both a cognitive and behavior technique. First, clients are taught to test the validity of their thoughts by asking if their thoughts are valid. Second, clients are taught to test their beliefs against objective reality. Clearly, monitoring dysfunctional thoughts against objective reality is behavioral.

EXPOSURE THERAPY, like hypothesis testing, has cognitive and behavioral dimensions. Imaginary exposure is the first step toward desensitizing clients to anxiety and stress; and second, in vivo exposure, clients expose themselves to situations that produce anxiety and stress.

BEHAVIORAL REHEARSAL is the therapeutic use of role-playing of techniques that clients will use in actual situations, and if clients can practice or rehearse new skills with a variety of individuals, such as in group therapy, the transfer of skills to real situations increases. Finally, clients can cognitively rehearse new skills, and this can add with skills generalization.

DIVERSION is a behavioral technique used to distract and divert clients' attentions from negative and dysfunctional cognitions. This technique can include a variety of strategies such as physical activity, work, play activity, mental imagery, meditation, hypnosis, social contact, and so on.

ACTIVITY SCHEDULING is when clients set up routines to offset emotions like depression. Essentially, clients are encouraged to engage in activities and to rate such activities on a 0 to 10 scale in terms of mastery and pleasure experienced. Finally, such data provides clients with a wealth of information about daily activities.

GRADED TASK ASSIGNMENT is the gradual increase of tasks for clients. Clients are encouraged to take steps in an incremental fashion toward tasks. For example, if a client fears socializing, perhaps at first, he or she would be encouraged to observe social groups and to later slowly engage with such groups.

In summary, cognitive therapy uses a variety of cognitive and behavioral techniques. As this writer stressed, cognitive and behavioral techniques overlap and with many cognitive techniques, there are parallel behavioral techniques. Finally, the goal of cognitive therapy is to aid clients with modifying their faulty cognitive profiles, and the scientific method of experimentation is used to get clients to test the validity of their beliefs.

Role of Therapist

Guided discovery or behavioral experiments are used to get clients to modify dysfunctional cognitions. For example, experiments are employed whereby a client tests certain beliefs and draws conclusions from those data. In contrast to Ellis and some REBT therapists, clients are not cajoled into accepting new self-enhancing beliefs; in fact, the therapist encourages the client to consider data and relevant alternatives.

Cognitive therapy tends to encourage **collaborative empiricism,** or a collaborative relationship between the therapist and client. The client is actively involved in determining the goals of therapy and the two—client and therapist—become co-investigators in conducting behavioral and cognitive experiments (Beck & Emery, 1985).

Socratic dialogue, or skillful questioning, is the most used technique in cognitive therapy, and it is used to encourage new learning, to identify and clarify concerns, and to explore dysfunctional cognitions.

Therapeutic Relationship

As previously stated, therapeutic relationship is collaborative. Clients are assessed from a cognitive perspective and the client and therapist clarify therapeutic goals. With severe depression, often, the therapist is more active and directive and clients are taught how thoughts, behaviors, and feelings affect each other.

Many clients enter cognitive therapy believing in **subjective reasoning** or assuming that feelings are objective and factual. Cognitive therapists show clients how "**hot cognitions**" or strong cognitions affect emotional functioning and produce extreme emotions.

During the initial phase of therapy, Levels I and II skills are used to establish a relationship. Toward the end of each session, clients are often asked for feedback of what they liked or disliked; this process of receiving feedback enhances the collaborative relationship and it allows for therapeutic alterations to fit clients' individual preferences.

During the middle phases of therapy, the focus shifts from just mainly Levels I and II counseling skills to exploring clients' maladaptive patterns of thinking and the therapist teaches clients about **automatic thoughts**—thoughts that occur spontaneously and are at a nonconscious level. Also during this phase, clients are given homework assignments to monitor automatic thoughts and clients are encouraged to become more self-reliant and are alerted to the fact that therapy is time limited.

Even though therapy depends on clients' concerns, unipolar depression can usually be successfully treated in fifteen to twenty-five sessions, while moderately severe depression usually requires four to five weeks of biweekly sessions and later may require ten to fifteen weekly sessions (Beck & Weishaar, 1995; Dobson, 1989). Once clients leave therapy, it is not uncommon for them to return to therapy for booster sessions.

Beck differs from Ellis in that he views the therapeutic relationship as critical for therapy to proceed, but unlike Carl Rogers, Beck does not see therapeutic relationships as necessary and sufficient for therapeutic growth to occur.

In summary, cognitive therapists use collaborative empiricism, Socratic dialogue, and guided discovery to forge a therapeutic relationship with clients. Beck and Ellis differ in their therapeutic styles—since Ellis tends to be more forceful, directive, persuasive, and confrontive, while Beck uses more Socratic dialogue and structure than Ellis. In addition, cognitive therapy is more inductive and REBT is more deductive. Cognitive therapy tends to allow clients to discover cognitive distortions and other dysfunctional thoughts on their own. Finally, Beck believes that each emotional disorder has its own cognitive profile, while Ellis believes that emotional problems are the result of irrational beliefs and not just errors in processing information.

Multicultural Applications and Limitations

Beck (1995) claims that cognitive therapy is effective with clients with different educational levels, income, and background. Like other cognitive-behavioral approaches, one would expect to find that cognitive therapy has many applications for minority groups; however, this writer would like to see studies investigating the effects of cognitive therapy with minority clients. The reader is aware that a paucity of studies have investigated the effects of REBT with minority clients, but as far as this writer is aware of, studies with specific minority groups as the focus of research have been conducted with cognitive therapy. Moreover, this writer believes that some of the more cognitively based techniques may be difficult for some minority clients to follow. Nevertheless, the fact that cognitive therapy is short-term and has behavioral aspects suggests that it may be applicable for some minority clients.

Critique

COMPREHENSIVENESS. Because cognition is primary with cognitive therapy, other dimensions of human functioning are overlooked or are secondary, like behaviors. Clearly, multimodal behavior therapy, rational-emotive behavior therapy (REBT), and Bandura's social learning theory is more comprehensive and expansive than cognitive therapy. Even in comparison to psychoanalysis and some psychodynamic approaches, cognitive therapy is lacking in not explaining human development. Moreover, cognitive therapy, unlike developmental psychology, does not explain human development and is not a comprehensive theory.

PRECISION AND TESTABILITY. Since concepts are operationally defined and easily testable, cognitive therapy has outstanding precision and testability, and like other cognitive-behavioral approaches, it encourages precision and testability.

PARSIMONY. Cognitive therapy is parsimonious and uses few concepts to explain psychological constructs and is probably the most concise of the traditional cognitive-behavioral approaches.

EMPIRICAL VALIDITY. Beck (1995) reported that cognitive therapy has been tested extensively since 1977. Controlled studies and meta-analysis have found that cognitive therapy is effective in treating unipolar depression, generalized anxiety disorder (Butler, Fennell, Robson, & Gelder, 1991), panic disorder (Barlow, Craske, Cerney, & Klosko, 1989; Beck, Sokol, Clark, Berchick & Wright, 1992; Clark, Salkorskis, Hackmann, Middleton, & Gelder, 1992), social phobia (Gelernter et al., 1991; Heimberg et al., 1990), substance abuse (Woody et al., 1983), eating disorders (Agras et al., 1992; Fairburn, Jones, Peveler, Hope, & Doll, 1991; Garner et al., 1993), couples and marital therapy (Baucom, Sayers, & Seher, 1990), obsessive-compulsive disorder (Salkovkis & Kirk, 1989), posttraumatic stress disorder (Dancu & Foa, 1992; Parrott & Howes, 1991), personality disorders (Beck et al., 1990; Layden, Newman, Freeman, & Morse, 1993; Young, 1990), chronic pain (Miller, 1991; Turk, Meichenbaum, & Genest, 1983), hypochondriasis (Warwick & Salkovskis, 1989), and schizophrenia (Chadwick & Lowe, 1990; Kindgom & Turkington, 1994; Perris, Ingleton, & Johnson, 1993). For more complicated disorders like obsessive-compulsive, posttraumatic stress disorder, personality disorder, and schizophrenia, cognitive therapy is an adjunctive treatment (Simons, Murphy, Levine, & Wetzel, 1986).

Beck and Weishaar (1995) stated that eighty-six of ninety-nine studies supported the cognitive therapy notion of unipolar depression, and thirty of thirty-four studies endorsed the theory of cognition distortions and biased informational processing underlying depression. When cognitive therapy is compared to antidepressant medication, it is found to be superior or equal to antidepressant medication (Blackburn, Bishop, Glen, Whalley, & Christie, 1981; Dobson, 1989). In addition, Beck and Weishaar stated that six studies compared drug use alone and in combination with cognitive therapy, and four studies found the combination approach to be superior (Blackburn et al., 1981; Blackburn, Eunsun, & Bishop, 1986; Maldonado, 1982; Teasdale, Fennell, Hibbert, & Amies, 1984), but only two studies found drugs alone to be equal to the combined treatment (Murphy, Simons, Wetzel, & Lustman, 1983; Simons, Murphy, Levine, & Wetzel, 1986). In conclusion, there appears to be greater improvement with cognitive therapy over time (Antonuccio, 1995).

HEURISTIC VALUE. Cognitive therapy helped stimulate the cognitive movement within psychology, and, currently, cognitive-behavioral therapy is the major paradigm within psychology. Cognitive therapy was one of the first cognitive-behavioral therapies to use manualized treatments and led the way for manualized treatments within cognitive-behavioral therapies. Even though cognitive therapy is the treatment of choice for unipolar depression, it has influenced the treatment of anxiety disorders, personality disorders, substance abuse disorders, and family therapy. Finally, cognitive therapy has had excellent heuristic value.

APPLIED VALUE. Cognitive therapy has excellent applied value, and as previously stated, it has been used to treat a variety of psychological disorders such as unipolar depression, anxiety, trauma, and so on.

SUMMARY

Cognitive therapy is an outstanding treatment for unipolar depression, and even though REBT predates it, cognitive therapy developed independently from REBT. Like other cognitive-behavioral therapies, cognitive therapy utilizes Level III counseling skills, and it expanded the scope of behavior therapy by focusing on cognition and by moving beyond the stimulus-response theories of neobehaviorism. Finally, cognitive therapy emphasizes that clients' feelings can be changed by changing clients' cognitions.

Glossary of Key Terms

Activity scheduling. A behavioral strategy that establishes routine activities or behaviors for clients.

Arbitrary inference. Drawing conclusions through subjective reasoning.

Automatic thoughts. Thoughts that are spontaneous and nonconscious and do not require cognitive resources or attention.

Behavioral rehearsal. Applying cognitive skills to actual situations, often done through role-playing as the first phase.

Catastrophizing. Exaggerating the meaning of situations.

Cognitive distortions. Errors in the processing of information.

Cognitive shift. A biased shift in the processing of information.

Cognitive triad. The negative view that a depressed client has about the self, world, and the future.

Decatastrophizing. A what-if technique that helps insulate clients from the consequences of what they fear.

Dichotomous thinking. A cognitive distortion in which a client sees things in black and white terms.

Graded-task assignment. Gradually increasing the difficulty of assigned tasks for clients.

Hot cognitions. Strong thoughts that produce powerful feelings.

Magnification. Exaggerating the meaning of an event.

Overgeneralization. A cognitive distortion in which clients construct general rules from isolated events.

Personalization. A cognitive distortion in which clients assume personal responsibility for events that are not within their control.

Reattribution. Reexamining the perceived causes of events. This is a process of getting clients to reinterpret their cognitive attributions.

Schema. A cognitive theory that assumes that clients have general rules and constructs of how the world should operate.

Selective abstraction. A cognitive distortion in which clients make interpretations and conclusions from isolated events.

Sociotrophy. A personality style in which a client has desires for closeness, dependency, and social support.

Subjective reasoning. Clients attempt to reason through their emotions and error of assuming that emotions are objective and factual.

Review Questions

1. Compare and contrast cognitive therapy with other cognitive behavioral theories.
2. Discuss and provide examples of automatic thoughts, cognitive distortions, and core beliefs.
3. Describe the empirical evidence that supports cognitive therapy as a treatment for depression.
4. Explain why Joseph Wolpe was a major opponent of cognitive therapy and the cognitive movement within psychology.
5. Compare and contrast cognitive therapy with other models of depression.

Beck Institute

GSB Building
City Line and Belmont Avenues, Suite 700
Bala Lynwyd, PA 19004–1610
Telephone: (610) 664-3020
Fax: (610) 664-4437
E-mail: beckinst@gim.net
Website: http://www.beckinstitute.org

Journals

Journal of Cognitive Psychotherapy: An International Quarterly, edited by Dr. Robert Leahy.
American Institute for Cognitive Therapy
30 East 60th Street, Suite 1107

New York, NY 10022
Telephone: (212) 308-2440
E-mail: AICT@aol.com
Website: www.cognitivetherapyNYC.com

Cognitive Therapy and Research
Kluwer Academic/Plenum Publishers
Kluwer Law International
233 Spring St. Floor 7
New York, NY 10013-1522
Telephone: (212) 620-8000
Website: http://www.sci.sdsu.edu/CAL/CTR.html

Assess Instruments

The following instruments can be ordered from The Psychological Corporation, 555 Academic Court, San Antonio, TX, 78204-9990. Telephone: 1-800-228-0752.

Beck Depression Inventory and Manual
Beck Anxiety Inventory
Beck Hopelessness Scale
Beck Scale for Suicidal Ideation

Chapter 9

COGNITIVE-BEHAVIOR MODIFICATION

CHAPTER OVERVIEW

Donald Meichenbaum attempted to bridge the gap between cognitive-semantic therapists, or we would call them cognitive-behavioral or cognitive therapists such as George Kelly, Jerome Frank, Albert Ellis, Aaron Beck, and Jerome L. Singer, and the technology of behavior therapy. Meichenbaum placed his emphasis on inner speech and images and how to conceptualize them. Essentially, he wanted to know which constructs best explain what goes on in our heads, and he referred to attributions, appraisals, interpretations, self-reinforcements, beliefs, and defense mechanisms as internal dialogue.

Meichenbaum oppugned traditional behavior therapy because it lacked a cognitive dimension. Even though his approach is not an overarching theoretical approach, like the theories of Ellis, Beck, and Lazarus, he stated that his theoretical position is closer to that of Beck and he offers clients methods and phases of coping with anxiety, anger, trauma, pain, and other psychological issues (Meichenbaum, 1977, 1994).

Specifically, Meichenbaum developed cognitive-behavior modification, self-instructional training, and stress inoculation, but slightly differently from Ellis, Beck, and Lazarus, he believes that a client's internal dialogue, self-statements, or self-talk affect his or her feelings and behavior. As previously stated, Meichenbaum emphasizes how clients can cope with anxiety, stress, anger, pain, and posttraumatic stress, and so on. Even though he uses cognitive restructuring, according to his theoretical approach, the goal is to modify clients' self-verbalizations (Meichenbaum, 1985, 1986, 1993a, 1993b).

KEY CONCEPTS

In 1969, Meichenbaum started **cognitive-behavior modification (CBM)** (Meichenbaum, 1969). CBM states that behaviors change as the result of inner speech, cognitive structures, expectations, inferences, other behaviors, and outcomes. In many regards, Meichenbaum's theory is similar to that of Beck, and Meichenbaum, like Beck, adopted an information processing theory to explain cognitive-behavior modification. Meichenbaum found that when self-talk was added to behavioral techniques like systematic desensitization, these techniques were more effective and he found that cognitive processes responded to the same rules that applied to behavior therapy—mainly classical and operant conditioning.

Unlike Ellis and some REBT practitioners, Meichenbaum tends not to use direct and vigorous techniques to confront clients, and his focus is to help clients be aware of what they say to themselves on a covert level. As stated several times, theoretically CBM is similar to cognitive therapy or Beck's approach, but since it stresses primarily cognitions and behaviors, it is not as comprehensive as Lazarus's multimodal behavior therapy.

Meichenbaum starts therapy by assessing clients' levels of functioning in terms of their ability to cope with their problems and he asks a series of questions to determine the appropriate cognitive-behavioral strategies. For example, perhaps he would ask clients the following: "What have you been doing to cope with your concerns?" "Which forms of self-talk could you be using that prevent you from effectively coping?" "Are you doing things that are self-defacing?" It is apparent that Meichenbaum's approach is a problem centered one.

In 1969, Meichenbaum developed the term **self-talk** when he noticed that schizophrenics improved when they learned to modify their unhealthy self-talk and started his work with self-statements. Later, he developed a treatment manual on self-instructional training and PTSD (Meichenbaum, 1997, 1994).

Self-instructional training was developed from a method used by the French pharmacist Emile Coué for self-improvement with self-instructional training. Clients are taught a variety of self-control procedures such as self-monitoring, self-planning, self-evaluation, and techniques for cognitive restructuring. For the details of Coué's influence on psychotherapy, see Sapp (2000).

According to Kalodner (1995), self-instructional training is a method of charting or monitoring self-statements and replacing unhealthy self-statements with healthy ones. For example, a client may be taught the following: I can handle being divorced from my wife, even though I do not like this situation, and every day I will be able to handle things better. The initial part of this process is practicing self-affirmations in nonstressful situations and later using them during stressful and anxious situations.

Stress inoculation training (SIT) is the psychological analogy of inoculating clients against stress, and the goal is to gain psychological resistance to stress. More specifically, SIT is a group of eclectic cognitive-behavioral techniques that includes psychoeducational instructions, Socratic questioning, classical conditioning, operant conditioning, imaginal exposure, and cognitive restructuring.

There are three phases to SIT: conceptualization, skills acquisition and rehearsal, and application and follow-through. During the **conceptualization phase** the client is given in lay terms the explanations for why he or she responds to stressful events. Meichenbaum points out that during this phase, the conceptual framework for therapy should match the clients' expectations; thus, capitalizing on clients' expectancies and the placebo effects. The conceptualization phase is also when Levels I and II counseling skills are implemented. One goal of this phase of treatment is for the client and therapist to develop a working alliance. This is similar to the collaborative relationship stressed by Beck. Another goal of this phase of psychotherapy is to assess antecedents and consequences of stressful situations. For example, antecedents may be assessed by asking, "Describe when you become tense and anxious." "Can you describe situations that make you feel stressed?" "Are there any events that precede your anxiety attacks?" "After you have a panic attack, what happens next?" "What are the outcomes of being stressed out?" "How do you feel when you have an anxiety attack?" The third goal of this phase is to use guided imagery or **imagery-based recall** to guide a client through a stress event. Guided imagery allows the therapist to assess the client's cognitions, affects, and behaviors when imagining the stressful event. Moreover, during this phase, clients monitor thoughts, feelings, and behaviors. Finally, the therapist and client determine which techniques may be used during the skills acquisition and rehearsal phase.

Meichenbaum and Deffenbacher (1988) and Meichenbaum (1994) reported teaching a variety of coping skills during the skills and acquisition phase such as problem solving skills, relaxation skills, cognitive restructuring skills, and so on. Meichenbaum presents skills as techniques that can generalize to a variety of situations. He teaches clients how to anticipate stressful events and to have well-learned skills as automatic responses.

The **application and follow-through phase** of SIT is the continuation of skills generation to the real world. Clients are encouraged to practice skills learned in previous phases in real situations. Again, the use of imagery helps clients bridge the foundation between behavior and cognitive techniques. Clients are urged to practice coping strategies in actual situations and they learn to make adjustments.

The final phase of SIT is **follow through**. It is when clients are prepared for the possibility that treatment effects can weaken over time. Clients are prepared for mistakes and are taught how to cope with mistakes by giving themselves affirmative statements such as, "Okay, I have made some mistakes, but this is not the end of the world and I have to regroup and continue moving forward." "I can handle these setbacks, even though I would have preferred continued progress." "I will figure out how to get things back on track." Because

SIT is a cyclical form of therapy, at times clients need booster sessions. Finally, SIT is a series of methods for teaching clients how to cope with a variety of concerns such as anxiety, stress, reactive depression, anger, pain, and trauma.

THERAPEUTIC PROCESS

Therapeutic Goals

The goal of cognitive-behavior modification is to bridge the gap between behavioral and cognitive dimensions and to show clients how to restructure negative self-talk. First, clients learn how to monitor self-verbalizations and later they learn to modify these verbalizations and to cope with difficult life situations. Finally, within cognitive-behavior modification, the major emphasis is on the clients' self-verbalizations.

Role of Therapist

In some respects, Meichenbaum is similar to both Ellis and Beck, but he reports that his theoretical position is close to that of Beck in that he believes that the therapeutic relationship is crucial for therapy to progress and a fair amount of time is spent on Levels I and II counseling strategies. But unlike nondirective therapy, once the client and therapist have a strong therapeutic alliance, Level III counseling strategies are employed. Finally, cognitive-behavior modification tends not to be as forceful and vigorous as REBT and it tends not to use an expansive array of disputing interventions.

Therapeutic Relationship

As stated repeatedly, Meichenbaum uses Levels I and II counseling strategies during the conceptualization phase and unlike Ellis, he has faith in the beneficial effects of the therapeutic alliance between client and therapist; however, unlike nondirective and some psychodynamic therapists, Meichenbaum is active, directive, and engaging.

Multicultural Applications and Limitations

There is mounting research that the effects of racism, sexism, and homophobia can produce learned helplessness. If minority clients can inoculate themselves with a sense of control, then it is possible that these groups can develop an optimistic explanatory cognitive style and enhancements in overall mental health (Lee, 1996). Without a doubt, an inflexible therapist could overly emphasize minority clients' cognitive dimensions and fail to address subtle and overt acts of racism, sexism, and homophobia. The major strength of cognitive-behavior modification is its ability to help minority clients deal with a racist, sexist, and homophobic society.

Critique

COMPREHENSIVENESS. Clearly cognitive-behavior modification is not as comprehensive as social learning theories and it has not adequately addressed the social issues of America such as racial discrimination. Without a doubt, coping is a good strategy, but if the United States is to deal with its variety of minority groups, social justice has to occur. Even though cognitive-behavior modification developed through the continuity assumption of cognitive-behavioral theories, it is possibly more comprehensive than cognitive therapy but less comprehensive than REBT, multimodal behavior therapy, and social learning theories. Finally, by focusing solely on cognitions and behaviors, cognitive-behavior modification is not comprehensive and it fails to take into account social psychological variables.

EMPIRICAL VALIDITY. Meichenbaum (1972, 1979, 1990a, 1990b, 1994) has provided empirical support for the cognitive-behavior modification for anxiety disorders, test anxiety, post-traumatic stress disorder, generalized anxiety disorders, dental phobias, headaches, type-A behavior, lower back pain, and anger-control disorders. In summary, cognitive-behavior modification has excellent empirical validity.

PRECISION AND TESTABILITY. Cognitive-behavior modification is a concise theory and has few concepts. Many of the concepts are operationally defined in cognitive-behavioral terms; therefore, cognitive-behavior modification has excellent precision and testability.

HEURISTIC VALUE. Meichenbaum has had strong heuristic value with his theory and like Ellis, Beck, and Lazarus is an architect of cognitive-behavioral therapies. Currently, cognitive-behavior modification is being applied to the treatment of traumas and it emphasizes treatment generalization as part of a treatment package.

APPLIED VALUE. Cognitive-behavior modification has outstanding applied value. For example, it has been used as a supplement to systematic desensitization and has been applied to issues of anger control, reactive depression, anxiety disorders, and health concerns.

SUMMARY

The central goal of cognitive-modification is to teach clients coping and problem solving skills and to show them how to be inoculated against stress. Unlike cognitive therapy and REBT, cognitive-behavior modification attempts to change clients' self-talk or self-statements. Finally, unlike REBT, cognitive-behavior modification is not as directive, confrontive, forceful, and vigorous in attacking clients' irrational self-verbalizations.

Glossary of Key Terms

Cognitive-behavior modification. Techniques for inoculating clients to stress that were developed by Donald Meichenbaum.

Imagery-based recall. The use of guided imagery to assess clients' thoughts, feelings, and behaviors related to stressful events.

Internal dialogue. The covert messages and possibly nonconscious statements that occur at a cognitive level.

Self-affirmations. Positive self-talk that prepares clients to cope with stress.

Self-instructional training. A cognitive-behavioral method of changing clients' negative self-talk into positive self-talk.

Self-talk. The covert and automatic thoughts, messages, images, and so on that clients activate at a covert level.

Stress inoculation training. Cognitive-behavioral strategies that are used to inoculate clients against stress.

Review Questions

1. Compare and contrast cognitive-behavior modification with social learning theories, Adlerian therapy, REBT, multimodal behavior therapy, and cognitive therapy.
2. Critique cognitive-behavior modification from a social justice vantage point. In addition, address multicultural applications and limitations.

Chapter 10

PERSONAL CONSTRUCTS PSYCHOTHERAPY

CHAPTER OVERVIEW

Unlike many of the other cognitive-behavioral approaches discussed within this text, George Kelly (1905–1967) took an intellectual and scholarly approach to counseling. Kelly's **personal construct theory** explores how clients create cognitive constructs about their environments (Schultz & Schultz, 2001). As opposed to drives, reinforcement, or motivation, Kelly described how clients organized their worlds and how as scientists, they tested their hypotheses against the real world. Even though Ellis, Beck, Meichenbaum, and Lazarus credited Kelly as influencing their thinking, Kelly actually resisted being categorized as behavioral or psychoanalytic.

KEY CONCEPTS

George Alexander Kelly's (1905–1967) theory is based on **personal constructs** that means clients are capable of altering their interpretation of events. Kelly believed the way clients respond to things is connected with the way they interpret events. This concept is related to teleology. As the readers may remember, this concept is one of the important concepts of Adler's Individual Psychology, which emphasized goals and purposes and the ends and purposes that clients chose to fulfill themselves (Bannister, 1977).

Constructive alternativism is a concept that clients can change their minds about events, or they can change their interpretations (Rychlak, 1989; Liebert & Speigler, 1990; Sapp, 1997a; Schultz & Schultz, 2001).

Kelly used the term **superordinate construct** to indicate that one construct can control or limit another construct. For example, obtaining an advanced degree within psychology limits or controls one's life in a number of ways. For example, graduate studies will control or limit the number of social events that one can attend. In general, if one is pursuing full-time studies, studying and being a student will be the dominant activity within one's life.

Kelly believed that as opposed to fixed and rigid thinkers, clients were constantly shifting and changing their world views based on new information. Moreover, as previously stated, Kelly believed that clients were like scientists who tested hypotheses and made adjustments and alterations in thinking based on new data.

For Kelly, the word **construct** did not have a colloquial meaning, but rather a bipolar meaning and that constructs are organized and constructed in terms of similarities and differences. For example, to say that a fruit is an apple is to imply that it is not a peach. Constructs are manipulated by construing, interpreting, making abstracts, and finding meaning about events (Soffer, 1993). In addition, clients arrange constructs in an ordinal fashion within their cognitive worlds, which means that constructs are hierarchical. For example, a client with a rigid personality structure may see people as good or bad as a means to control other constructs such as "good people" believe in God and obey God, while "bad people" obey the devil and are not God-fearing.

Interestingly, Kelly stated that clients use constructs in a convenient way. This suggests that concepts have breadth and clients use concepts to maintain their underlying beliefs. Moreover, clients are able to assimilate new elements about a construct which means constructs are **permeable;** however, normally constructs are not totally permeable but flexible enough for clients, depending on personality style, to produce changes within their cognitive systems. In summary, the more flexible a client's personality style, the more permeable constructs will be, but clients with rigid personality styles tend to have difficulty assimilating new information within their cognitive styles. **Preemptive constructs,** which are ones used by rigid thinkers, lead to polarized or dichotomous thinking.

Constellatory constructs can explain why stereotypes occur. For example, once we categorize someone into a certain ethnic or cultural group, we tend to stereotype or to attribute a constellation of traits to that individual. In summary, constellatory constructs permit elements to belong to several realms, but once a realm is chosen, the elements become fixed like the example given about stereotypes.

Propositional constructs allow the most flexible forms of thinking, and they leave elements open for modifications and adjustments. Kelly suggested that clients must balance preemptive constructs between propositional constructs because the overreliance on preemptive constructive thinking can lead to rigid and dogmatic beliefs, while overreliance on propositional constructive thinking can result in indecisiveness.

The basic theorem underlying Kelly's theory is that clients' cognitive processes are assimilated and accommodated by clients' expectations (Kelly, 1955). Kelly stated that clients seek information that supports or fails to support their expectations, and clients are incessantly modifying their cognitive views based on external experiences. From a personal constructs view, a psychological disorder is the result of clients' repetitively using invalid constructs. In addition, psychological disturbances result when clients cannot tolerate changes in their personal constructs or core roles. **Core roles** are roles that clients play that maintains their self-concepts and philosophies of life and they are resistant to changes.

KELLY'S COROLLARIES

1. **Construction Corollary**—clients make predictions concerning events by conceptualizing them as recurring themes.
2. **Choice Corollary**—clients choose one of two dichotomized constructs in terms of the one that best validates their construct system.
3. **Dichotomy Corollary**—a client's cognitive system has a limited number of bipolar or dichotomous constructs.
4. **Range Corollary**—the range of convenience of a construct is limited.
5. **Organizing Corollary**—constructs are ordinally arranged so that they facilitate the client's anticipation of events.
6. **Experience Corollary**—a client's construct system can continuously change as he or she construes similar events.
7. **Modulation Corollary**—the more permeable a client's cognitive construct system, the greater the probability of change within his or her cognitive system.
8. **Fragmentation Corollary**—clients employ a variety of cognitive construct systems and subsystems that are incompatible; therefore, newer constructs are not necessarily extensions of older constructs.
9. **Individuality Corollary**—each client has an idiosyncratic set of personal constructs; therefore, clients can differ in how they interpret the same event.
10. **Commonality Corollary**—when clients employ similar constructs, they are likely to construe events in similar ways.
11. **Sociality Corollary**—socialization or social interactions involve one person construing how another person views a role; therefore, playing a social role involves anticipating the way another expects a social role to be played.

EMOTIONS

Kelly stated that **emotions** were changes and awareness within clients' cognitive systems. Anxiety is when a client does not have response expectancies that predict the future and events are outside the range of convenience; thus, events cannot be predicted nor processed. To summarize, negative emotions are the clients' inability to conceptualize or construct an event.

ACTION STRATEGIES

Fixed-role therapy and The Role Construct Repertory Test (Rep Test) are the two major action strategies. **Fixed-role therapy** is when a client plays the roles of imagery persons whose cognitive constructs are the opposite of theirs. From information gathered from psychotherapy, the therapist writes or constructs fixed roles for his or her clients in which the clients act out these roles during therapy. This writer has found the following exercise useful during therapy. On three sheets of paper, have the client, who will role play, write down three statements with which he or she would agree. The client should only write out statements that state crystal clear positions on some issues. Next, the therapist shuffles the sheets of paper and randomly chooses one. Third, the therapist has the client write out as many arguments as he or she can against the statement the therapist chose blindly. Now, discuss with the client his or her responses. Finally, repeat the process for the remaining statements.

Sapp (1997a) described the **Rep Test** as a means to elicit role constructs by having the client compare and contrast individuals within his or her life. **Sorting** is the process of comparing and contrasting.

Sapp explained the process for the Rep Test as the following. Names of significant others within the clients' lives are written across the top of the Rep Test grid. Clients determine how two individuals within the grid are alike and different from a third person. During the sorting, clients are instructed to circle three names. To the right of the three names endorsed, clients are asked to write in grids the ways in which the two significant others are similar and different from the third significant other. Xs are placed in the two circles in which significant others are alike. In a separate column, clients are asked to write, within the grids, ways in which the two significant others differed from the third.

To summarize, there are four steps to the Rep Test. First, clients provide the names of 15 significant people and then assign an Arabic numeral to the names. Second, clients determine how the three significant others with circles in their grids are similar, two people, and different, how the two similar people differ from the third; these are written in the similarity and difference column.

Third, clients consider the next three people from the sort. Fourth, clients repeat step two and move to the next sort.

The following is an example of a Client's Rep Grid:

CLIENT'S REP GRID

Role		Similarity	Difference
1. Self			
2. Mother			
3. Father			
4. Brother			
5. Sister			
6. Spouse			
7. Ex-girlfriend			
8. Ex-boyfriend			
9. Ex-friend			
10. Attractive Person			
11. Depressed Person			
12. Unhappy Person			
13. Employer			
14. Happy Person			
15. Good Person			

THERAPEUTIC PROCESS

Therapeutic Goals

The goals of personal constructs psychotherapy is to teach clients to act as scientists and to test hypotheses. Like cognitive therapy, another goal is to change the way clients think and process information. In contrast to cognitive therapy, a computer analogy is not used to represent cognitions but like other cognitive-behavioral therapies, the goals are to change clients' cognitions.

Role of Therapist

Like other cognitive-behavioral approaches, personal constructs therapists construct experiments that allow clients to explore their degree of choice. By exploring choice, in some respects, personal constructs psychotherapy is similar to phenomenology and humanism. In contrast, to these philosophical positions, personal constructs psychotherapists are almost totally cognitive and practically do not pay attention to learning, developmental psychology, affect, motivations, needs or even behavior. In addition, personal constructs therapists work with **sociality,** or the ability of clients to play roles with each other. Finally, like other cognitive-behavioral therapies, personal constructs therapists are active, directive, and psychoeducational (Rychlak, 1990).

Therapeutic Relationship

Like phenomenological theories such as Adlerian, personal constructs therapists start therapy by exploring the internal world of the client, and they try to view things through clients' cognitive lenses. Unlike Ellis, they tend to use Levels I and II counseling skills and similar to Beck, they tend to implement collaborative empiricism, and they assist clients with designing and implementing experiments (Neimeyer, 1986). In other words, clients are taught to function as scientists. Therapists are the teachers who use Level III counseling skills. Stated somewhat differently, therapists operate as research supervisors and clients function as student researchers. The relationship between therapists and clients is interactional; clients have expertise with their experiences, while therapists have expertise with testing the validity of experiences and with evaluating experiences.

The issues of transference are construed differently within personal constructs psychotherapy. Unlike Ellis and other cognitive-behavioral therapists, Kelly thought that clients construe therapists through lenses of transference, but, unlike Freud and some psychodynamic therapists, Kelly did not view transference as pathological, but as adaptive. Likewise, Kelly proposed the term **secondary transference** to describe the adaptive feature of transference where clients learn to view the roles of therapists as flexible and able to be revised, validated, and redefined. Moreover, clients are taught to have tentative response expectancies of therapists and they are taught to test their transference expectancies against reality. Unlike traditional psychoanalysis, the blank-screen procedure is not employed since it encourages stereotyping therapists, but what are used are a variety of Level III counseling techniques such as role enactments, modifying clients' range of convenience constructs, and modifying the meanings of constructs.

Multicultural Applications and Limitations

An argument can be made that, like other cognitive-behavioral therapies, personal constructs psychotherapy has many applications for Latinos, African Americans, American Indians, Asians, and other cultural groups, but what is lacking is data that show the multicultural efficacy of personal constructs psychotherapy. Clearly, the strong cognitive dimension of this therapy does not allow the intensive exploration of racism, sexism, social class discrimination, family issues, and other salient features which are pertinent to cultural groups within the United States. In conclusion, one difficulty some cultural groups will have with this therapy is the minor role that affects plays.

Critique

COMPREHENSIVENESS. Personal constructs psychotherapy is an intellectual approach to psychotherapy and it is ahistorical in that it does not describe the developmental process in which clients develop into rational beings. In many respects, this therapy is similar to the approach of Beck, and even though personal constructs psychotherapy employs secondary transference, it does not intensively explore historical and nonconscious and motivational influences.

PARSIMONY. Personal constructs psychotherapy is parsimonious almost to a fault, and it does not use learning, motivation, and level of consciousness to explain behavior. Because clients are perceived as scientists who test hypotheses, this is an intellectual and cognitive form of psychotherapy.

EMPIRICAL VALIDITY. Neimeyer (1986) claimed that there are about 1,000 empirical studies investing personal constructs psychotherapy. In addition, a great deal of research has supported the use of the Rep Test and there is general support for several of Kelly's propositions. For example, there is support for Kelly's ideas that clients with schizophrenia have disordered thought. The major drawback to the empirical validity is that most of the studies are correlational or nonexperimental. Sophisticated experimental research is needed to support the postulates of Kelly's theory (Sapp, 1997a).

PRECISION AND TESTABILITY. Personal constructs psychotherapy has excellent precision and testability, and in comparison to other cognitive-behavioral therapies, it has clear propositions that can be easily tested. Being an excellent theory, personal constructs psychotherapy has many hypotheses that can be easily derived from the theoretical framework.

HEURISTIC VALUE. Unlike the United States, personal constructs psychotherapy is stronger in Canada, Israel, Europe, and Australia. For example, during the 1980s, the Centre for Personal Construct Psychology was established in England, and the *International Journal of Personal Construct Psychology* started publication in the 1980s. In the 1990s, the first volume of a series entitled *Advances in Personal Construct Psychology* was published (Shultz & Shultz, 2001).

APPLIED VALUE. Kelly's theory has applications to vocational psychology. For example, vocational psychologists can use the Rep Test to measure clients' attitudes towards certain careers. In addition, businesses have used the Rep Test to measure consumers' attitudes toward certain products. In summary, personal constructs psychotherapy has application to counseling psychology, business, occupational counseling, and vocational psychology. Finally, Kelly's theory has outstanding applied value.

SUMMARY

Personal constructs psychology is a theory of human thought and reasoning. Kelly did not derive nor develop his theory from existing theories; therefore, he did not view his theory as cognitive, affective, or conative. Kelly did not accept that all constructs would be coterminous within the bounds of personality theories. In reality, Kelly's theory is a paradox. First, it is almost completely cognitive, yet it pays minimal attention to cognition, affection, motivation, needs, and behavior; but within the same vein, it subsumes all aspects of the personality with individual controlling constructs such as feelings, behavior, motivation, and so on.

In some respects, Kelly was a humanist in that he viewed the universe as consisting of integrated parts. As previously alluded to, Kelly's position is narrow and broad and it is an adventurous theory that cannot be easily pigeonholed. Personal constructs psychotherapy has broad applications to counseling psychology, clinical psychology, multicultural counseling, and industrial organizational psychology. Finally, this theory is a constructivist one, and it is a sophisticated system of psychotherapy.

Glossary of Key Terms

Constellatory construct. A construct that permits elements from several constructs to coexist simultaneously; nevertheless, after elements are chosen in a particular fashion, the other elements become fixed. This suggests that there are some automaticity aspects once a client chooses certain constructs.

Construct. A mental abstraction that explores similarities and differences of elements.

Constructive alternativism. A term that extends beyond radical determinism and it suggests that clients can change their interpretations about events from the past.

Fixed-role therapy. Almost a form of psychodrama in which clients play particular roles from a specified period of time. The goal is to show clients that roles do not have to be rigid or fixed.

Individual corollary. The notion that clients' intraindividually construct their reality and that there are vast individual differences to clients' realities.

Permeability. The idea that new elements can penetrate clients' ranges of convenience.

Preemptive construct. A form of cognitive distortion in which clients view elements as categorical, and polarized thinking leads to viewing one aspect of an element.

Propositional construct. A divergent manner of thinking that leaves elements open to change.

Range of convenience. A broad spectrum of events in which constructs can be applied. Constructs that have broad elements tend to have a wider range of convenience and breadth.

Role Construct Repertory Test (Rep Test). A test used to explore the constructs that are important to clients.

Self-characterization. A technique like the Rep Test used to assess clients' construct systems. For example, clients can be asked to write a character sketch in which they play the principal roles.

Sociality corollary. The observation that people from the same culture tend to construe events in a similar way. This proposition describes how people are able to construe each other's constructs.

Superordinate construct. Constructs that control other constructs.

Journal of Constructivist Psychology. This journal publishes theoretical, empirical, and methodological developments in such diverse topics of constructivism as personal construct theory, structural-developmental and social constructionist approaches, constructivist family therapy, and narrative psychology. The editor of this journal is Dr. Robert A. Neimeyer, Dept. of Psychology, University of Memphis, Memphis, TN, 38152, USA (b.neimeyer@mail.pscy.memphis.edu). Subscription to the quarterly publication can be arranged through Taylor Francis, 1900 Frost Road, Suite 101, Bristol, PA 19007–1598; phone (800) 821-8312; fax (215) 785-5515. Personal subscriptions are $75/year; institutional $155.

North American Personal Construct Network (NAPCN). NAPCN membership is open to anyone worldwide. NAPCN organizes a biennial conference, and members receive a newsletter, discounted rates for NAPCN conferences, and a subscription to the *Journal of Constructivist Psychology.*

For 2000, regular memberships are $66 US or $100 CDN for persons in North America. Student memberships are $36 US or $55 CDN for students in North America and also include subscriptions to the journal and newsletter. Members from outside North America are also welcome, but there is an added charge to cover overseas postage on journal subscriptions. Regular memberships are $76 US and student memberships are $46 US for persons from outside North America.

The membership is substantially less than an individual subscription to the *Journal of Constructivist Psychology* if it were ordered directly from the publisher. If one joins NAPCN after the journal subscription year commences, new members will receive that year's back issues.

Dues payments should be in check or money order payable to NAPCN. They should be mailed to Stephanie Harter, Ph.D., Psychology Department, Box 42051, Texas Tech University, Lubbock, TX 79409–2051, USA. Please include your name, affiliation, address, and email for membership database.

Inquiries can also be sent to Stephanie Harter, NAPCN Treasurer, at steph.harter@ttu.edu.

To contribute to *The Constructivist Chronicle,* contact the editor, Jonathan Raskin, at raskinj@matrix.newpatlz.edu.

European Personal Construct Association (EPCA). EPCA comprises over twelve separate country groups and, currently, just over 100 members. It has supported the development of strong national groups in Germany (membership varies between sixty and 100) and Ireland (currently forty strong). This association tends to branch off from its services as the national dimension develops. It has some sixty-odd UK members, and fulfills a particularly valuable service for smaller countries groupings like Spain, Portugal, the Netherlands, Scandinavia, and the Yugoslav regions, acting through a group of national representatives.

Inquiries about EPCA membership should be sent to the Membership Secretary, Ann Howard, Kent Cottage, The Drive, Belmont, Surrey SM2 7DH; about EPCA overall to the Convenor, Pam Denicolo (P.M.Denicolo@reading.ac.uk), Community Studies, Bulmershe Court, University of Reading, Reading, Berks; and the Newsletter to John Fisher at John.M.Fisher@compuserve.com.

PCP International Conferences. The 2003 PCP International Congress will be held in Europe. EPCA is deciding between Huddersfield, UK and Israel.

The 2005 PCP International Congress will be held in North America to commemorate the fiftieth anniversary of the publication of Kelly's

The Psychology of Personal Constructs. NAPCN will organize this in Columbus, Ohio, where Kelly spent many years as a Professor of Clinical Psychology.

A website for Personal Construct Psychology is located at: http://repgrid.com/pcp/.

Review Questions

1. How does Kelly's theory differ from REBT, multimodal behavior therapy, cognitive therapy, cognitive-behavior modification, and Adlerian therapy?
2. Is there a relationship between Kelly's theory and automaticity theory?
3. Describe some multicultural applications of personal construct psychology.
4. Discuss the relationship between personal construct theory and constructivism within behavior therapy.
5. Kelly believed that clients are generally rational. Do you agree?
6. Describe some multicultural and business applications of the Rep Test. Could there be advantages and disadvantages in using the Rep Test?

Chapter 11

TRANSACTIONAL ANALYSIS

CHAPTER OVERVIEW

Transactional analysis (TA), even though it did not develop from traditional behavioral therapy, is a Level III nontraditional cognitive-behavioral form of psychotherapy. Eric Berne developed TA as an alternative and challenge to psychoanalysis. Unlike psychoanalysis, Berne developed TA with a humanistic-existential flavor where humans can choose as opposed to being determined by their destinies. Finally, TA has much in common with traditional and nontraditional cognitive-behavioral approaches.

BIOGRAPHICAL SKETCH

Eric Berne (1910–1970) was born in Montreal, Canada. He obtained his medical degree from McGill University in Canada, and moved to the United States to start his psychiatric residency training.

Berne began his psychoanalytic training in 1941, and during 1946, he trained under Erik Erickson. In 1947, Berne published *The Mind in Action,* his first book. In 1949, he published his work outlining the following ego states: parent (exteropsyche), adult (neopsyche), and child (archaepsyche) from neurosurgical research that showed when parts of the brain were stimulated electrically, patients reexperienced anterior events as though they were present events.

Berne published *Transactional Analysis in Psychotherapy* in 1961 and in 1964, he published *Games People Play.* Both books were best-sellers. During the 1960s, Berne developed a strong following, especially in San Francisco.

Berne borrowed the term **life script** from Adler and this term describes how clients make decisions earlier in their life that have future outcomes. In essence, early decisions determine how clients will live their lives, but unlike

Freud, Berne stressed that clients choose life scripts. Steiner (1971) described in his book, *Scripts People Live,* how Berne was affected by his own life script, which prognosticated an early death.

Like many popular theorists, Berne was not without psychological difficulties. For example, Poidevant and Lewis (1995) described Berne as detached, rigid, stern, and as an individual with difficulty in giving and receiving love. Moreover, they depicted Berne as shy, a workaholic, and a person who spent little time with enjoyable activities and intimacy with others. Unfortunately, very similarly to his mother, Berne died of coronary failure at the age of 60, and leaving behind eight published books and sixty-four journals and/or magazine articles (Harris, 1969; Garfield, 1994).

DEVELOPMENTAL PERSPECTIVE OF HUMAN NATURE

Even though TA uses similar terms that are somewhat related to psychoanalysis; in contrast to psychoanalysis, it is not intrapsychic and is not deterministic, but it has cognitive-behavioral, affective, and humanistic dimensions (Poidevant & Lewis). One apparent connection between TA and psychoanalysis is the ego states called the parent (P), adult (A), and child (C), which are behavioral analogues of the superego, ego, and id (Emerson, Bertoch, & Checketts, 1994; Hazell, 1989; Horwitz, 1982).

Klein (1980) proposed a personality theory that described how the three ego states developed, and, as the reader remembers these are the parent, adult, and child. The following are the developmental stages for the development of ego states:

Stage 1: Birth–Age 1

From birth, infants are born with all **natural child (NC)**. NC is dependent, egocentric, lovable, spontaneous, and carefree. Attachment theorists and TA theorists believe that physical and emotion stroking is important to meet the developmental needs of infants during this period. After six months, the **little professor** or the adult within the child develops, and it will later develop into the adult ego state. Characteristics of the little professor include being intuitive, inquisitive, and exploratory. Also during this period, two other parts of the child ego state develop: the **free child (FC)** and **adaptive child (AC)**. The **free child** is curious, playful, intuitive, and hyperactive with spontaneity. In contrast, the **adaptive child** is friendly, conforming, compliant, compromising, and at times nonconforming.

In summary, the child ego state initiates the development of feelings within clients. Almost through an evolutionary process, the child ego state differentiates several subparts that need nurturance for a balanced development.

Stage 2: Ages 1–3

During phase two, the adult ego states continue to develop through social interactions, especially with adults and parents, and through restrictions imposed by parents within the child's environment, and the adult and parent ego states continue to develop and differentiate.

The **adult** and **parent** ego states are more rigid and inflexible than the child ego state. In addition, the adult ego state is rational, objective, unemotional, and reality based. With extreme forms, it can process, manipulate data like a computer, and it is the problem solving part of the personality.

In comparison to the adult, the parent ego state is the most rigid and inflexible and it is shaped by social influences. Like the child ego state, the parent ego state has subparts—nurturing parent and critical parent. The **nurturing parent** embodies all the ideals of a perfect parent, usually a mother, who nurtures, encourages, comforts, and offers positive strokes or positive reinforcement. In contrast, within the other extreme, the **critical parent** ego state is programmed to control aspects of the child ego state intraindividually and child ego states within others. In essence, the critical parent ego state has an attraction or affinity to control child ego states within itself or within others.

In summary, the adult and parent ego states are pliable until about six years of age, and Berne believed, like attachment theorists, that children and the development of ego states require healthy and positive strokes from parents and society to ensure healthy psychological development. Finally, also during this period, children who are two years of age develop a pattern of temper tantrums.

Stage 3: Ages 3–6

According to this theory, the adult and parent ego states need continued stroking to continue to development. Children, during this phase, continue to acquire language, and they acquire toilet skills and basic bathing skills.

Stage 4: Age 6

Around the age of six, children have strongly developed parent, adult, and child ego states and at times children within this developmental phase will display attributes and mannerisms of adults.

Stage 5: Ages 6–12

During phase five, education, training, and experience leads to additional development of the adult ego state, and children start learning more facts and how to deal with their environment within a factual manner. Affective development takes a secondary role to the development of cognition.

Stage 6: Ages 13–16

This is a period of tension and struggle for adolescents, and they tend to use sexual development, and a disregard for rules and structure as a means to their intraindividual parental ego states and the ego states of their parents. During this phase, adolescents become locked into child ego state and their parents are locked into the critical parent ego state. To summarize, during stage six, adolescents tend to rebel and their parents tend to be judgmental and punitive.

Stage 7: Late Adolescence

This phase is the latter period of adolescence and the ego states are more balanced during stage seven then the previous stages. There is more collaborative work among the three ego states during later adolescence, and the adult ego state tends to moderate between the child and parent ego state.

Stage 8: Adulthood

If the natural child can successfully differentiate into the adaptive and free child and the child ego state develops into the adult ego state and the parent ego state develops from social interaction into nurturing and critical parent subparts, the three ego states can be balanced. The lack of balance results into unhealthy psychological development and an immature and non-autonomous stance toward life. Finally, the end result can be positive psychological development or unhealthy psychological development. See Figure 11.1 for a pictorial display of the ego states.

STRUCTURAL ANALYSIS

The first phase of TA is teaching clients **structural analysis,** or becoming aware of the functioning of the parent, adult, and child ego states. Through

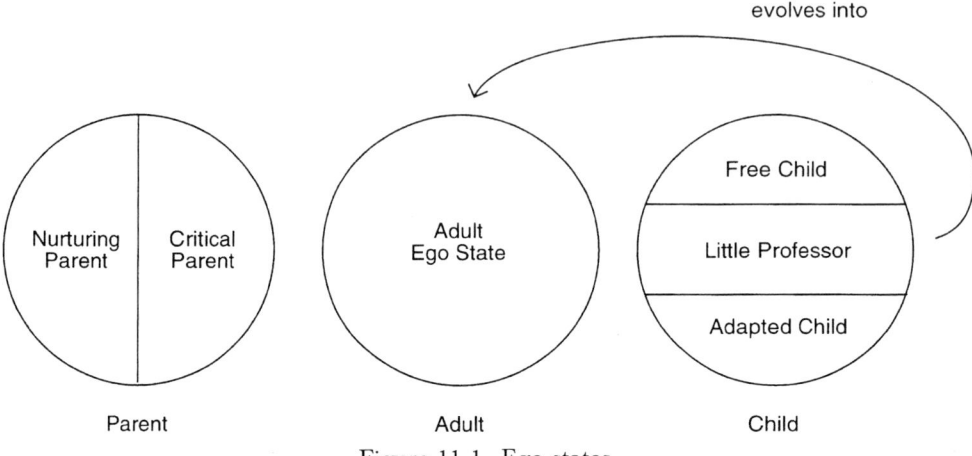

Figure 11-1. Ego states.

training and practice, clients are taught to identify the functioning of their ego states. Two inflexible aspects of clients learning about structural analysis are contamination and exclusion. **Contamination** is when ego states mix with each other. For example, the parent and child ego states become contaminated and the adult and child can mix, as well as the contamination of the adult by the parent and child. **Exclusion** is the blocking out of an ego state. For example, **constant parent** blocks out both the adult and child ego states. Clients with constant parents tend to be rigid, morality-bound, demanding, commanding, judgmental, and inflexible. Clients with constant parents tend to repeat rituals and cannot vary from their constant parents and they assume that things are either black or white and answers are either right or wrong, and for these clients grey areas do not exist.

The **constant adult** blocks or excludes the parent and child ego states, and clients with this personality orientation tend to lack spontaneity, tend to appear robotic, tend to show a limited range of feelings, and they tend to be objective, and concerned with outcomes, results, facts, and not the process of enjoyment or the process of doing things for the sake of enjoyment.

The **constant child** excludes the parent and adult ego states, and within extreme forms can result in antisocial personality disorders or clients who lack a conscience. The personality orientation of constant child is "me" and only "me," and there is a disregard for the rights, values, and concerns of others. The diagnosis of dependent personality disorder can be the result of a mild form of constant child, and the features of this style of personality are desires to take care of others, and submissiveness and clinging behaviors. Clients who tend to use the constant child personality style tend to refuse to grow up and they want to escape responsibility.

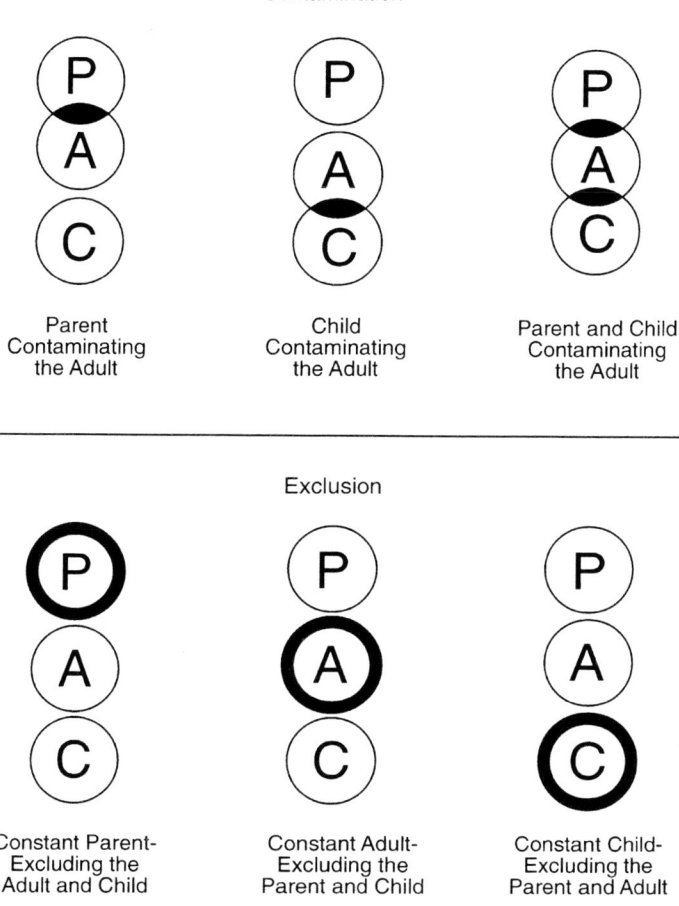

Figure 11-2. Contamination and exclusion.

TA therapists teach clients **boundary work** to demarcate or decontaminate the boundaries of each ego state and to detect exclusion. In summary, the first aspect of structural analysis is to teach clients about ego states. Next, clients are taught boundary work and to decontaminate ego states and to detect the exclusion of ego states (McGrath, 1994). Figure 11.2 has diagrams that illustrate contamination and exclusion.

TRANSACTIONS

Simply stated, transactional analysis (TA) is the interaction between at least two people. For example, when two people greet each other is a transaction.

Saying "hello" is the transactional analysis (TA) stimulus, and the person responding in a similar manner is called the transactional analysis (TA) response. A **transaction** is the basic unit of human communication, and it is just the stimulus and response between ego states of two people. In addition, transactions can have social and psychological meanings or levels. The **social meaning** of a transaction is the overt or **manifest** meaning, and the **psychological meaning** of a transaction is the covert, latent, or hidden meaning of a transaction.

Berne (1961) described the following three transactions: complementary, crossed, and ulterior. **Complementary transactions** are ones where the vectors or arrows are parallel and the ego state responses come from the same ego state that served as a stimulus. For example, complementary transactions can be the following:

$$P \rightleftarrows P, A \rightleftarrows A, C \rightleftarrows C, P \rightarrow C, C \rightarrow P, C \rightarrow A, A \rightarrow C, \text{ and } A \rightarrow P, P \rightarrow A.$$

Complementary transactions, unlike games, are not attempts to avoid intimacy and are forms of contact that can continue indefinitely. Figure 11.3 illustrates parent $\rightleftarrows$ parent transaction, adult $\rightleftarrows$ adult transaction, and child $\rightleftarrows$ child transaction with the following three complementary transactions, identifying the ego states:

1. Ted: We need to talk.
   Paul: Sure, let us talk after work.
2. Mary: You should not be such a jerk.
   Jane: Kiss my ass, bitch.
3. Peter: Let us go swimming!
   Jack: That is a good idea. Let us go!

1. $A \rightleftarrows A$
2. $P \rightleftarrows P$
3. $C \rightleftarrows C$

Crossed transactions occur when arrows or vectors are crossed. In other words, the stimulus transaction comes from one ego state, and the response transaction comes from another ego state. Stated slightly differently, the ego state that is addressed does not respond and communication stops. For example, with the following three transactions, explain why the transactions are crossed:

1. Bill: Can I have a kiss?
   Mary: Can't you see that I have work to do?
2. Jill: Where is my bag?
   Jane: How should I know?

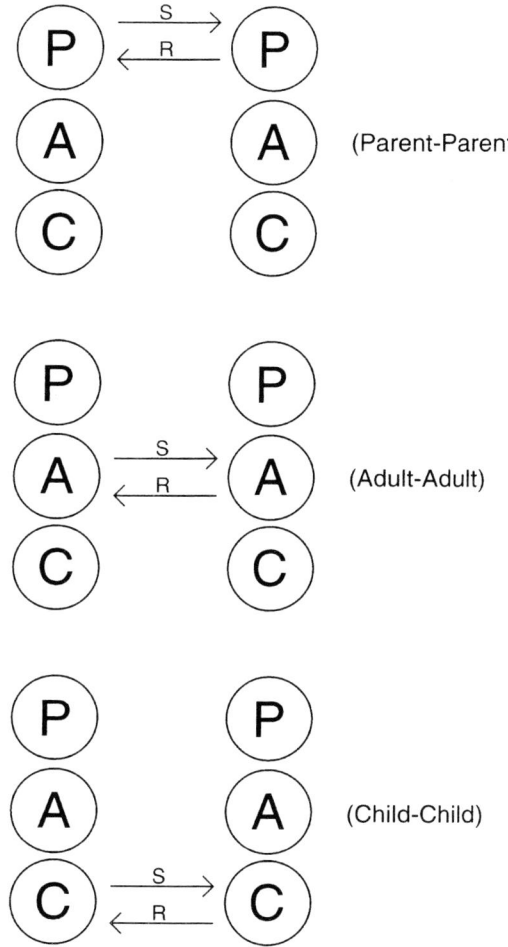

Figure 11-3. Complementary transactions.

3. Mary: When are we going to make love?
   John: Do I seem like a sex machine?

Answers:

1. Bill starts with a stimulus from his child ego state and Mary gives a parental response.
2. Jill's stimulus comes from her adult ego state and Jane responds from the child ego state.
3. Mary's stimulus comes from her child ego state and John's response is from his parental ego state.

Figure 11.4 depicts two crossed transactions.

Ulterior transactions have both social and psychological meanings simultaneously, or dual level transactions that are necessary for psychological

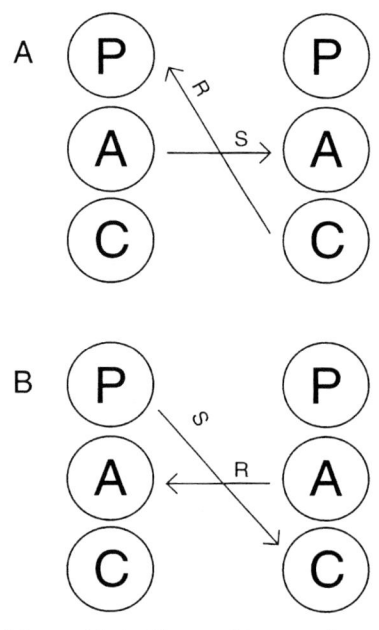

Figure 11-4. Crossed transactions.

games. TA therapists believe that understanding the meanings or messages of communication is the key to understanding behavior. Figure 11.5 depicts an ulterior transaction. An example of an ulterior transaction could be as follows:

Ken: This was a wonderful night.
Barb: Would you like a drink in my house?
Ken: Let us do it.
Barb: I think you know what I want.
Ken: I am taking my clothes off.
Barb: Help me with mine.

In summary, Ken and Barb used dual-level transactions to communicate that they were interested in each other and that they wanted sex.

ANALYSIS OF PSYCHOLOGICAL GAMES

As previously alluded to, games are used to avoid intimacy and they are the ongoing transactions between at least two people in which the players

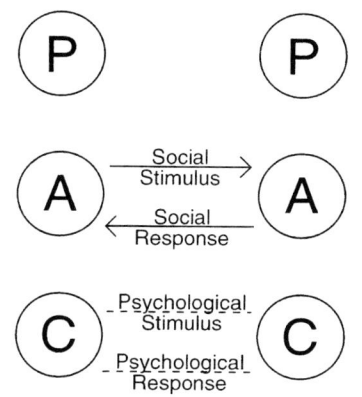

Figure 11-5. Ulterior transactions.

transact dual-level transactions that have overt and covert meanings and often, but not always, end with negative feelings (Berne, 1964).

Berne described games as having three levels: first-degree, second-degree, and third-degree. **First-degree games** are games where no one gets hurt and they are socially acceptable. For example, the previous example of Ken and Barb would be an example of a first-degree game that was harmless and fun. In addition, harmless practical jokes would be examples of first-degree games.

Second-degree games, unlike first-degree games, are more costly psychologically and they frequently result in someone getting hurt or psychologically slapped. **Third-degree games** are the most severe ones and they end in payoffs such as death, murder, divorce, and so on. One difficulty with games is that the roles can switch. Karpman (1968) describes this process of switching with the Karpman's drama triangles that describe three interchangeable roles: victim, rescuer, and persecutor. The **victim role** is a client's dramatic display of being weak, helpless, and irresponsible. The client is feigning weakness to trap the therapist into assuming the dramatic role of **rescuer,** but as soon as the therapist takes on this dramatic role, the client assumes the role of **persecutor** and condemns the therapist for not being a perfect savior, and at this point, the therapist becomes the victim, and the switching of roles continues. Figure 11.6 depicts the Karpman's drama triangle.

Rackets are the residuals or emotional aftermath from games, and often rackets are learned from parents and significant others and they are carried into adulthood. In addition, through conditioning, rackets become automatic and can become habitual feelings following games. For example, clients can have sadness rackets, depression rackets, shame rackets, anxiety rackets,

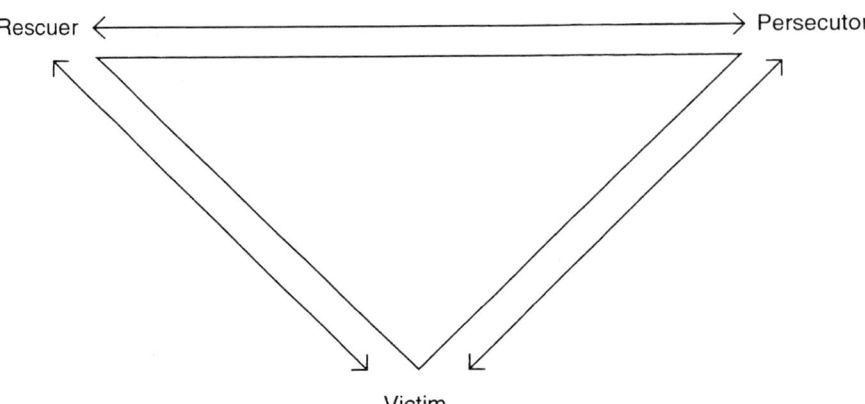

Figure 11-6. Karpman's drama triangle.

anger rackets, and so on. Often clients will cognitively see their rackets as self-defeating, but they are ingrained within a client's life script and are difficult to change. Sapp (1997a) described how rackets can be exchanged for **trading** or **collection stamps**. For example, TA would theorize that clients who have nervous breakdowns or attempt suicide have accumulated rackets and cash them in for psychological or physical pain. In contrast, clients can collect **positive stamps** and trade these in for positive and self-enhancing activities like vacations, relaxation, and so on.

SCRIPT ANALYSIS

As previously stated, Berne believed that children strive for **strokes,** or the recognition of their existence. In addition to being only psychological strokes, there can be physical strokes such as touching, hugging, kissing, and so on. Strokes can be both positive and negative; **positive strokes** connote like of another, while negative strokes connote dislike of another on a verbal or nonverbal level. Moreover, strokes can be **unconditional** or expressed liking of another without stipulations and conditional strokes is expressed liking of another with stipulations.

Berne and Goulding and Goulding (1978, 1979) differed on how they viewed clients' life scripts. For example, Berne believed that clients' life scripts were influenced by early stroking from parents. In contrast, the Gouldings believed that **injunctions** influence one's life script; however, they did not believe that injunctions were automatically scripted within one's head, but rather from the contact that children invent or misinterpret messages from their parents. Moreover, the Gouldings pointed out injunctions may be appropriate during childhood but inappropriate during adulthood. According to the Gouldings, based on earlier decisions, clients make certain decisions that influence their life scripts. In contrast, Berne suggested that clients were scripted by their parents. Explicitly, injunctions are the negative messages communicated to the child ego states of children, and they originate from the parent ego states of clients' parents.

Corey (1991) and Sapp (1997a) listed the following 10 injunctions:

1. Don't	6. Don't exist.
2. Don't be.	7. Don't enjoy.
3. Don't succeed.	8. Don't be a child.
4. Don't be outstanding.	9. Don't be emotional.
5. Don't be you.	10. Don't cry.

Within the Gouldings' framework, children assume that injunctions from their parents are things to refrain from doing. This notion is similar to Adler's view of life script, which was based on clients' misperceptions and misinterpretations. The Gouldings believed that the parent of the opposite gender communicates injunctions, and just as injunctions start with "don't," in contrast, **counterinjunctions** or **counterscripts** are parental messages denoted by "shoulds, oughts, and dos." Counterinjunctions are as difficult to live by as injunctions. TA therapists have clients explore injunctions and counterinjunctions and make new decisions that provide autonomy and personal responsibility over one's life (Goulding & Goulding, 1978, 1979). Finally, as Adler suggested and restated by Berne, one's life script is a conscious and nonconscious guide through one's life, and as TA therapists stress, strokes, injunctions, counterinjunctions, and early decisions influence clients' life scripts.

BERNEIAN OR TRADITIONAL TRANSACTIONAL ANALYSIS APPROACH

Berne's traditional approach to TA includes five interventions or techniques: (1) basic life positions, (2) structural analysis, (3) transactional analysis, (4) game analysis, and (5) life script analysis.

Harris (1969) described four life positions: (1) I'm OK–you're OK; (2) I'm OK–you're not OK; (3) I'm not OK–you're OK; and (4) I'm not OK–you're not OK.

The first life position is one of a "winner." These individuals value relationships, function effectively interpersonally and professionally, and they are constructive problem solvers. Overall, the "I'm OK–you're OK" life position has a positive attitude toward life and is emotionally healthy.

The "I'm OK–you're not OK" is an arrogant life position, and clients with this life position tend to fit what Rotter referred to as an external locus of control. These individuals' reinforcements and punishments are the results of external influences and these clients will play the role of victims. Clients who were abused as children are overly presented within this life position as well as criminals and individuals with antisocial personality disorders.

The third life position, "I'm not OK–you're OK" occurs when clients rely heavily on their adapted child personalities. These individuals tend to compensate for feelings of inferiority by seeking social acceptance to cover feelings of insecurity, powerlessness, and worthlessness.

The fourth life position, "I'm not OK–you're not OK" is the most destructive position. Individuals who would commit mass murder and tend to commit suicide would fit this life pattern. Since these individuals are suspicious of personal relationships, life is futile. Treatment with these individuals tends to be difficult, but if these individuals can learn not to exclude the adult ego state and not vacillate between the parent and child ego states, treatment is possible. Even though this life position is resistant to treatment, if the exclusion of the adult ego state can be corrected, therapeutic change can occur.

As previously stated, structural analysis is when clients learn to identify and be aware of their ego states—parent, adult, and child. The goal of structural analysis is to balance out the client's ego states and to get the client to move freely among ego states. Therapists use boundary work to uncontaminate the ego states. If a client understands structural analysis, he or she will more freely move among the ego states and avoid ego exclusion.

Transactional analysis allows clients to understand how transactions occur between people. Therapists use game analysis to show clients how closed and ulterior transactions can affect interactions and result in games. In summary, game analysis permits clients to see how games occur and how to minimize them. Finally, **life script analysis** allows the client to understand his or her life script and to see how early decisions affect current experiences.

Game analysis is the analysis of transactions between at least two people. The client and therapist determine if transactions are complementary, crossed, and ulterior. Finally, therapists use game analysis to teach clients how crossed and ulterior transactions can lead to games.

Life-script analysis allows clients to understand their life positions and to see how early decisions affect current decisions. Essentially, life scripts are clients nonconscious plans that are based on fantasies and early childhood experiences.

GOULDINGS' REDECISIONAL THEORY

The Gouldings (Goulding & Goulding, 1979) developed their **redecisional theory** by combining Gestalt techniques, psychodrama, which is a form of group therapy developed by J.L. Moreno in which clients dramatically act out roles as a way of obtaining understanding and emotional release using family therapy and TA. The Gouldings provided TA with an affect component by integrating Gestalt techniques and psychodrama techniques with TA.

The basic premise of redecisional theory is that early childhood decisions can be reversed. The therapeutic process involves regression of a client to a childhood scene and then having the client reexperience the scene while using the adult ego state and making adult decisions. The emotional aspect of this procedure is done through the child ego state, then through the adult ego state, the client makes a new decision and thinks differently, feels differently, and behaves differently. After the client reexperiences an early childhood event, the therapist has to help the client with behavioral experiences that reinforce and support the new decisions. Suppose a client had the following injunctions: don't be; don't be close; don't be important. Which would be some possible decisions a client could have made and which would be some possible redecisions?

TA AND FAMILY THERAPY

McClendon (1977) combined TA with family therapy and developed a four-stage model of therapy. During stage one, each family member is able to communicate his or her feelings. In addition, the therapist can negotiate contracts among family members and family members can express their desires (Garfield, 1994).

During stage two, the therapist determines which family member has the most power. The strategy is to change the client with the most power first, then to change the next family member with the most power. The process continues until all family members renegotiate their power. In addition, during this phase, therapists can return to stage one to more fully explore the family dynamics.

At stage three, the therapist uses a variety of action strategies such as analyzing life scripts, analyzing rackets, and analyzing early childhood injunctions. This lays the foundation for stage four which focuses on changing the structure of the family.

With stage four, the therapist works toward changing the family structure into a harmonious one. Moreover, every family member is permitted to express his or her desires. Finally, the therapist tries to get family members to integrate individual members' goals and family goals.

OTHER ACTION STRATEGIES

As previously stated, TA is a Level III theory with many action strategies such as structural analysis, transactional analysis, game analysis, and redecisional therapy. In addition, reparenting, shifting energy within egograms, contracts, family modeling, and analysis of rituals and pasttimes are other action strategies or Level III strategies.

Reparenting has a variety of approaches. For example, the Gouldings (1978, 1979) believed that clients could rewrite their own life scripts with the help of their strong parent ego states that are internal or intraindividual. Wissink (1994), using quasiexperimental methodology, validated that the Gouldings' approach could increase self-esteem of participants who participated in a self-parenting program.

In contrast to the Gouldings' approach, Schiff (1969, 1970, 1975) developed a different approach to reparenting. First, clients are regressed to earlier childhood experiences, then the therapist provides nurturing and reparenting experiences to the client. In contrast to the Gouldings' approach, with the Schiff approach, reparenting is done by the therapists playing the roles of surrogate parents. Jacobs (1994) argued that this form of reparenting can put a client at additional risk and should only be done under careful supervision or within a long-term treatment facility.

Teaching clients how to **shift energy** among the parent, adult, and child ego states is another way for a therapist to show clients how to produce changes. Techniques that were previously discussed such as script analysis, structural analysis, and game analysis can also be used to show clients how to shift energy among ego states. Therapists can use **egograms** for diagnostic purposes and if clients can shift energy from overactive ego states to lower active ego states, the experience is often reported to be exhilarating. Figure 11.7 depicts a relatively balanced egogram and a relatively unbalanced egogram. Within the relatively unbalanced egogram, decreases can be made within the critical parent, adapted child, and natural child ego states. In addition, the nurturing parent ego state could be increased. Finally, egograms can be used as action strategies and for diagnostic purposes (Dusay & Dusay, 1989).

Like traditional cognitive-behavioral approaches to psychotherapy, TA is a contractual form of psychotherapy, and Dusay and Dusay (1989) described the following four components of a contract: mutual assent, competency, legal objective, and consideration.

Mutual assent is the mutual agreement between the client's adult ego state and therapist's adult ego state to engage in a contract. It is believed that contracts help clients to become committed and they help to prevent games.

Within contracts, therapists agree to provide services that they are trained to provide, which is referred to as **competency.** Moreover, the therapist-client

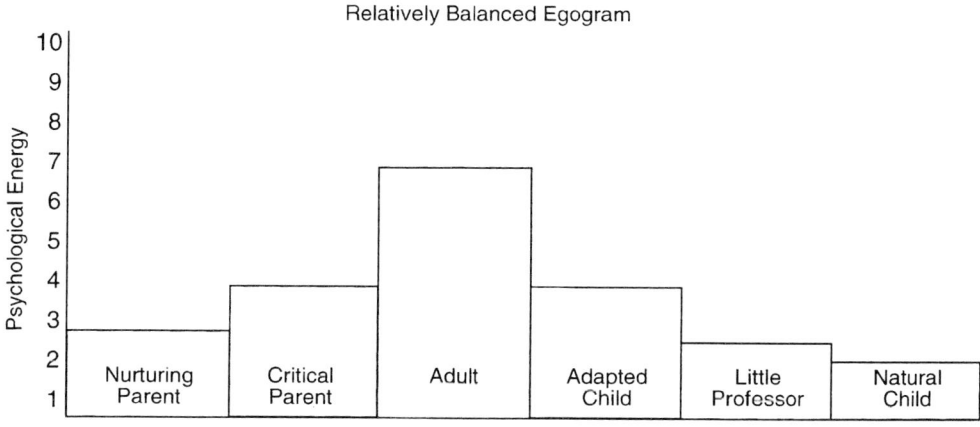
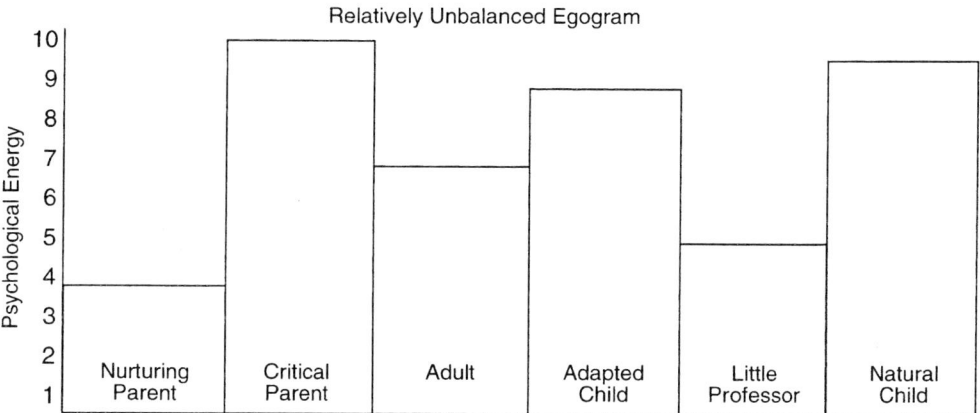

Figure 11-7. Egograms.

relationship is a collaborative one in that clients are not told what to do, nor forced to do things. Finally, clients have to be competent in achieving their goals.

Contracts must have **legal aims** or **objectives.** First, contracts must fall within ethical limits, and clients and therapists must agree to the goals of contracts; and finally, contracts have to be measurable and attainable.

Consideration is the last aspect of a contract and it involves encouraging the client to commit, focus, and be involved within the therapeutic process. In summary, consideration entails the client showing commitment to the therapeutic process.

Family modeling is an action strategy that occurs within the context of a group. Therapists assist clients in recreating and reexperiencing events from the past with group members as substitutes for family members. The strength of this technique is that clients become actors, directors, and producers of their reexperienced events.

TA therapists also use the **analysis of rituals and pastimes** as an action strategy. Essentially, clients' life scripts are analyzed in terms of how clients spend their time. For example, clients who are anxious may withdraw and engage in ritualistic worry type patterns of thinking and may feel stroke deprived.

NEW DEVELOPMENTS WITHIN TRANSACTIONAL ANALYSIS

Joines and Stewart (2002) have integrated **object relations** and **self psychology** into transactional analysis. According to St. Clair (2000), Sigmund Freud first used the term object to refer to that which will satisfy a need. More broadly, objects refer to significant others or significant things within clients' lives. In addition, objects refer to interpersonal relationships and indicate inner residues of historical relationships that shape clients' current interactions and relationships (Kernberg, 1975; St. Clair, 2000).

Object relations and **self psychology** theorists are scholars, other than the psychoanalysts such as Carl Jung, Erickson, Otto Rank, and others who separated from Freud when he was alive, who see themselves in the psychodynamic mainstream, but they alter the mainstream in a variety of ways. Object relations and self psychology theorists include, but are not limited to Melanie Klein, W.R.D. Fairbairn, D.W. Winnicot, Margaret Mahler, Edith Jacobson, Otto Kernberg, Heinz Kohut, and Stephen A. Mitchell. Moreover, object relations theorists explore the early formation and differention of psychological structures, images of the self and others, and how these structures have lasting effects on clients. More specifically, self psychology was lead by Heinz Kohut. He investigated how early relationships form the self. In summary, self psychologists give more emphasis to the self than they do to the ego instincts, or self representations. Finally, Joines and Stewart described how to make personality assessments and diagnoses using object relations and self psychology into transactional analysis (Sullivan, 1953, 1964; Kohut, 1971, 1977; Krausz, 1993).

THERAPEUTIC PROCESS

Therapeutic Goals

One goal of TA is for clients to learn that they can rewrite their life scripts and to learn that they are not scripted. Moreover, another goal is for clients to realize that they make new decisions and take charge of their lives. In addition, TA has the following goals:

- Teach clients the vocabulary of TA.
- For clients to learn to move freely among ego states.
- For clients to learn that at times boundaries are necessary among ego states.
- Understand the nature of games.

Role of Therapist

TA therapists are active, directive like traditional cognitive-behavioral therapists, and they stress the importance of a collaborative and contractual relationship with clients. In addition, clients are taught to rely on their own adults and not the adults of therapists. Likewise, contracts are made on an adult to adult level. Like other cognitive-behavioral approaches, Level III counseling strategies are an integrative part of the roles of therapists. Finally, unlike traditional cognitive-behavioral approaches, the terminology of traditional learning theories is not part of TA.

Therapeutic Relationship

TA involves a contract on an adult-adult level between therapist and client, and therapists work in a collaborative manner with clients while using action strategies and being directive.

Multicultural Applications and Limitations

TA can be used to show clients how to break cultural injunctions such as "Don't disrespect the family; don't be selfish;" and so on. TA offers structure so that ethnic groups can see how early decisions affect current behavior, and this approach has techniques that can empower ethnic groups. The major multicultural limitation of TA is moving too quickly with ethnic minority clients and providing too much specialized terminology which can be overwhelming. Coupled with the fast paced nature of this therapy, minority clients may terminate prematurely from therapy. Finally, another multicultural and general limitation of TA is that it does not stress the affective domain and may need to be combined with Gestalt therapy or psychodrama, like the Gouldings have done.

COMPREHENSIVENESS. Berne imitated Freud by developing a theory that talks about three dimensions of the self: parent, adult, and child which are similar to Freud's superego, ego, and id, respectively. Even though Berne imitated Freud, he was more influenced by Adler, especially Adler's notion of inferiority feelings which is similar to TAs notion of "not being OK." Moreover, Adler discussed how clients have lifestyles and life goals, while Berne described scripts, stamps, and rackets, which are similar terms. Likewise, individual psychology is a social psychology and TA, based on transactions, is also primarily a socially-based theory.

TA is not as comprehensive as psychoanalysis or Erickson's psychosocial theory of developmental psychology, but Klein (1980) has added to the developmental psychological aspect of TA; however, social learning theories are more comprehensive than TA from a social psychological perspective, but TA is more comprehensive than some traditional and nontraditional cognitive-behavioral therapies.

PARSIMONY. TA has complex terminology and even though TA therapists say that the theory is easy to learn, the subparts of the ego states can become complex and the diagrams and charts can be confusing. Finally, TA is not parsimonious.

EMPIRICAL VALIDITY. TA has empirical validity, but is lacking in systematic quantitative research that controls for threats to internal validity, because most of the research on TA is correlational research.

Prochaska (1984) stated that TA has effects similar to behavior therapy, and he reported that TA has been found to lend to improved behavior with juvenile delinquents, alcoholics, and outpatients with anxiety, sexual disorders, and adjustment disorders. Moreover, Allen and Allen (1989) found that stroke deprivation was correlated with anxiety, depression, adjustment disorders, and poor health. Likewise, Horwitz (1982) found a positive association between stroking and wellness, and Hazell (1989) reported that TA combined with REBT was effective in reducing anxiety and stress. Finally, Douglas (1986), with adolescents, found that suicide attempts were due to dysfunctional parental relationships and stroke deprivation (Schiff, 1969, 1970, 1975).

PRECISION AND TESTABILITY. TA needs research that tests the reliability and validity of items used as dependent variables. In addition, research that provides confidence intervals around population reliability coefficients is needed. Moreover, confidence intervals around effects sizes derived from true-experimental designs is also needed. Finally, TA rates low in the area of precision and testability.

HEURISTIC VALUE. TA has strong heuristic value. For example, it has influenced Gestalt therapy and psychodrama and currently object relations and self psychology is being integrated within TA. Finally, other approaches, such as Person-Centered, have incorporated TA in order to broaden comprehensiveness.

APPLIED VALUE. TA has been applied to help juvenile delinquents, alcoholics, clients experiencing anxiety disorders, mood disorders, and adjustment disorders. Moreover, TA has applications to industrial organizational psychology, the world of business, marriage and family counseling, group counseling, and for suicide prevention (Erskine, 1994; Evans, 1994; Fischer, 1993; Freedman, 1993; Gard, 1993; Garfield, 1993; James, 1994; Krausz, 1993; Lester, 1994; McClendon & Kadis, 1994; Sapp, 1997a). Finally, TA has excellent applied value.

SUMMARY

In some respects, TA is an extension of Adlerian therapy with aspects of psychoanalysis and communications theory. It points out that often people operate ritualistically during transactions. Unlike traditional cognitive-behavioral forms of psychotherapy, TA did not originate from academic psychology and it started as primarily a cognitive form of psychotherapy. This is why the Gouldings added affective techniques to TA. Due to the fact that various therapists practice TA differently, it is an eclectic form of therapy. Moreover, as previously stated, it has applications to the business; for example, individuals within the business world are being taught to communicate more effectively using TA techniques.

The major difficulty this writer has with TA is the assumption that humans need strokes. Clearly, babies and children need strokes to develop appropriately, but adults do not need strokes in order to survive. Adults may desire strokes, but they are not a necessity and adults are capable of self-reinforcement and can lead fruitful lives without strokes from others.

Glossary of Key Terms

Adult. This ego state is the TA analogue to the ego. It is the objective, unemotional, rational aspect of the personality.

Child. The TA analogue of the id. It is egocentric, spontaneous, and is dependent with the following three subcomponents: free child, little professor, and adapted child.

Complementary transactions. Transactions in which the vectors of communication are parallel.

Contamination. A form of structural analysis in which ego states overlap or are mixed.

Critical parent. A subcomponent of the parent ego state that is fault-finding, harsh, and critical.

Crossed transactions. Transactions in which the vectors of communication are nonparallel or crossed.

Ego states. The parent, adult, and child personality patterns.

Exclusion. A form of structural analysis in which a given ego state is prevented from functioning.

Game analysis. The analyses of ongoing transactions that are meant to avoid intimacy and can have several layers that support decisions made earlier in life.

Injunctions. Verbal and nonverbal forms of communication usually communicated to children in the form of "Don't."

Karpman's drama triangle. A theory that explains games that involves three players: victims, rescuers, and persecutors.

Life positions. A term related to the Adlerian terms of lifestyle and life goals and are the basic stances clients take concerning the ways they see themselves and others.

Nurturing parent. A subpart of the parent ego state that offers positive reinforcement and nurturance.

Object Relation Theory. A theory related to psychoanalysis. An object is a significant person, place, or thing from the past. During the 1950s and 1960s, object relations theorists dominated psychoanalysis. This theory describes the process clients undergo to separate psychologically from their parents during childhood.

Parent. The TA analogue of the superego. It develops from significant others.

Rackets. Habitual feelings that clients use, regardless if they are appropriate. These feelings are usually the products of games during early childhood.

Redecision therapy. A version of redecision therapy developed by the Gouldings that integrates Gestalt therapy, psychodrama, and behavior therapy with TA. A premise of this theory is that early childhood decisions are reversible.

Reparenting. A regressive form of therapy in which the client is regressed to an earlier time period and given positive parental messages by the therapist.

Self Psychology. A branch of psychoanalysis that gives primary emphasis to the self.

Script analysis. A Level III technique in which the basic life positions of clients are identified and analyzed.

Stroke. A form of reinforcement that can be a verbal or nonverbal form of recognition.

Structural analysis. A Level III procedure in which clients become aware of their ego states.

Transactional analysis. A form of psychotherapy developed by Berne that analyzes communication between people.

Transactional Analysis Associations and Journal

The United States of America Transactional Analysis Association is located at the following address and website:

USATAA, 4810 Sutcliff Avenue
San Jose, CA 95118–2341
Telephone: (408) 723–8231
Fax: (408) 723–8235
E-mail: info@usataa.org
Website: http://www.usataa.org/

The International Transactional Analysis Association is located at:

436 14th Street, Suite 1301
Oakland, CA 94612–2710
Telephone: (510) 625–7720
Fax: (510) 625–7725
Office hours: 7:00 a.m. to 4:00 p.m. PST

The following are contacts for The International Transactional Analysis Association:

Johnathon Wagner, Chair USA
jonathon@itaa-net.org

Gianpiero Petriglieri, ITALY
gianpiero@itaa-net.org

Elisabeth Clearly, IRELAND
elisabeth@itaa-net.org

Jessica Leong, SINGAPORE
jessica@itaa-net.org

Robin Maslen, AUSTRALIA
robin@itaa-net.org

Elaine Frances, Webmaster
webmaster@itaa-net.org

Transactional Analysis Journal is an international journal that is published quarterly. The International Transactional Analysis Association has guidelines for becoming a certified clinical member, the international conference, and training videos.

Review Questions

1. Compare and contrast TA's notion of strokes and REBT behavior therapy interpretations of reinforcement.

2. Describe how TA can be classified as a cognitive-behavioral therapy, humanistic therapy, and a communication theory.
3. Compare and contrast the Gouldings' approach to reparenting to Jacqui Schiff's (1969, 1970, 1975) approach that was developed for severely disturbed and psychotic clients in residential treatment facilities.
4. How could objection relations and self psychology be integrated within TA?

Chapter 12

REALITY THERAPY

CHAPTER OVERVIEW

William Glasser published his original book on reality therapy, entitled *Reality Therapy* in 1965. During the 1970s, Glasser stated that control theory underlies reality therapy. During the 1990s, Glasser (2000) added choice theory to reality therapy (James & Gilliland, 2003).

Glasser was trained as a psychiatrist. Reality therapy, like the nonacademically-based other Level III cognitive-behavioral approaches to psychotherapy, is not connected with the Association for the Advancement of Behavior Therapy (AABT), but reality therapy is similar to Adlerian therapy, transactional analysis, rational-emotive behavior therapy, multimodal behavior therapy, cognitive therapy, cognitive-behavior modification, personal constructs psychotherapy, social learning theory, and behavior therapy. Very similar to transactional analysis, reality therapy is humanistic and existential, and it rejects the disease model of mental illness and it is a reaction to historical therapies such as psychodynamic, self psychology, object relations theory, and short-term dynamic therapy and Jungian approaches.

It was stated in Chapter 1 that reality therapy has an effect size of .75, which is a point estimate, based on twenty-one studies, but with a 95 percent confidence interval around the population effect size of $-.0722$ to $.8083$. This range around the population effect size suggests that reality therapy can be harmful as well as beneficial. In addition, the power value reported for the reality therapy effect size was .38, which is low power. As stated in Chapter 1, according to Stevens (2002), power values greater than .70 are adequate and greater than .90 are excellent.

BIOGRAPHICAL SKETCH

During 1956, while completing his psychiatric residency with G.L. Harrington at the University of California, Glasser gained recognition for helping chronic psychotics and delinquent adolescent girls (James & Gilliland). Glasser spelled out the tenets of reality therapy in his first book, *Mental Health or Mental Illness?* Glasser coined the term reality therapy in 1964 (Glasser, 1964). He challenged the practice of psychoanalysis and he stated that clients must fulfill their needs in a responsible manner (Glasser, 1961, 1965, 1969).

School systems embraced reality therapy following the publication of *Schools Without Failure* (Glasser, 1969). In Los Angeles, the Glasser Institute for Reality Therapy of the Education Training Center and the William Glasser LaVerne College Center were established to eliminate school failure. Glasser had several publications that focused on schools, *Control Theory in the Classroom* (1986) and *The Quality School: Managing Students Without* (Glasser, 1986, 1990a, 1990b, 1999).

When Glasser published *Stations of the Mind* in 1981, he discussed a personality construct called behavior—the control of perception psychology. Glasser stated, according to control theory, clients use their brains to control their perceptions since they cannot control their environments totally. In 1984, Glasser wrote three books building on this concept: *Stations of Mind, Taking Effective Control of Your Life,* and *Control Theory: A New Explanation of How We Control Our Lives*. The major axiom of Glasser's work is that clients can only control themselves, not others.

In *Control Theory,* Glasser expanded on his theory of psychological needs: survival, love and belonging, power, fun, and freedom (Glasser, 1984, 1986, 1989; Wubbolding, 1997). Within Glasser's 1998 book, *Choice Theory: A New Psychology of Personal Freedom,* Glasser stated that clients choose everything that they do, including mental illnesses, diseases, and so on. Glasser and Wubbolding both expanded on choice theory and described how it could work with a variety of client problems (Glasser, 2000; Wubbolding, 2000). Glasser and Wubbolding stated that meaningful interpersonal relationships are central to good mental health and the choices clients make determine their quality. Clients can create good relationships by taking responsibility of themselves and trying not to control others.

Currently, Glasser is the president of The William Glasser Institute in Los Angeles. The institute provides training, certification, services to the public, and it publishes the *International Journal of Reality Therapy*.

A NONDETERMINISTIC VIEW OF HUMAN NATURE

It was previously stated that reality therapy was a reaction to the psychodynamic therapies, especially the deterministic view of traditional psychoanalysis, and reality therapy is a humanistic existential approach like rational emotive behavior therapy (REBT) and transactional analysis, but it deviates from these approaches by seeing behavior as **total,** and it involves **doing, thinking, feeling,** and **physiology.** Reality therapy states that clients are not victims of their pasts and they are not dominated by unconscious influences (Glasser, 1972, 1984, 1986, 1990a, 1994; Glasser & Wubbolding, 1995).

Choice theory states that a therapist must connect with a client's **inner quality world** and establish a phenomenological and trusting relationship with the client. The reader may notice that this is similar to Adler's notion of starting counseling by establishing a primary relationship with a client that is trusting and meaningful. The client's inner quality world is a window into how he or she would like things to be psychologically.

According to Glasser (2000), clients have **inner mental pictures** that represent their quality worlds and they fall within three categories. First, they involve inner mental pictures of people that clients want most; second, things that clients want and prize the most; and third, ideas or systems of beliefs that guide behavior (James & Gilliland, 2003). Glasser believes that each client has his or her own unique quality world. In addition, clients have a **world view** that is an acquired view of the world. This notion is similar to cognitive attributions that cognitive-behavioral therapists discussed. In summary, a client's **quality world** is unique and is analogous to the transactional analysis notion of life script and the Adlerian concept of life style and life tasks. Finally, a client's quality world is equivalent to his or her unique psychological DNA.

Glasser (2000) argues that **external control psychology,** in contrast to control psychology, operates by using external controlling strategies such as blaming, criticizing, punishing, nagging, pressuring, labeling, complaining, and so on. Glasser believes that clients must replace external control psychology with behaviors and techniques that strengthen and support relationships. In contrast to external control psychology, clients have to learn to love, support, negotiate, encourage, trust, and nurture, and sustain relationships.

James and Gilliland (2003) described ten axioms that drive freedom within the choice theory. The **first axiom** is that a client can only control his or her behavior and not that of others. **Axiom two** states that people can only give us information and how we deal with information is a matter of personal choice. **Axiom three** states that all psychological problems are relationship problems, and Glasser borrows his notion of needs from the psychologist Abraham Maslow (1908–1970). In addition, Glasser's notion of control theory is similar to Maslow's theory of self-actualizing, and as the reader may remember, Maslow was influenced by Adler. **Axiom four** states that problem relationships are always part of clients' current lives.

Axiom five states that the past does not determine current behavior and that current relationships affect current behaviors. **Axiom six** restates that clients are driven by what Glasser refers to as genetic needs: survival, love and belonging, power, freedom, and fun. Both Adler and Maslow would describe a self-actualized person as one who has maximized human or personal potentialities.

Axiom seven states that clients satisfy their needs by satisfying pictures within their quality worlds. **Axiom eight** states that all behavior is total behavior and it is made up of four inseparable components: acting, thinking, feeling, and physiology. This axiom is similar to the notion of psychological interactionism from REBT that states that feeling, thinking, and behaving occur simultaneously and are not separate components.

Axiom nine states that all total behavior is described verbally such as infinitives and gerunds. For example, clients are not depressed, but they are choosing to be depressed and they are depressing and clients are not suffering from anxiety, but they are choosing anxiety.

Finally, **axiom ten** states that clients can control their feelings and physiology indirectly through what they choose to do or think. In essence, all behaviors are chosen.

Wubbolding (1995) stated that **quality time** is an important part of clients' development and it is determined by their interests. He described the following activities as important for clients' growth and development:

- Effortful. Growth activities require effort. For example, watching a television program requires little effort, while exercising requires a reasonable degree of effort.
- Awareness. When clients are aware of others, growth and development are enhanced.
- Repetition. Growth activities must be repeated. For example, frequently talking with good friends can deepen and enhance such relationships.
- Void of criticism and blaming. When engaging in social activities, they should be free of criticism, blaming, and complaining.
- Need fulfillment of all persons. Social activities must be geared toward the interests of everyone involved. For example, teenage children would probably not want to attend a disco concert that celebrated the 1970s.
- Performed for a restricted period of time. Activities that enhance growth require a certain time period for development to occur.

It was William Powers (1973) adapted **control theory,** a theory that describes how the brain operates, so it could be adapted to the applications of mental health. Glasser and Wubbolding (1995) believe that the brain operates like a thermostat, and it attempts to control behavior as a way to control the external world so it fits the internal quality world. In essence, the brain operates to fulfill needs.

APPLICATIONS TO MENTAL HEALTH

Glasser and Wubbolding (1995) discussed mental health in terms of regressive and positive stages. **Regressive stages,** also called a **failure identity,** are ineffective ways that clients attempt to fulfill their needs. There are three phases to the failure identify. During phase one, clients have attempted to fulfill their needs, were unsuccessful, and they withdraw. With phase two, clients have continued to meet certain goals and they experience more frustration than phase one. They begin to have negative thoughts and feelings such as depressing, angering, and anxietying. Corey (1996) called these paining behaviors. As the reader may remember, Glasser and Wubbolding use the "ing" suffix because they believe that clients choose depression and anxiety as opposed to being depressed, angered, or anxious.

Phase three is the extreme end of regression where clients use ineffective ways to fulfill needs. For example, clients may have negative addictions to drugs, alcohol, and work and use these ineffective ways to fulfill their needs. Finally, regressive phases are the opposites of positive or effective phase, and positive phases lead to success identities.

Positive stages or phases, or success identities, are effective ways clients use to fulfill needs. Like regressive phases, there are three with positive stages, too. During phase one, clients commit to change, and during phase two clients have positive symptoms. For example, they use effective choices to fulfill their needs. In addition, clients are emotionally healthy by meeting their needs and they learn to contribute to society. Moreover, during this phase, clients' cognitions are rational and clients accept responsibility for things they can change and they accept things that are resistant to change. In terms of feelings, clients experience patience, tolerance, hope, and other positive feelings. In terms of physiology, clients exercise, eat properly, and take care of their bodies.

Phase three is the **positive addictions phase;** they enhance mental health and they satisfy needs. Glasser described two positive addictions—running and meditation. In contrast to regressive addictions, positive addictions are not self-destructive, and they consist of choosing a noncompetitive behavior for twelve to eighteen months for at least forty-five minutes per day. Finally, Glasser pointed out that positive and negative phases are continuous variables and not absolute discrete categories. This suggests that clients can vacillate between negative and positive addictions.

To reiterate, choice theory is a system of brain functioning that is an underpinning of reality therapy. This theory was popularized by Norbert Wiener (1948), a mathematics professor at Harvard University; however, Wubbolding (1991, 1995) described five principles that underlie reality therapy.

First, clients have five innate needs: belonging, power, fun or enjoyment, freedom, and survival. Wubbolding assumes that these needs are transcultural and universal and motivate all behavior.

Second, the differences among what clients want and they perceive they are getting are the sources of behavior at a given moment. This principle has several implications. First, clients' needs are conscious and not unconscious conflicts. In addition, this principle does not embrace determinism, nor total environmentalism. In other words, the past does not control the present, and clients are not victims of their environments.

Third, all clients' behaviors are total behaviors that consist of doing, thinking, feeling, and physiology. As previously stated, this principle is similar to the REBT principle of psychological interactionism. This principle suggests that all human behavior is teleological or purposeful, and all behaviors function by closing the gap between what clients want at certain periods of times with perceptions of what they think they are getting. Therefore, total behavior is expressed by words that end in "ing." Fourth, human behaviors originate from within; therefore, clients are responsible for their behaviors and they can choose effective or ineffective behaviors.

Fifth, clients view the world through a filtering system that functions as a screening lens, and clients make judgments based on their perceptions; therefore, one goal of reality therapy is to explore the practicality of clients' perceptions.

THERAPEUTIC PROCESS

Therapeutic Goals

The overall goal of reality therapy is for clients to effectively fulfill their needs without affecting the needs of others, but in order for clients to facilitate effective need fulfillment, they must use total behavior and do things that lead to need fulfillment. Moreover, clients must make choices about which behaviors fulfill needs and which behaviors are regressive. In addition, usually clients learn to make incremental changes in their behaviors, and it is through encouragement, an Adlerian technique through the therapist that clients effectively change their thinking, feelings, and physiology.

Role of Therapist

Reality therapy therapists, like Adlerian therapists, seek to establish collaborative and trusting relationships with clients. Glasser sees relationships or the lack of relationships as core psychological issues, and it is through the relationship that therapists connect with clients. One way therapists can connect and become involved with clients is by employing Levels I and II counseling skills. Once a positive and trusting relationship is established with clients, reality therapists, like other cognitive-behavioral therapies, use Level III counseling skills, specifically the use of skillful questioning to help clients determine if their current behaviors garner what they want. In addition, clients are taught choice theory and taught to develop success identities.

Therapeutic Relationship

According to choice theory, involvement, the relationship between client and therapist, is a critical precursor to change. Unlike person-centered therapy, involvement is necessary for change to occur, but is not sufficient; hence, therapeutic movement occurs through total behavior—clients change their behaviors. This notion is in line with Adlerian therapy and traditional and other nontraditional cognitive-behavioral therapies.

During the 1980s, Corey (1982) described the following eight characteristics of reality therapy:

Characteristics of Reality Therapy

1. Rejection of the medical model of mental illness.
2. Focuses on total behavior in contrast to feelings and attitudes.
3. Present focused.
4. Determines if clients' behaviors are getting them what they want.
5. De-emphasis on transference.
6. Stresses conscious functioning and not the unconscious nor preconscious personality functioning.
7. Clients are allowed to experience the natural consequences of their behaviors, and therapists do not punish clients.
8. Clients are encouraged to accept personal responsibility for their behaviors.

Also during the 1980s, Glasser (1984) described the following eight steps of reality therapy:

> **Eight Steps of Reality Therapy**
>
> 1. Establish relationships with clients.
> 2. Focus on the clients' current behaviors.
> 3. Have clients evaluate their behaviors.
> 4. Have clients construct an action plan and action strategies.
> 5. Have clients commit to action plans.
> 6. Do not accept excuses from clients.
> 7. Do not punish clients.
> 8. Never give up on clients.

Sapp (1997a) summarized these steps as the following. During step one, Levels I and II counseling skills are used to create a therapeutic atmosphere of empathy, congruence, and positive regard for the client.

During step two, therapists focus on skillful questioning to focus on clients' current behaviors. For example, the therapist may ask, "Are your current behaviors helping you to achieve your wants and goals? Are the things you are doing effective?"

With step three, therapists get the client to determine if their behaviors are getting them what they want. Therapists encourage clients to evaluate their behaviors. Again, therapists use skillful questioning such as "Are your behaviors effective? Are your behaviors working for you?"

In step four, therapists help clients develop specific and measurable action plans. Wubbolding (1995) stated that effective plans have at least eight qualities characterized by the acronym SAMIICCC or SAMI^{2}C^3.

> **Eight Characteristics of an Effective Plan**
>
> 1. S. Simple: The plan is simple.
> 2. A. Attainable: The plan is attainable within a reasonably short period of time.
> 3. M. Measurable: The plan is concrete, explicit, and specific.
> 4. I. Immediate: When possible, the plan is enacted immediately.
> 5. I. Involvement: The client and therapist are involved within a therapeutic relationship.
> 6. C. Control: The client controls the plan.
> 7. C. Commitment: The client is committed to the plan.
> 8. C. Consistent: The client repeatedly uses the plan.

During step five, if clients can commit to a plan, they can take personal responsibility for their total behaviors. With step six, if clients do not follow through with plans, therapists do not accept excuses but use skillful questioning to determine why the plans failed. This is a form of confrontation.

Step seven involves allowing clients to experience the natural consequences of their behaviors. Reality therapists do not use punishment because they do not want to reinforce a failure identity. During the final step, stage eight, reality therapists never give up on clients. They have high frustration tolerance even with extremely resistant clients.

Wubbolding (1995) stated that reality therapy is not a series of steps and should not be conducted in a mechanical fashion. He stated that reality therapy is a cycle and can be entered at any point. He developed the WDEP system to describe the cycle of reality therapy.

W is the assessment of clients wants, desires, and commitment to therapy. Wubbolding listed the following five levels of commitment:

1. I am not thrilled about being here.
2. I want the results, but I do not want to go through the process.
3. I will try.
4. I will do my best.
5. I will do whatever the task requires.

These levels of commitment are hierarchical. Higher levels represent higher levels of commitment than lower levels.

At **D**, therapists assess what clients are doing, and **E** is where therapists help clients evaluate their behaviors, wants, perceptions, level of commitment, and plans. Finally, **P** is a plan. Glasser and Wubbolding (1995) believe that clients must have plans based on self-realizations.

To reiterate, the cycle of reality therapy is abbreviated by WDEP. W is the assessment of clients' wants, perceptions, and commitment to change. D is total behavior, and it is composed of doing, thinking, feeling, and physiology. Point E is the assessment of the effectiveness of clients' behaviors, and Ps are the plans clients formulate to obtain their needs.

Wubbolding (1995) stressed the importance of Levels I and II counseling skills during the early phases of reality therapy and he listed five interventions abbreviated by **ABCDEFG**. AB means always be. The five interventions are as follows:

1. Always be courteous.
2. Always be determined.
3. Always be enthusiastic.
4. Always be firm.
5. Always be genuine.

Even though therapists cannot perform these five interventions 100 percent of the time, Wubbolding stated that therapists should be aware of these principles when conducting reality therapy.

Wubbolding also listed fourteen principles of reality therapy. The principles are as follows:

Fourteen Principles of Reality Therapy

1. Suspend judgment.
2. Do what is unexpected.
3. Employ humor.
4. Use immediacy when appropriate by sharing aspects of yourself with clients.
5. Be yourself.
6. Notice metaphors, since clients may communicate through metaphors.
7. Watch for themes that connect clients' issues.
8. Focus on the client, and summarize the components of the WDEP.
9. Let clients experience the consequences of their behaviors.
10. Become comfortable with silence.
11. Maintain high standards of ethics.
12. Be repetitious.
13. Create suspense and be spontaneous.
14. Remember and maintain boundaries within the counseling relationship.

The five interventions listed are necessary to build strong therapeutic relationships with clients and the fourteen principles of reality therapy are the building blocks for the WDEP system. In summary, reality therapy has evolved over the years and has incorporated sensible counseling process skills from the general area of counseling psychology.

Multicultural Applications and Limitations

Glasser (2000) and Wubbolding, Al-Rashidi et al. (1998) stated that therapists should demonstrate competencies in multicultural counseling, awareness, knowledge, and experience. Choice theory assumes that there are several characteristics that are common across various cultures such as the five basic needs. If these assumptions are true, reality therapy should offer diverse clients a means of changing their behaviors, cognitions, and feelings.

LaFontaine (1994, 1995) stated that choice theory does not address issues related to gay, lesbian, bisexual, and transsexual issues of youth, and she recommended that choice theory and reality therapy make adaptations and expand in order to address diverse sexual orientations. Likewise, Cunningham (1995) expressed concerns regarding reality theory's emphasis on the European world view of individualism. This framework includes linear thinking, fragmentations of clients from their families and cultures, and a neglect of clients' traditional cultural roots.

Sapp (1997a) also stated that reality therapy has multicultural limitations. For example, he stated that it does not address language differences of American Indians, African Americans, Latinos, and Asian Americans. Since language influences clients' ways of thinking and cultural identity, therapists have to take language differences of various groups into account during psychotherapy. Even minority clients who are fluent in English may experience confusion due to the nuances of various English words. In addition, reality therapy does not discuss acculturation. For example, minority clients who are first, second, or third generation will experience various degrees of acculturation. This writer has observed through psychotherapy practice that many minority clients tend to synthesize their cultures with American culture.

Finally, there is a major gap in the reality of racism, sexism, and homophobia that is not addressed by reality therapy. Homophobia, racism, sexism, and classism can oppress clients' identities and senses of self-worth. In conclusion, reality therapy can be adapted within a multicultural context, but, as a theory, it has several multicultural limitations.

Critique

COMPREHENSIVENESS. Since the mid-1960s to the present, reality therapy has expanded with control theory, choice theory, and the WDEP system. Reality therapy has been a major challenge to the medical model of mental illness and it has made many contributions to education. From a developmental psychological perspective, it does not provide a framework for human development, nor for the development of emotional disorders. Even choice theory does not offer a thorough explanation of the various social and psychological phases that humans move through, and referring to the role of innate needs as the major explanatory construct is inadequate. In terms of comprehensiveness, reality therapy is not as comprehensive as transactional analysis. Because reality therapy does not address the details of social and psychological development, it rates low in comprehensiveness.

PARSIMONY. Reality therapy is the most parsimonious nontraditional cognitive-behavioral, existential, and humanistic theory, and it does not include unnecessary concepts. The theory is economical and common sense based.

EMPIRICAL VALIDITY. Two empirical articles suggested that reality therapy is effective within schools (Hawes, 1971; Glasser & Zunin, 1973). Hawes found that "Schools Without Failure" programs were effective in improving internal locus of control with African American children in grades three through six. In addition, students reported improvements in time spent on tasks, assimilation and accommodation of information, and social interactions of other students and teachers. Glasser and Zunin found that reality therapy was effective in reducing classroom discipline and in improving academic achievement. Radtke, Sapp, and Farrell (1997) conducted a meta-analysis on reality therapy. They found an effect size of .75 with twenty one studies. Even though reality had a medium effect size, many of the studies used in the meta-analysis used inexperienced therapists. Several of the treatments were brief, and many of the clients did not meet a DSM-IV T-R diagnosis. Finally, several of the studies violated the selection threat to internal validity.

Glasser and Wubbolding have made many claims about reality therapy, but the meta-analysis by Radtke, Sapp, and Farrell found that reality therapy had applications mainly for school-based issues. In order to explore the claims of reality theorists, experimental studies are needed. In addition, from the meta-analysis by Radtke, Sapp, and Farrell, the 95 percent confidence interval for the population effect was $-.0722$ (lower limit) and .8083 (upper limit). This suggests that reality therapy can be harmful as well as beneficial, and the power value for the 95 percent confidence interval was .38, indicating low power. In summary, additional meta-analyses, experimental, and quasi-experimental studies are needed to explore the efficacy of reality therapy.

PRECISION AND TESTABILITY. Terms such as success identity, failure identity, choice theory, power, freedom, fun, and the physiological need for survival, but operational definitions are not provided. Neither Glasser nor Wubbolding have emphasis hypothesis testing; therefore, reality therapy rates low in the area of precision and testability. Unlike academic forms of behaviorism, reality therapy has not been subjected to intense experimentation.

HEURISTIC VALUE. Glasser has been controversial by challenging the medical model of emotional disorders such as schizophrenia, manic depressive disorders, and so on. After almost forty years of reality therapy, it is still not clear if it has sparked strong heuristic interest. Reality therapy is familiar to counseling psychologists, but it has been popular within the general area of psychology. This is probably due to the lack of experimental evidence for this therapy. Unlike Ellis's REBT, other researchers within psychology have not been that interested in researching reality therapy. It is hoped that in the future reality therapy will stimulate researchers into action. In summary, reality therapy has not had high heuristic value within the general area of psychology.

APPLIED VALUE. Recently, Glasser has expanded reality therapy to marriage and family counseling, the workplace environment, and community relationships. In addition, reality therapy has been applied to delinquents, prison settings, drug and alcohol addicts, clients with disabilities, PTSD, depression, anxiety, eating disorders, and so on. In summary, reality therapy has applied value for families, groups, couples, schools, prisons, rehabilitation counseling organizations, and so on.

SUMMARY

In terms of constructs, reality therapy is a nontraditional form of cognitive-behavioral psychotherapy that uses constructs, and it is a cyclical therapy whereby therapists establish relationships or involvement with clients, focus on total behaviors, help clients evaluate their behaviors, help clients develop plans, get clients to commit to plans, and therapists do not accept excuses. Reality therapy challenges the notion of mental illness; however, as discussed in Chapter 8, biochemical correlates have been found for depression, and it is believed that the hypothalamic-pituitary-adrenal (HPA) axis plays a role in depression. Finally, there are biological bases for a variety of mental disorders.

Glossary of Key Terms

Choice theory. A theory that states clients choose emotional disturbances.

Control theory. A theory that states clients use their brains to control the world around them.

Five internal forces or needs. These are universal needs and include belonging, power, fun, freedom, and survival.

Mental health. Regressive and positive ways of fulfilling needs.

Negative addictions. Behaviors that are not part of a failure identity and do not strengthen mental health.

Paining. Clients who choose misery and develop negative symptoms such as headaching, depressing, and anxietying.

Positive addictions. Behaviors that are part of a success identity and strengthen mental health such as jogging and meditation.

Quality time. The period of time that is needed for growth and psychological well being.

Quality world. The inner world that clients have in their minds of how to satisfy needs.

Total behavior. The four components—thinking, doing, feeling, and physiological—that control all behavior. A term that is similar to Ellis's notion of psychological interactionism.

WDEP system. Wants, doing, evaluation of behaviors, and specific plans that are part of the cycle of reality therapy.

Reality Therapy Websites

The William Glasser Institute website is located at: http://www.wglasser.com/
Telephone: (800) 899–0688; (818) 700–8000
Fax: (818) 700–0555
22024 Lassen Street, Suite 118
Chatsworth, California 91311
E-mail: wginst@wglasser.com

Center for Reality Therapy is located at: http://home.fuse.net/3templar/
Dr. Robert E. Wubbolding, Director
Sandra T. Wubbolding, Administrator
7672 Montgomery Road
Cincinnati, Ohio 45236–4258
Telephone: (513) 561–1911
Fax: (513) 561–3568
E-mail: wubsrt@fuse.net

There is also the *International Journal of Reality Therapy* and the editor is as follows:

Dr. Lawrence Litwack, Editor
The International Journal of Reality Therapy
650 Laurel Avenue #402
Highland Park, Illinois 60035
Telephone: (847) 681–0290
E-mail: llitwack@aol.com

Review Questions

1. Why has reality therapy not been accepted outside the area of education and counseling psychology?
2. How did Glasser challenge the medical theory of mental illness?
3. Glasser tends to emphasize control theory and Wubbolding tends to emphasize the WDEP. Why do you think this is the case?

Chapter 13

SUMMARY

Chapter 1 started with a discussion of psychotherapy efficacy research, and even though traditional cognitive-behavioral counseling approaches have large d effect sizes, confidence intervals suggest that the population parameters of d different from the point estimates and confidence intervals reveal that traditional cognitive-behavioral approaches have medium effect sizes. In addition, the SPSS control lines for confidence intervals around reliability indices were provided. The control lines for testing hypothesized values of the alpha coefficient against calculated values were also provided. Also, within Chapter 1, the theory of automaticity was introduced. This is a theory that connects brain and behavior, and it has sociocognitive aspects.

Chapter 2 presented criteria for critiquing traditional and nontraditional cognitive-behavioral theories of counseling. In addition, variables that are used in counseling research were discussed, and suppressor variables were described in detail. The various cultural groups that reside within the United States were described within this chapter.

Chapter 3 described Adlerian therapy as an analytic, behavioral, and cognitive form of psychotherapy and as a precursor to traditional and nontraditional cognitive-behavioral approaches.

Chapter 4 covered behavior therapies and the paradigms of the founders, Pavlov, Watson, and Skinner. The following five models or theories of behavior therapy were described: applied behavior analysis, neobehaviorism, cognitive-behavior therapy, social learning theory, and multimodal behavior therapy.

Chapter 5 covered the family of social learning theories. These theories are also called sociocognitive approaches, and these approaches expand behaviorism by including social and cognitive aspects of clients.

Chapter 6 discussed rational-emotive behavior therapy which is the original traditional cognitive-behavioral therapy. Ellis founded this approach and emphasized that it is a cognitive, behavioral, and emotive approach to psychotherapy.

Multimodal behavior therapy was covered in Chapter 7. Lazarus based this theory on technical eclecticism, and he believes in using techniques from theories without endorsing the individual theories. Lazarus emphasized that it is impossible to integrate vastly opposing theories and that many theories are epistemologically incompatible. By doing an assessment of clients' behaviors, affects, sensations, imageries, cognitions, interpersonal relationships, and biology/drugs, comprehensive intraindividual assessments of clients are done.

Cognitive therapy was covered in Chapter 8. The Becks' cognitive therapy gives primacy to cognitions and cognitive therapy is based on an informational processing theory of how clients process information. As opposed to trying to change clients' irrational beliefs like rational emotive behavior therapy, cognitive therapy tries to change the way clients process information. Moreover, cognitive therapy assumes that each disorder has its own profile. For example, disorders like anxiety and depression have separate profiles and require different approaches.

Chapter 9 covered cognitive-behavior modification, and Meichenbaum bridged the gap between cognitive-semantic therapists and cognitive therapists. He added the cognitive component to therapies like systematic desentization and operant conditioning. Essentially, clients are taught to modify their self-verbalizations.

In Chapter 10, personal constructs psychotherapy investigated how clients create cognitive constructs about their environments. This therapy is an intellectual approach to psychotherapy. Kelly did not view his theory as cognitive, affective, or conative, and he did not develop his theory from existing theories. In some ways Kelly's theory is a paradox; first, it is almost completely cognitive, and it pays minimal attention to cognition, affect, motivation, needs, and behavior.

Transactional analysis was discussed in Chapter 11. Unlike traditional cognitive-behavioral theories, transactional analysis did not develop from traditional behavioral therapy or learning theories. This theory is a contractual communications theory and it teaches clients to be aware of ego states and to move energy freely among ego states. Finally, object relations theory and self-psychology are new developments within transactional analysis.

Reality therapy was presented in Chapter 12. Like transactional analysis, this did not develop from traditional behavior theory or learning theories. This theory has much in common with Adlerian therapy. Finally, reality therapy is a nontraditional cognitive-behavioral and humanistic-existential approach to psychotherapy.

REFERENCES

Abram, J.L. (1983). Cognitive-behavioral strategies to induce and enhance a collaborative set in distressed couples. In A. Freeman (Ed.), *Cognitive therapy with couples and groups* (pp. 125–155). New York: Plenum.

Abramson, L.Y., Metalsky, G.I., & Alloy, L.B. (1989). Hopelessness depression: A theory-based subtype of depression. *Psychological Review, 96* (2), 358–372.

Agras, W.S., Rossiter, E.M., Arnow, B., Schneider, J.A., Telch, C.F., Raeburn, S.D., et al. (1992). Pharmacologic and cognitive-behavioral treatment for bulimia nervosa: A controlled comparison. *American Journal of Psychiatry, 149,* 82–87.

Allen, J., & Allen, B. (1989). Stroking: Biological underpinnings and direct observations. *Transactional Analysis Journal, 19,* 26–31.

Al-Rashidi, B., & Brickell, J. (1998). Multicultural awareness: Implications for reality therapy and choice theory. *International Journal of Reality Therapy, 17* (2), 4–6.

American Psychiatric Association. (1994). *Diagnostic and statistical manual of mental disorders* (4th ed.). Washington, DC: Author.

Ansbacker, H.L., & Ansbacker, R.R. (Eds.) (1956/1964). *The individual psychology of Alfred Adler: A systematic presentation in selections from his writings.* New York: Harper and Row.

Antonuccio, D. (1995). Psychotherapy for depression: No stronger medicine. *American Psychologist, 50* (6), 450–452.

Arlow, J.A. (2002). Psychoanalysis. In R.J. Corsini & D. Wedding (Eds.), *Current psychotherapies* (6th ed., pp. 15–50). Itasca, IL: F.E. Peacock.

Arazoz, D.L. (1981). Negative self-hypnosis. *Journal of Contemporary Psychotherapy, 12,* 45–52.

Axelson, J.A. (1990). *Counseling and development in a multicultural society* (2nd ed.). Belmont, CA: Brooks/Cole.

Axelson, J.A. (1993). *Counseling and development in a multicultural society* (3rd ed.). Belmont, CA: Brooks/Cole.

Baldwin, A.C., Critelli, J.W., Stevens, L.C., & Russell, S. (1986). Androgyny and sex role measurement: A personal construct approach. *Journal of Personality and Social Psychology, 51,* 1081–1088.

Bandura, A. (2000). Social cognitive theory: An agentic perspective. *Annual Review of Psychology, 52,* 1–26.

Balthazard, C.G., & Woody, E. (1989). Bimodality, dimensionality, and the notion of hypnotic types. *International Journal of Clinical and Experimental Hypnosis, 37,* 70–89.

Bandura, A. (1982). Self-efficacy mechanism in human agency. *American Psychologist, 37,* 122–147.

Bandura, A. (1983). Self-efficacy determinants of anticipated fears and calamities. *Journal of Personality and Social Psychology, 45,* 464–469.

Bandura, A. (1984). Recycling misconceptions of perceived self-efficacy. *Cognitive Therapy and Research, 8,* 231–255.

Bandura, A. (1985). Model of causality in social learning theory. In M.J. Mahoney & A. Freeman (Eds.), *Cognition and psychotherapy* (pp. 25–125). New York: Plenum.

Bandura, A. (1986). From thought to action: Mechanisms of personal agency. *New Zealand Journal of Psychology, 15,* 1–17.

Bannister, D. (Ed.) (1977). *New perspectives in personal construct theory.* New York: Academic Press.

Barabasz, A., & Barabasz, M. (1996). Neurotherapy and alert hypnosis in the treatment of attention deficit/hyperactivity disorder. In I. Kirsch & J.W. Rhue (Eds.), *Casebook of clinical hypnosis* (pp. 271–292). Washington, DC: American Psychological Association.

Barabasz, A., Barabasz, M., Jensen, S., Calvin, S., Trevisan, M., & Warner, D. (1999). Cortical event-related potentials show the structure of hypnotic suggestions is critical. *International Journal of Experimental Hypnosis, 47,* 5–22.

Barber, T.X. (1969). *Hypnosis: A scientific approach.* New York: Van Nostrand Reinhold. (Reprinted 1995, Northvale, NJ: Jason Aronson).

Barber, T.X. (1999). A comprehensive three-dimensional theory of hypnosis. In I. Kirsch, A. Capafons, E. Cardeña, & S. Amigo (Eds.), *Clinical hypnosis and self-regulation: Cognitive-behavioral perspectives* (pp. 3–14). Washington, DC: American Psychological Association.

Barber, T.X. (2000). A deeper understanding of hypnosis: Its secrets, its nature, its essence. *American Journal of Clinical Hypnosis, 42* (3)/42 (4), 208–272.

Bargh, J.A. (1994). The four horsemen of automaticity: Awareness, intention, efficiency, and control in social cognition. In R.S. Wyer & T.K. Srull (Eds.), *Handbook of social cognition* (2nd ed., pp. 1–40). Hillsdale, NJ: Erlbaum.

Bargh, J.A., & Gollwitzer, P.M. (1994). Environmental control of goal-oriented action: Automatic and strategic contingencies between situations and behavior. *Nebraska Symposium on Motivation, 41,* 71–124.

Bargh, J.A., & Barndollar, K. (1996). Automaticity in action: The unconscious as repository of chronic goals and motives. In P.M. Gollwitzer & J.A. Bargh (Eds.), *The psychology of action: Linking cognition and motivation to behavior,* pp. 457–481. New York: Guilford.

Barlow, D., Craske, M., Cerney, J.A., & Klosko, J.S. (1989). Behavioral treatment of panic disorder. *Behavior Therapy, 20,* 261–268.

Barrett, D. (1990). Deep trance subjects: A schema of two distinct subgroups. In R.G. Kunzendorf (Ed.), *Mental imagery* (pp. 101–112). New York: Plenum Press.

Barrett, D. (1996). Fantasizers and dissociators: Two types of highly hypnotizables, two different imagery styles. In R.G. Kunzendorf, W.P. Spanos, & B. Wallace (Eds.), *Hypnosis and imagination* (pp. 123–135). Amityville, NY: Baywood.

Bartis, S.P., & Zamansky, H.S. (1990). Cognitive strategies in hypnosis: Toward resolving the hypnotic conflict. *International Journal of Clinical and Experimental Hypnosis, 38,* 168–182.

Bartlett, F.C. (1932). *Remembering.* New York: Columbia University Press.

Baucom, D., Sayers, S., & Scher, T. (1990). Supplementary behavioral marital therapy with cognitive restructuring and emotional expressive training: An outcome investigation. *Journal of Consulting and Clinical Psychology, 58,* 636–645.

Bauer, S.R., Sapp, M., & Johnson, D. (2000). Group counseling for rural at-risk high school students. *The High School Journal, 83* (2), 41–50.

Beal, D., Kopec, A.M., & DiGiuseppe, R. (1996). Disputing clients' irrational beliefs. *Journal of Rational Emotive and Cognitive Behavior Therapy, 14* (4), 215–229.

Beck, A.T. (1976). *Cognitive therapy and the emotional disorders.* New York: International University Press.

Beck, A.T., Brown, G., Berchick, R.J., Stewart, B.L., & Steer, R.A. (1990). Relationship between hopelessness and ultimate suicide: A replication with psychiatric outpatients. *American Journal of Psychiatry, 147* (2), 190–195.

Beck, A.T., & Emery, G. (1985). *Anxiety disorders and phobias: A cognitive perspective.* New York: Basic Books.

Beck, A.T., Freeman, A., & Associates. (1990). *Cognitive therapy of personality disorders.* New York: Guilford Press.

Beck, A.T., Kovacs, M., & Weissman, A. (1979). Assessment of suicide intention: The scale for suicidal ideation. *Journal of Consulting and Clinical Psychology, 47,* 343–352.

Beck, A.T., Rush, J., Shaw, B., & Emery, G. (1979a). Interview with a depressed and suicidal patient. In D. Wedding & R.J. Corsini (Eds.), *Cognitive therapy of depression* (pp. 225–243). New York: Guilford Press.

Beck, A.T., Rush, J., Shaw, B.F., & Emery, G. (1979b). *Cognitive therapy of depression.* New York: Guilford Press.

Beck, A.T., Schuyler, D., & Herman, I. (1974). Development of the suicidal intent scales. In A.T. Beck, H.L.P. Resnik, & D.J. Lettieri (Eds.), *The prediction of suicide* (pp. 45–56). Bowie, MD: Charles Press.

Beck, A.T., Sokol, L., Clark, D.A., Berchick, R.J., & Wright, F.D. (1992). A crossover study of focused cognitive therapy for panic disorder. *American Journal of Psychiatry, 149* (6), 778–783.

Beck, A.T., Steer, R.A., Kovacs, M., & Garrison, B. (1985). Hopelessness and eventual suicide: A 10-year study of patients hospitalized with suicidal ideation. *American Journal of Psychiatry, 412,* 552–563.

Beck, A.T., Ward, C.H., Mendelsohn, M., Mock, J.E., & Erbaugh, J.K. (1961). An inventory for measuring depression. *Archives of General Psychiatry, 4,* 561–571.

Beck, A.T., & Weishaar, M.E. (1995). Current psychotherapies. In R.J. Corsini & D. Wedding (Eds.), *Cognitive therapy* (5th ed., pp. 229–261). Itasca, IL: F.E. Peacock.

Beck, A.T., Weissman, A., Lester, D., & Trexler, L. (1974). The measurement of pessimism: The hopelessness scale. *Journal of Consulting and Clinical Psychology, 42,* 861–865.

Beck, J.S. (1995). *Cognitive therapy: Basics and beyond.* Spring Street, New York: Guilford Press.

Becker, J. (1987). *Behavior therapy.* Santa Monica, CA: Association for Advanced Training in Behavioral Sciences.

Beere, D.B. (1992). More on EMDR. *The Behavior Therapist, 15* (8), 179–180.

Bergin, A.E., & Garfield, S.C. (Eds.) (1994). *Handbook of psychotherapy and behavior change* (4th ed.). New York: Wiley.

Berne, E. (1961). *Transactional analysis in psychotherapy*. New York: Grove Press.

Bird, K.D. (2002). Confidence intervals for effect sizes in analysis of variance. *Educational and Psychological Measurement, 62,* 197–226.

Birnbaum, F. (1935). The Individual Psychological Experimental School in Vienna. *American Journal of Individual Psychology, 12,* 1–11.

Blackburn, I.M., Bishop, S., Glen, A.I.M., Whalley, L.J., & Christie, J.E. (1981). The efficacy of cognitive therapy in depression: A treatment trial using cognitive therapy and pharmacotherapy, each alone and in combination. *British Journal of Psychiatry, 139,* 181–189.

Blackburn, I.M., Eunsun, K.M., & Bishop, S. (1986). *A two-year naturalistic follow-up of depressed patients treated with cognitive therapy, pharmacotherapy, and a combination of both.* Unpublished manuscript. Royal Edinburgh Hospital, Scotland.

Bootzin, R.R., Bower, G.H., Zajonc, R.B., & Hall, E. (1986). *Psychology today: An introduction* (6th ed.). New York: Random House.

Bottone, P. (1957). *Alfred Adler: A portrait from life*. New York: Vanguard Press.

Bowers, K.S. (1992). Imagination and dissociation in hypnotic responding. *International Journal of Clinical and Experimental Hypnosis, 40,* 253–275.

Burnett, M.C., & Pulvino, C.J. (1990). Pro-tech, a multimodal group intervention for children with reluctance to use computers. *Elementary School Guidance and Counseling, 24,* 281–288.

Butler, G., Fennell, M., Robson, D., & Gelder, M. (1991). Comparison of behavior therapy and cognitive-behavior therapy in the treatment of generalized anxiety disorder. *Journal of Consulting and Clinical Psychology, 59,* 167–175.

Cautela, J.R. (1967). *The token economy: A review and evaluation*. New York: Plenum Press.

Chadwick, P.D.J., & Lowe, C.F. (1990). Measurement and modification of delusional beliefs. *Journal of Consulting and Clinical Psychology, 58,* 225–232.

Clark, D.M. (1989). Anxiety states: Panic and generalized anxiety. In K. Hawton, P.M. Salkovskis, J. Kirk, & D.M. Clark (Eds.), *Cognitive-behavior therapy for psychiatric problems: A practical guide* (pp. 52–96). New York: Oxford University Press.

Coe, W.C., & Sarbin, T.R. (1991). Role theory: Hypnosis from a dramaturgical and narrational perspective. In S.J. Lynn & J.W. Rhue (Eds.), *Theories of hypnosis: Current models and perspectives* (pp. 303–323). New York: Guilford Press.

Cohen, J. (1977). *Statistical power analysis for the behavioral sciences*. New York: Academic Press.

Colby, K.M. (1951). On the disagreement between Freud and Adler. *American Imago, 8,* 229–238.

Connery, D.S. (1982). *The inner source: Exploring hypnosis with Dr. Herbert Spiegel*. New York: Holt, Rinehart, and Winston.

Corey, G. (1982). *Theory and practice of counseling and psychotherapy* (3rd ed.). Pacific Grove, CA: Brooks/Cole.

Corey, G. (1991). *Theory and practice of counseling and psychotherapy* (4th ed.). Pacific Grove, CA: Brooks/Cole.

Corey, G. (1995). *Theory and practice of group counseling* (4th ed.). Pacific Grove, CA: Brooks/Cole.

Corey, G. (1996). *Theory and practice of counseling and psychotherapy* (5th ed.). Pacific Grove, CA: Brooks/Cole.

Corey, G. (2001). *Theory and practice of counseling and psychotherapy* (6th ed.). Pacific Grove, CA: Brooks/Cole.

Corey, G. (2004). *Theory and practice of group counseling* (6th ed.). Pacific Grove, CA: Brooks/Cole.

Cormier, W., & Cormier, L. (1991). *Interviewing strategies for helpers: A guide to assessment and evaluation* (3rd ed.). Pacific Grove, CA: Wadsworth.

Cormier, W.H., & Cormier, L.S. (1998). *Interviewing strategies for helpers: Fundamental skills and cognitive behavioral interventions* (4th ed.). Pacific Grove, CA: Brooks/Cole.

Corsini, R.J., & Wedding, D. (Eds.) (1989). *Current psychotherapies* (4th ed.). Itasca, IL: R.E. Peacock.

Crasilneck, H.B., & Hall, J.A. (1985). *Clinical Hypnosis: Principles and application* (2nd ed.). Orlando, FL: Grune and Stratton.

Crawford, H.J., Kendel, T., & Vendemia, J.M.C. (1998). The nature of hypnotic analgesia: Neurophysiological foundation and evidence. *Contemporary Hypnosis, 15,* 22–23.

Cunningham, L.M. (1995). Control theory, reality therapy, and cultural bias. *Journal of Reality Therapy, 15,* 15–32.

Dancu, C.V., & Foa, E.B. (1992). Posttraumatic stress disorder. In A. Freeman & F.M. Dattilio (Eds.), *Comprehensive casebook of cognitive therapy* (pp. 79–88). New York: Plenum Press.

Dasgupta, N., McGhee, D.E., Greenwald, A.G., & Banaji, M.R. (2000). Automatic preference for white Americans: Eliminating the familiarity explanation. *Journal of Experimental Social Psychology, 36* (3), 316–328.

Dattilio, F.M. (1994). Paradoxical intention as a proposed alternative in the treatment of panic disorders. *Journal of Cognitive Psychotherapy, 8* (1), 33.

Day, W.F. (1980). The historical antecedents of contemporary behaviorism. In R.W. Rieber & K. Salzinger (Eds.), *Psychology: Theoretical-historical perspectives* (pp. 203–262). New York: Academic Press.

Day, W.F. (1983). On the difference between radical and methodological behaviorism. *Behaviorism, 11,* 89–102.

de Shazer, S. (1991). *Putting difference to work.* New York: W.W. Norton.

DiGiuseppe, R., speaker (1990). *What do I do with my anger: Hold it in or let it out.* Cassette recording. New York: Institute for Rational-Emotive Therapy.

Dinkmeyer, D.C., Dinkmeyer, D.C., Jr., & Sperry, L. (1987). *Adlerian counseling and psychotherapy* (2nd ed.). Columbus, OH: Charles E. Merrill.

Dixon, M., Brunet, A., & Laurence, J.R. (1990). Hypnotizability and automaticity: Toward a parallel distributed processing model of hypnotic responding. *Journal of Abnormal Psychology, 99,* 336–343.

Dixon, M., & Laurence, J.R. (1992). Hypnotic susceptibility and verbal automaticity: Automatic and strategic processing differences in the Stroop color-naming task. *Journal of Abnormal Psychology, 101,* 344–347.

Dobson, K.S. (1989). A meta-analysis of efficacy of cognitive therapy for depression. *Journal of Consulting and Clinical Psychology, 57* (3), 414–419.

Douglas, L. (1986). Is adolescent suicide a third-degree game and who is the real victim? *Transactional Analysis Journal, 16*, 165–169.

Dryden, W. (1987). *Counseling individuals: The rational-emotive approach.* Philadelphia: Taylor and Francis.

Dryden, W., & DiGiuseppe, R. (1990). *A primer on rational-emotive therapy.* Champaign, IL: Research Press.

Dryden, W., & Hill, L.K. (1993). *Innovations in rational-emotive therapy.* Newbury Park, CA: Sage.

Dusay, J.M., & Dusay, K.M. (1989). In R.J. Corsini & D. Wedding (Eds.), *Current psychotherapies* (4th ed., pp. 405–453). Itasca, IL: F.E. Peacock.

Edmonston, W. F., Jr. (1981). *Hypnosis and relaxation: Modern verification of an old equation.* New York: Wiley.

Edwards, L., & Sapp, M. (2002). Reoperationalizing adaptive regression during hypnosis. *The Australian Journal of Clinical Hypnotherapy and Hypnosis, 23* (2), 115–129.

Ellenberger, H.F. (1970). *The discovery of the unconscious: The history and evolution of dynamic psychiatry.* New York: Basic Books.

Ellis, A. (1962). *Reason and emotion in psychotherapy.* New York: Lyle Stuart.

Ellis, A. (1973). *Humanistic psychotherapy.* New York: McGraw-Hill.

Ellis, A. (1977). The basic clinical theory of rational-emotive therapy. In A. Ellis & R. Grieger (Eds.), *Handbook of rational-emotive therapy* (Vol. 1, pp. 3–34). New York: Springer.

Ellis, A. (1985). *Overcoming resistance: Rational-emotive therapy with difficult clients.* New York: Springer.

Ellis, A. (1989). Rational-emotive therapy. In R.J. Corsini & D. Wedding (Eds.), *Current psychotherapies* (4th ed., pp. 197–238). Itasca, IL: F.E. Peacock.

Ellis, A. (1992a). Do I really hold that religiousness is irrational? *American Psychologist, 47* (3), 428–429.

Ellis, A. (1992b). Group rational-emotive and cognitive-behavior therapy. *International Journal of Group Psychotherapy, 42* (1), 63–80.

Ellis, A. (1993). Fundamentals of rational-emotive therapy. In W. Dryden & L.K. Hill (Eds.), *Innovations in rational-emotive therapy* (pp. 1–32). Newbury Park, CA: Sage.

Ellis, A. (1994a). A corrective note on O'Donohue and Szymanski's study of logical analysis and REBT's use of empirical hypothesis testing as well as logical analysis. *Journal of Rational-Emotive Therapy, 12* (1), 73–76.

Ellis, A. (1994b). Radical behavioral treatment of private events: A response to Michael Dougher. *The Behavior Therapist, 17* (9), 219–221.

Ellis, A. (1995). Changing rational-emotive therapy (RET) to rational emotive behavior therapy (REBT). *Journal of Rational Emotive and Cognitive Behavior Therapy, 13* (2), 85–89.

Ellis, A. (2001). Reasons why rational emotive behavior therapy is relatively neglected in the professional and scientific literature. *Journal of Rational Emotive and Cognitive Behavior Therapy, 19*, 67–74.

Ellis, A. (2003). Similarities and differences between rational emotive behavior therapy and cognitive therapy. *Journal of Cognitive Psychotherapy: An International Quarterly, 17* (3), 225–240.

Ellis, A., Abrams, M., & Dengelegi, L. (1992). *The art and science of rational eating.* New York: Barricade Books.

Ellis, A., & Bernard, M.E. (1985). *Clinical applications of rational-emotive therapy.* New York: Plenum Press.

Ellis, A., & Dryden, W. (1987). *The practice of rational emotive therapy.* New York: Springer.

Ellis, A., & Dryden, W. (1991). *A dialogue with Albert Ellis: Against dogma.* Stony Stratford, England: Open University Press.

Ellis, A., & Dryden, W. (1997). *The practice of rational emotive behavior therapy* (2nd ed.). New York: Springer.

Ellis, A., & Dryden, W. (1990). *The essential Albert Ellis: Against dogma.* Stony Stratford, England: Open University Press.

Ellis, A., & Grieger, R. (Eds.) (1986). *Handbook of rational-emotive therapy* (Vol. 2). New York: Springer.

Ellis, A., & Velten, E. (1992). *When AA doesn't work: Rational steps for quitting alcohol.* New York: Barricade Books.

Emerson, J., Bertoch, M.R., & Checketts, K.T. (1994). Transactional analysis ego-state functioning, psychological distress, and client change. *Psychotherapy, 31* (1), 109–113.

Epstein, N. (1982). Cognitive therapy with couples. *American Journal of Family Therapy, 10,* 5–16.

Erickson, M.H. (1980). Hypnosis: A general review. In E.L. Rossi (Ed.), *The collected papers of Milton H. Erickson on hypnosis* (Vol. 3, pp. 13–20). New York: Irvington. (Original work published in 1941.)

Erickson, M.H. (1967). *Advanced techniques of hypnosis and therapy.* New York: Grune and Stratton.

Erickson, M.H. (1958). Hypnosis in painful terminal illness. *American Journal of Clinical Hypnosis, 1,* 117–121.

Erickson, M.H. (1944). The method employed to formulate a complex story for the induction of an experimental neurosis in a hypnotic subject. *Journal of General Psychology, 31,* 67–84.

Erickson, M.H., & Rossi, E.L. (1979). *Hypnotherapy: An exploratory casebook.* New York: Irvington.

Erskine, R.G. (1994). Shame and self-righteousness: Transactional analysis perspectives and clinical interventions. *Transactional Analysis Journal, 24* (2), 86–102.

Evans, K.R. (1994). Healing shame: A Gestalt perspective. *Transactional Analysis Journal, 24* (2), 103–108.

Fairburn, C.G., Jones, R., Peveler, R.C., Hope, R.A., & Doll, H.A. (1991). Three psychological treatments for bulimia nervosa: A comparison trial. *Archives of General Psychiatry, 48,* 463–469.

Fakouri, M.E., & Hafner, J. (1994). Adlerian-oriented early recollection studies: What do we ask? *Individual Psychology, 50* (2), 170–172.

Fan, X., & Thompson, B. (2001). Confidence intervals about score reliability coefficients, please: An EPM guidelines editorial. *Educational and Psychological Measurement, 61* (4), 517–531.

Farrell, W., Sapp, M., Johnson, J., & Pollard, D. (1994). Assessing college aspirations among at-risk high school students: A principal component analysis. *The High School Journal, 77* (4), 294–303.

Fischer, G.P. (1993). The changing organizational parent. *Transactional Analysis Journal, 23* (2), 70–76.

Fish, J.M. (1992). EMDR workshop and openness. *The Behavior Therapist, 15* (8), 180.

Fisher, R.A. (1928). *Statistical methods for research workers* (2nd ed.). London: Olviver and Boyd.

Frank, J.D. (1986). What is psychotherapy? In S. Bloch (Ed.), *An introduction to psychotherapy* (pp. 5–45). New York: Oxford University Press.

Frankl, V.E. (1959). *Man's search for meaning: An introduction to logotherapy.* New York: Washington Square Press.

Frankl, V.E. (1983). *The doctor and the soul.* New York: Vintage Books.

Freedman, L.D. (1993). TA tools for self-managing work teams. *Transactional Analysis Journal, 23* (2), 104–109.

Freeman, A. (1990). Cognitive therapy. In A.S. Bellack & M. Hersen (Eds.), *Handbook of comparative treatments for adult disorders* (pp. 64–87). New York: Wiley.

Freeman, A., Simon, K.M., Beutler, L.E., & Arkowitz, M. (Eds.) (1989). *Comprehensive handbook of cognitive therapy.* New York: Plenum Press.

Fromm, E. (1941). *Escape from freedom.* New York: Farrar and Reinhart.

Gambrill, D.K. (1994). Concepts and methods of behavioral treatment. In D. Granvold (Ed.), *Cognitive and behavioral treatment: Methods and applications* (pp. 33–57). Pacific Grove, CA: Brooks/Cole.

Gard, T. (1993). Transactional analysis for battered women. *Transactional Analysis Journal, 23* (3), 152–157.

Garfield, V. (1994). Ethical principles for work in organizations. *Transactional Analysis Journal, 23* (2), 60–65.

Garner, D.M., Rockett, W., Davis, R., Garner, M.V., Olmstead, M.P., & Eagle, M. (1993). Comparison of cognitive-behavioral and supportive-expressive therapy for bulimia nervosa. *American Journal of Psychiatry, 150,* 37–46.

Gelerntner, C.S., Uhde, T.W., Cimbolic, P., Arnkoff, D.B., Vittone, B.J., Tancer, M.E., et al. (1990). Cognitive-behavioral and pharmacological treatments of social phobia: A controlled study. *Archives of General Psychiatry, 48,* 938–945.

Gendlin, E.T. (1986). What comes after traditional psychotherapy research? *American Psychologist, 41,* 131–136.

Gerbode, F.A., & Moore, R.H. (1994). Beliefs and intentions in RET. *Journal of Rational-Emotive Therapy and Cognitive-Behavior Therapy, 12* (1), 27–46.

Gerler, E.R., Drew, N.S., & Mohr, P. (1990). Succeeding in middle school: A multimodal approach. *Elementary School Guidance and Counseling, 24,* 263–271.

Glasser, W. (1961). *Mental health or mental illness?* New York: Harper and Row.

Glasser, W. (1965). *Reality therapy.* New York: Harper and Row.

Glasser, W. (1969). *Schools without failure.* New York: Harper and Row.

Glasser, W. (1972). *The identity society.* New York: Harper and Row.

Glasser, W. (1984). Reality therapy. In R. Corsini (Ed.), *Current psychotherapies* (3rd ed., pp. 320–353).

Glasser, W. (1986). *Control theory in the classroom*. New York: Harper and Row.

Glasser, W. (1989). Control theory in the practice of reality therapy. In N. Glasser (Ed.), *Control theory in the practice of reality therapy: Case studies* (pp. 1–15). New York: Harper and Row.

Glasser, W. (1990a). *The basic concepts of reality therapy* [chart]. Canoga Park, CA: Institute for Reality Therapy.

Glasser, W. (1990b). *The quality school*. New York: Harper and Row.

Glasser, W. (1999). *The quality school*. New York: Harper and Row.

Glasser, W. (2000). *Reality therapy in action*. New York: Harper Collins. (Also reissued and titled as *Counseling with Choice Theory: The new reality therapy*.)

Glasser, W., & Wubbolding, R. (1995). Reality therapy. In R. Corsini & D. Wedding (Eds.), *Current psychotherapies* (5th ed., pp. 293–321). Itasca, IL: F.E. Peacock.

Glasser, W., & Zunin, L. (1973). In R. Corsini (Ed.), *Current psychotherapies* (pp. 302–339). Itasca, IL: F.E. Peacock.

Golden, W.L., Dowd, E.T., & Friedberg, F. (1987). *Hypnotherapy: A modern approach*. New York: Pergamon Press.

Goulding, M., & Goulding, R. (1979). *Changing lives through redecision therapy*. New York: Brunner/Mazel.

Goulding, R., & Goulding, M. (1978). *The power is in the patient: A TA/Gestalt approach to psychotherapy*. San Francisco: TA Press.

Granvold, D.K. (Ed.) (1994). *Cognitive and behavioral treatment: Methods and applications*. Pacific Grove, CA: Brooks/Cole.

Guidano, V.F. (1987). *Complexity of the self*. New York: Guilford Press.

Guidano, V.F., & Liotti, G. (1983). *Cognitive processes and emotional disorders*. New York: Guilford Press.

Hackett, G. (1995). Self-efficacy in career choice and development. In A. Bandura (Ed.), *Self-efficacy in changing societies* (pp. 232–258). Cambridge, England: Cambridge University Press.

Hajzler, D.J., & Bernard, M.E. (1991). A review of rational-emotive education outcome studies. *School Psychology Quarterly, 6* (1), 27–46.

Hamburg, S.R. (2000). Antidepressants are not placebos. *American Psychologist, 55* (7), 761–762.

Hammond, D.C. (1992). *Hypnotic induction and suggestion: An introductory manual*. Des Plaines, IL: American Society of Clinical Hypnosis.

Harris, T. (1969). *I'm OK – You're OK*. New York: Harper and Row.

Hawes, R. (1971). Reality therapy in the classroom. *Dissertation Abstracts International*, University of Pacific, 32A, 2483.

Hazell, J. (1989). Drivers as mediators of stress response. *Transactional Analysis Journal, 19,* 212–222.

Heckhausen, J., & Schulz, R. (1995). A life-span theory of control. *Psychological Review, 102,* 284–304.

Heimberg, R.G. (1990). Cognitive-behavior therapy (for social phobia). In A.S. Bellack & M. Hersen (Eds.), *Comparative handbook of treatments for adult disorders* (pp. 203–218). New York: Wiley.

Hensel, C.S., Sapp, M., Farrell, W., & Hitchcock, K. (2001). A survey of members of ASCH, SCEH, and Division 30, and if they reported using hypnosis to treat depression. *Sleep and Hypnosis, 3* (4), 152–168.

Herrnstein, R.J., & Murray, C.A. (1994). *The bell curve: Intelligence and class structure in American life.* New York: Free Press.

Hilgard, E.R. (1973). A neodissociation interpretation of pain reaction in hypnosis. *Psychological Review, 80,* 396–411.

Hilgard, E.R. (1994). Neodissociation theory. In S.J. Lynn & J.W. Rhue (Eds.), *Dissociation: Clinical and theoretical perspectives* (pp. 83–104). New York: Guilford Press.

Hoffman, E. (1994). *The drive for self: Alfred Adler and the founding of Individual Psychology.* Reading, MA: Addison-Wesley.

Horney, K. (1945). *Our inner conflicts.* New York: W.W. Norton.

Horwitz, A. (1982). The relationship between positive stroking and self-perceived symptoms of distress. *Transactional Analysis Journal, 12,* 218–221.

Huddleston, J.E., & Engles, D.W. (1986). Issues related to the use of paradoxical techniques in counseling. *Journal of Counseling and Human Service Professions, 1,* 127–133.

Hull, C.L. (1952). *A behavior system.* New Haven, CT: Yale University Press.

Iverson, G.L. (1994). Will the real behaviorism please stand up? *The Behavior Therapist, 17* (8), 191–194.

Jacobs, A. (1994). Theory as ideology: Reparenting and thought reform. *Transactional Analysis Journal, 24* (1), 39–55.

Jacobson, E. (1938). *Progressive relaxation.* Chicago: University of Chicago Press.

James, N.L. (1994). Cultural frame of reference and intergroup encounters: A TA approach. *Transactional Analysis Journal, 24* (3), 206–210.

James, R.K., & Gilliland, B.E. (2003). *Theories and strategies in counseling and psychotherapy* (5th ed.). Boston: Allyn and Bacon.

Joines, V., & Stewart, I. (2002). *Personality adaptations: A new guide to human understanding in psychotherapy and counseling.* Nottingham: Lifespace.

Kalodner, C.R. (1995). Cognitive-behavioral theories. In D. Capuzzi & D.R. Gross (Eds.), *Counseling and psychotherapy* (pp. 371–381). Englewood Cliffs, NJ: Merrill.

Karpman, S. (1968). Script drama analysis. *Transactional Analysis Bulletin, 26,* 16–22.

Kazdin, A.E., & Wilson, G.T. (1978). *Evaluation of behavior therapy: Issues, evidence, and research strategies.* Cambridge, MA: Ballinger.

Keat, D.B. (1990). Change in child multimodal counseling. *Elementary School Guidance and Counseling, 24,* 248–262.

Kelly, G. (1955). The psychology of personal constructors (Vols. 1–2). New York: W.W. Norton.

Kendall, P.C. (1992). *Anxiety disorders: Cognitive-behavioral interventions.* Needham Heights, MA: Allyn and Bacon.

Kendall, P.C., & Hammen, C. (1998). *Abnormal psychology: Understanding human problems* (2nd ed.). Boston: Houghton-Mifflin.

Kernberg, O.F. (1975). *Borderline conditions and pathological narcissism.* New York: Jason Aronson.

King, B.J., & Council, J.R. (1998). Intentionality during hypnosis: An ironic process analysis. *The International Journal of Clinical and Experimental Hypnosis, 45,* 295–312.

Kingdon, D.G., & Turkington, D. (1994). *Cognitive-behavioral therapy of schizophrenia.* New York: Guilford Press.

Kirsch, I. (1990). *Changing expectations: A key to effective psychotherapy.* Pacific Grove, CA: Brooks/Cole.

Kirsch, I. (1991). The social learning theory of hypnosis. In S.J. Lynn & J.W. Rhue (Eds.), *Theories of hypnosis: Current models and perspectives* (pp. 439–465). New York: Guilford Press.

Kirsch, I. (1997). Response expectancy and application: A decennial review. *Applied and Preventive Psychology* (6), 69–79.

Kirsch, I., Burgess, C.A., & Braffman, W. (1999). Attentional resources in hypnotic responding. *The International Journal of Clinical and Experimental Hypnosis, 47,* 175–191.

Kirsch, I., & Council, J.R. (1992). Situational and personality correlates of suggestibility. In E. Cromm & M. Nash (Eds.), *Contemporary hypnosis research* (pp. 267–292). New York: Guilford Press.

Kirsch, I., & Lynn, S.J. (1995). The altered state of hypnosis: Changes in the theoretical landscape. *American Psychologist, 50* (10), 846–858.

Kirsch, I., & Lynn, S.J. (1995). Social-cognitive alternatives to dissociation theories of hypnotic involuntariness. *Review of General Psychology, 2,* 66–80.

Kirsch, I., & Lynn, S.J. (1998). Dissociation theories of hypnosis. *Psychological Bulletin, 123,* 100–115.

Kirsch, I., & Lynn, S. J. (1999). Automaticity in clinical psychology. *American Psychologist, 54,* 504–515.

Kirsch, I., Montgomery, G., & Sapirstein, G. (1995). Hypnosis as an adjunct to cognitive behavioral psychotherapy: A meta-analysis. *Journal of Consulting and Clinical Psychology, 63,* 214–220.

Kirsch, J., & Sapp, M. (2000). Hypnotizability and inattention with college students. *The Australian Journal of Clinical Hypnotherapy and Hypnosis, 21,* 13–38.

Klein, M. (1980). *Lives people live: A textbook of transactional analysis.* New York: Wiley.

Kohut, H. (1971). *The analysis of the self.* New York: International Universities Press.

Kohut, H. (1977). *The restoration of the self.* Madison, CT: International Universities Press.

Kopec, A.M., Beal, D., & DiGiuseppe, R. (1994). Training in RET: Disputational strategies. *Journal of Rational-Emotive Therapy and Cognitive-Behavior Therapy, 12* (1), 47–60.

Krausz, R.R. (1993). Organizational scripts. *Transactional Analysis Journal, 23* (2), 77–86.

Kroger, W.S. (1977). *Clinical and experimental hypnosis in medicine, dentistry, and psychology* (2nd ed.). Philadelphia: J.B. Lippincott.

Kroger, W.S., & Fezler, W.D. (1976). *Hypnosis and behavior modification: Imagery conditioning.* Philadelphia: J.B. Lippincott.

LaFontaine, L. (1994). Quality schools for gay and lesbian youth: Lifting the cloak of silence. *Journal of Reality Therapy, 14,* 16–28.

LaFontaine, L. (1995). Basic needs and sexuality: Is something missing in reality therapy/control theory? *Journal of Reality Therapy, 15,* 32–36.

Lambert, M.J., & Bergin, A.E. (1994). The effectiveness of psychotherapy. In A.E. Bergin & S.L. Garfield (Eds.), *Handbook of psychotherapy and behavior change* (4th ed., pp. 143–189). New York: Wiley.

Lancaster, B.P. (1999). Defining and interpreting suppressor effects: Advantages and limitations. In B. Thompson (Ed.), *Advances in social science methodology* (Vol. 5, pp. 139–148). Stamford, CT: JAI Press.

Laurence, J.R., & Perry, C. (1983). Hypnotically created pseudomemories among highly hypnotizable subjects. *Science, 222,* 523–524.

Layden, M.A., Newman, C.F., Freeman, A., & Morse, S.B. (1993). *Cognitive therapy of borderline personality disorder.* Needham Heights, MA: Allyn and Bacon.

Lazarus, A. (1980). *Multimodal life history questionnaire.* Champaign, IL: Research Press.

Lazarus, A.A. (1976). *Multimodal behavior therapy.* New York: Springer.

Lazarus, A.A. (1986). Treating agoraphobia: Behavioral/multimodal perspectives. *Psychotherapy in Private Practice, 4,* 11–23.

Lazarus, A.A. (1989a). Brief psychotherapy: The multimodal model. *Psychology – A Journal of Human Behavior, 26* (1), 6–10.

Lazarus, A.A. (1989b). The case of George. In D. Wedding & R.J. Corsini (Eds.), *Case studies in psychotherapy* (pp. 227–238). Itasca, IL: F.E. Peacock.

Lazarus, A.A. (1989c). *The practice of multimodal therapy.* Baltimore: Johns Hopkins University Press.

Lazarus, A.A. (1990a). Multimodal applications and research: A brief overview and update. *Elementary School Guidance and Counseling, 24* (4), 243–247.

Lazarus, A.A. (1990b). Can psychotherapists transcend the shackles of their training and superstitions? *Journal of Clinical Psychology, 46* (3), 351–358.

Lazarus, A.A., & Lazarus, C.N. (1991). *Multimodal Life History Inventory.* Champaign, IL: Research Press.

Lazarus, A.A. (1992). The multimodal approach to the treatment of depression. *American Journal of Psychotherapy, 46* (1), 50–57.

Lazarus, A.A. (1995). Multimodal therapy. In R.J. Corsini & D. Wedding (Eds.), *Current psychotherapies* (pp. 503–544). Itasca, IL: F.E. Peacock.

Lazarus, A.A., & Beutler, L.E. (1993). On technical eclecticism. *Journal of Counseling and Development, 71,* 381–385.

Lazarus, A.A., Beutler, L.E., & Norcorss, J.C. (1992). The future of technical eclecticism. *Psychotherapy, 29* (1), 11–20.

Lee, C. (1996). M.C.T. Theory and implications for indigenous healing. In D.W. Sue, A.E. Ivey, & P. Pederson (Eds.), *A theory of multicultural counseling and therapy* (pp. 86–96). Pacific Grove, CA: Brooks/Cole.

Lester, D. (1994). Psychotherapy for suicidal clients. *Death-Studies, 18* (4), 361–374.

Lewinsohn, P.M., Clarke, G.W., Hops, H., & Andrews, J. (1990). Cognitive-behavioral treatment for depressed adolescents. *Behavior Therapy, 21,* 385–401.

Libet, B. (1985). Unconscious cerebral initiative and the role of conscious will in voluntary action. *Behavioral and Brain Sciences, 8,* 529–566.

Liebert, R.M., & Spiegler, M.D. (1990). *Personality: Strategies and issues* (6th ed.). Pacific Grove, CA: Brooks/Cole.

Linehan, M.M., Dimeff, L., & Reynolds, S.K. (2002). Dialectical behavior therapy versus comprehensive validation therapy plus 12-step for the treatment of opioid dependent women meeting criteria for borderline personality disorder. *Drug and Alcohol Dependence, 67* (1), 13–26.

Livneh, H., & Wright, P.E. (1995). Rational-emotive therapy. In D. Capuzzi & D.R. Gross (Eds.), *Counseling and psychotherapy: Theories and interventions* (pp. 325–352). Englewood Cliffs, NJ: Merrill.

Lynn, S.J. (1992). A non-state of hypnotic involuntariness. *Contemporary Hypnosis, 9,* 21–27.

Lynn, S.J., & Rhue, J.W. (1991). *Theories of hypnosis: Current models and perspectives.* New York: Guilford Press.

Lynn, S.J., & Rhue, J.W. (Eds.) (1994). *Dissociation: Clinical and theoretical perspectives.* New York: Guilford Press.

Lyons, L.C., & Woods, P.J. (1991). The efficacy of rational-emotive therapy: A quantitative review of the outcome research. *Clinical Psychology Review, 11,* 357–369.

Mahoney, M.J. (1974). *Cognition and behavior modification.* Cambridge, MA: Ballinger.

Mahoney, M.J. (1988). The cognitive sciences and psychotherapy: Patterns in a developing relationship. In K. Kobson (Ed.), *Handbook of cognitive-behavioral therapies* (pp. 357–386). New York: Guildford Press.

Mahoney, M.J. (1991). *Human change processes: The scientific foundations of psychotherapy.* New York: Basic Books.

Maldonado, A. (1982). Cognitive and behavioral therapy for depression: Its efficacy and interaction with pharmacological treatment. *Revista de psicologia general y aplicada, 37* (1), 31–56.

Maniacci, M.P. (1996). Mental disorders due to a general medical condition and cognitive disorders. In L. Sperry & J. Carson (Eds.), *Psychopathology and psychotherapy: From DSM-IV diagnosis to treatment* (2nd ed., pp. 51–75). Muncie, IN: Accelerated Development.

Maqsud, M., & Rouhani, S. (1991). Relationships between socioeconomic status, locus of control, self-concept, and academic achievement of Botswana adolescents. *Journal of Youth and Adolescence, 20,* 107–114.

Marger, M.N. (2000). *Race and ethnic relations: American and global perspectives* (5th ed.). Belmont, CA: Wadsworth/Thomson Learning.

Marger, M.N. (2003). *Race and ethnic relations: American and global perspectives* (6th ed.). Belmont, CA: Wadsworth/Thomson Learning.

Marshall, G.W. (1991). A multidimensional analysis of internal health locus of control beliefs: Separating the wheat from the chaff? *Journal of Personality and Social Psychology, 61,* 483–491.

Martin-Causey, T., & Hinkle, J.S. (1995). Multimodal therapy with an aggressive preadolescent: A demonstration of effectiveness and accountability. *Journal of Counseling and Development, 73* (3), 305–310.

Marziali, E., Marmar, C., & Krupnick, J. (1981). Therapeutic alliance scales: Development and relationship to psychotherapy outcome. *American Journal of Psychiatry, 138,* 361–364.

Masson, J. (1984). Freud and the seduction theory. *The Atlantic, 253* (2), 33–60.

Maultsby, M. (1984). *Rational behavior therapy.* Englewood Cliffs, NJ: Prentice-Hall.

Maultsby, M.C. (1990). *Rational behavior therapy.* Appleton, WI: Rational Self-Help Aids/ACT.

May, R. (1983). *The discovery of being*. New York: W.W. Norton.

McClendon, R. (1977). My mother drives a pickup truck. In G. Barnes (Ed.), *Transactional analysis after Eric Berne* (pp. 99–113). New York: Harper.

McClendon, R., & Kadis, L.B. (1994). Shame and early decisions; Theory and clinical applications. *Transactional Analysis Journal, 24* (2) 130–138.

McGrath, G. (1994). Ethics, boundaries, and contracts: Applying moral principles. *Transactional Analysis Journal, 24* (1), 6–14.

Meichenbaum, D. (1969). The effects of instructions and reinforcement on thinking and language behaviors of schizophrenics. *Behavior Research Therapy, 7,* 101–114.

Meichenbaum, D. (1972). Cognitive modification of test-anxious college students. *Journal of Consulting and Clinical Psychology, 39,* 370–380.

Meichenbaum, D. (1977). *Cognitive-behavioral modification: An integrative approach*. New York: Plenum.

Meichenbaum, D. (1979). Cognitive-behavior modification: Future directions. In P.O. Sjoden, S. Bates, & W.S. Dockens, III (Eds.), *Trends in behavior therapy* (pp. 55–65). New York: Academic Press.

Meichenbaum, D. (1985). *Stress inoculation training*. New York: Pergamon Press.

Meichenbaum, D. (1986). Cognitive behavior modification. In F. H. Kanfer & A.P. Goldstein (Eds.), *Helping people change: A textbook of methods* (3rd ed., pp. 346–380). New York: Pergamon Press.

Meichenbaum, D. (1990a). Providing challenges. *Psychological Inquiry, 1* (4), 96–100.

Meichenbaum, D. (1990b). Cognitive perspectives on teaching self-regulation. *American Journal on Mental Retardation, 94* (4), 367–369.

Meichenbaum, D. (1993a). Changing conceptions of cognitive-behavior modification: Retrospect and prospect. Special section. Recent developments in cognitive and constructivist psychotherapies. *Journal of Consulting and Clinical Psychology, 61* (2), 202–204.

Meichenbaum, D. (1993b). The "potential" contributions of cognitive-behavior modification to literacy training for deaf students. *American Annals of the Deaf, 138* (2), 87–95.

Meichenbaum, D. (1994). *A clinical handbook/practical therapist manual for assessing and treating adults with post-traumatic stress disorder (PTSD)*. Waterloo, Ontario: Institute Press.

Meichenbaum, D.H., & Deffenbacher, J.L. (1998). Stress inoculation training. *The Counseling Psychologist, 16,* 69–90.

Miller, N.E., & Dollard, J.C. (1941). *Social learning and imitation*. New Haven, CT: Yale University Press.

Miller, P. (1991). The application of cognitive therapy to chronic pain. In T.M. Vallis, J.L. Howes, & P.C. Miller (Eds.), *The challenge of cognitive therapy: Application to nontraditional populations* (pp. 159–182). New York: Plenum.

Mosak, H.H. (1971). Lifestyle. In A.G. Nikelly (Ed.), *Techniques for behavior change* (pp. 77–81). Springfield, IL: Charles C Thomas.

Mosak, H.H. (1989). In R.J. Corsini & D. Wedding (Eds.), *Current psychotherapies* (pp. 65–118). Itasca, IL: F.E. Peacock.

Mosak, H., & Maniacci, M. (1999). *A primer of Adlerian psychology: The analytic-behavioral-cognitive psychology of Alfred Adler*. Philadelphia: Brunner/Mazel.

Mozdierz, G.L., & Greenblatt, R.L. (1994). Techniques in psychotherapy: Cautions and concerns. *Individual Psychology, 50* (2), 232–249.

Munuchin, S. (1974). *Families and family therapy.* New York: Basic Books.

Murphy, G.E., Simons, A.D., Wetzel, R.D., & Lustman, P.J. (1983). Cognitive therapy and pharmacotherapy: Singly and together in the treatment of depression. *Archives of General Psychiatry, 41,* 33–41.

Mylott, K. (1994). Twelve irrational ideas that drive gay men and women crazy. *Journal of Rational-Emotive Therapy and Cognitive-Behavior Therapy, 12* (1), 61–72.

Nash, M.R., (1987). What, if anything, is regressed about hypnotic age regression? A review of the empirical literature. *Psychological Bulletin, 102,* 42–52.

Neimeyer, R.A. (1986). Cognitive-behavioural approaches to psychotherapy. In W. Dryden & W.L. Golden (Eds.), *Personal construct therapy* (pp. 224–260). London: Harper and Row.

Nieves, L.C. (1978a). *College achievement through self-help.* Princeton, NJ: Educational Testing Service.

Nieves, L.C. (1978b). *The minority college student experience: A case for the use of self-control.* Princeton, NJ: Educational Testing Service.

Norman, D.A., & Shallice, T. (1986). Attention to action: Willed and automatic control of behavior. In R.J. Davidson & G.E. Schwartz, *Consciousness and self-regulation, 4,* 1–18. New York: Plenum Press.

Nosek, B.A., & Banaji, M.R. (2003). Understanding and using the implicit association test: I. An improved scoring algorithm. *Journal of Personality and Social Psychology, 85* (2), 197–216.

Okeke, B.I., Draguns, J.G., Skeku, B., & Allen, W. (1999). Culture, self, and personality in Africa. In Y.T. Lee, C.R. McCauley, & J.G. Draguns (Eds.), *Personality and person perception across cultures* (pp. 139–162). Mahwah, NJ: Erlbaum.

Orgler, H. (1963). *Alfred Adler, the man and his work: Triumph over the inferiority complex.* New York: Liveright.

Orne, M.T. (1959). The nature of hypnosis: Artifact and essence. *Journal of Abnormal and Social Psychology, 58,* 277–299.

Orne, M.T. (1979). On the simulating subject as a quasi-control group in hypnosis research: What, why, and how. In E. Fromm & R.E. Shor (Eds.), *Hypnosis: Developments in research and new perspectives* (2nd ed. pp. 519–565). Chicago: Aldine.

Padesky, C.A., & Beck, A.T. (2003). Science and philosophy: Comparison of cognitive therapy and rational emotive behavior therapy. *17* (3), 211–224.

Parrot, C.A., & Howes, J.L. (1991). The application of cognitive therapy to post-traumatic stress disorder. In T.M. Vallis, J.L. Howes, & P.C. Miller (Eds.), *The challenge of cognitive therapy: Applications to non-traditional populations* (pp. 85–109). New York: Plenum Press.

Pashler, H.E. (1998). *The psychology of attention.* Cambridge, MA: The MIT Press.

Paul, G.L. (1967). Outcome research in psychotherapy. *Journal of Consulting Psychotherapy, 31,* 109–188.

Pedhazur, E.J. (1997). *Multiple regression in behavioral research: Explanation and prediction* (3rd ed.). Fort Worth, TX: Harcourt Brace College Publishers.

Pekala, R.J., Kumar, V.K., & Marcano, G. (1995). Hypnotic types: A partial replication concerning phenomenal experience. *Contemporary Hypnosis, 12,* 194–200.

Perris, C., Ingelson, U., & Johnson, D. (1993). Cognitive therapy as a general framework in the treatment of psychotic patients. In K. T. Kuehlwein & H. Rosen (Eds.), *Cognitive therapy in action: Evolving innovative practice* (pp. 379–402). San Francisco: Jossey-Bass.

Piaget, J. (1926). *The language and thought of the child.* New York: Harcourt, Brace.

Piccione, C., Hilgard, E.R., & Zimbardo, P.G. (1989). On the degree of stability of measured hypnotizability over a 25-year period. *Journal of Personality and Social Psychology, 56,* 289–295.

Pitsch, E., Sapp, M., & McNeely, R.L. (2001). Effects of locus of control, hypnotizability, transcript type, and gender on vividness of imagination, hypnotic depth, and inner subjective experiences of automaticity. *The Australian Journal of Clinical Hypnotherapy and Hypnosis, 22* (1), 1–10.

Poidevant, J.M., & Lewis, A.L. (1995). Transactional analysis theory. In D. Dapuzzi & D. R. Gross (Eds.), *Counseling and psychotherapy: Theories and interventions* (pp. 297–324). Englewood Cliffs, NJ: Merrill.

Powers, R.L., & Griffith, J. (1987). *Understanding life-style. The psycho-clarity process.* Chicago: The American Institute of Adlerian Studies.

Powers, W. (1973). *Behavior: The control of perception.* New York: Aldine.

Premack, D. (1959). Toward empirical behavioral laws: In psychological reinforcement. *Psychological Review, 66,* 219–233.

Prochaska, J.O. (1984). *Systems of psychotherapy: A transtheoretical analysis.* Pacific Grove, CA: Brooks/Cole.

Puk, G. (1994). EMDR: The utility of clinical observation. *The Behavior Therapist, 17* (8), 201.

Radtke, L., Sapp, M., & Farrell, W.C. (1997). Reality therapy: A meta-analysis. *International Journal of Reality Therapy, 17* (1), 4–9.

Ray, W.L., & Oathes, D. (2003). Brain imaging techniques. *International Journal of Clinical and Experimental Hypnosis, 51* (2), 97–104.

Raz, A., & Shapiro, T. (2002). Hypnosis and neuroscience: A cross talk between clinical and cognitive research. *Archives of General Psychiatry, 59,* 85–90.

Rescorla, R.A. (1988). Pavlovian conditioning: It's not what you think it is. *American Psychologist, 43,* 151–160.

Rhue, J.W., Lynn, S.J., & Kirsch, I. (Eds.) (1993). *Handbook of clinical hypnosis.* Washington, DC: American Psychological Association.

Rosen, G.M. (1992). A note to EMDR critics: What you didn't see is only part of what you don't get. *The Behavior Therapist, 15* (9), 216.

Rosenthal, R. (1984). *Meta-analytic procedures for social research.* Beverly Hills, CA: Sage.

Rotter, J.B. (1954). *Social learning and clinical psychology.* Englewood Cliffs, NJ: Prentice-Hall.

Rotter, J.B. (1966). Generalized expectancies for internal locus of control reinforcement. *Psychological Monographs, 80,* (1–28, whole No. 609).

Rotter, J.B. (1967). A new scale for the measurement of interpersonal trust. *Journal of Personality, 35,* 651–665.

Rotter, J.B. (1971). Generalized expectancies for interpersonal trust. *American Psychologist, 26,* 443–452.

Rotter, J.B. (1980). Interpersonal trust, trustworthiness, gullibility. *American Psychologist, 35*, 1–7.

Rotter, J.B. (1982). *The development and application of social learning theory.* New York: Praeger.

Rotter, J.B. (1990). George Kelly and the concept of construction. *International Journal of Personal Constructs Psychology, 3* (1), 7–19.

Rotter, J.B. (1993). Expectancies. In C.E. Walker (Ed.), *The history of clinical psychology in autobiography* (Vol. 2, pp. 273–284). Pacific Grove, CA: Brooks/Cole.

Rychlak, J.F. (1990). George Kelly and the concept of construction. *International Journal of Personal Constructs Psychology, 3* (1), 7–19.

Ryckman, R.M. (1989). *Theories of personality* (4th ed.). Pacific Grove, CA: Brooks/Cole.

Salkovskis, P.M., & Kirk, J. (1989). Obsessional disorders. In K. Hawton, P.M. Salkovskis, J. Kirk, & D.M. Clark (Eds.), *Cognitive-behavior therapy for psychiatric problems: A practical guide* (pp. 129–168). New York: Oxford University Press.

Sapp, M. (1990). Psychoeducational correlates of junior high school at-risk students. *The High School Journal, 73* (4), 232–234.

Sapp, M. (1991). Hypnotherapy and test anxiety: Two cognitive-behavioral constructs. *The Australian Journal of Clinical Hypnotherapy and Hypnosis, 12* (1), 25–33.

Sapp, M. (1992a). The effects of hypnosis in reducing test anxiety and improving academic achievement in college students. *The International Journal of Professional Hypnosis, 6* (1), 20–22.

Sapp, M. (1992b). Relaxation and hypnosis in reducing anxiety and stress. *The Australian Journal of Clinical Hypnotherapy and Hypnosis, 13* (2), 39–55.

Sapp, M. (1993). *Test anxiety: Applied research, assessment, and treatment interventions.* Lanham, MD: University Press of America.

Sapp, M. (1994a). Cognitive-behavioral counseling: Applications for African American middle school students who are academically at-risk. *Journal of Instructional Psychology, 21* (2), 161–171.

Sapp, M. (1994b). The effects of guided imagery in reducing the worry and emotionality components of test anxiety. *Journal of Mental Imagery, 18* (3&4), 165–180.

Sapp, M. (1995). Hypnosis: Applications for clients with physical disabilities who are seeking supported employment. *The Australian Journal of Clinical Hypnotherapy and Hypnosis, 16* (1), 1–8.

Sapp, M. (1996a). Irrational beliefs that can lead to academic failure for African American middle school students who are academically at-risk. *Journal of Rational-Emotive and Cognitive-Behavior Therapy, 14* (2), 123–134.

Sapp, M. (1996b). Potential negative sequelae of hypnosis. *The Australian Journal of Clinical Hypnotherapy and Hypnosis, 17* (2), 72–77.

Sapp, M. (1996c). Three treatments for reducing the worry and emotionality components of test anxiety with undergraduate and graduate college students: Cognitive-behavioral hypnosis, relaxation therapy, and supportive counseling. *Journal of College Student Development, 37* (1), 79–87.

Sapp, M. (1997a). *Counseling and psychotherapy: Theories, associated research, and issues.* Lanham, MD: University Press of America.

Sapp, M. (1997b). Hypnotizability scales: What are they, and are they useful? *The Australian Journal of Clinical Hypnotherapy and Hypnosis, 17* (11), 25–32.

Sapp, M. (1997c). Order effects for two measures of hypnotizability. *Perceptual and Motor Skills, 85* (3), 1042.

Sapp, M. (1997d). Theories of hypnosis. *The Australian Journal of Clinical Hypnotherapy and Hypnosis, 18,* 43–54.

Sapp, M. (1999). *Test anxiety: Applied research, assessment, and treatment interventions* (2nd ed.). Lanham, MD: University Press of America.

Sapp, M. (2000a). *Hypnosis, dissociation, and absorption: Theories, assessment, and treatment.* Springfield, IL: Charles C Thomas.

Sapp, M. (2000a). *Psychological and educational test scores: What are they?* Springfield, IL: Charles C Thomas.

Sapp, M. (2002b). Implications of Barber's three dimensional theory of hypnosis. *Sleep and Hypnosis, 4* (2), 70–76.

Sapp, M., Durand, H., & Farrell, W. (1995). Measures of actual test anxiety in educationally and economically disadvantaged college students. *College Student Journal, 29* (1), 65–72.

Sapp, M., & Evanow, M. (1998). Hypnotizability: Absorption and dissociation. *The Australian Journal of Clinical Hypnotherapy and Hypnosis, 19* (1), 1–8.

Sapp, M., & Farrell, W. (1994). Cognitive-behavioral interventions: Applications for academically at-risk and special education students. *Preventing School Failure, 38* (2), 19–24.

Sapp, M., Farrell, W., & Durand, H. (1995a). The effects of mathematics, reading, and writing tests in producing worry and emotionality test anxiety with economically and educationally disadvantaged college students. *College Student Journal, 29* (1), 122–125.

Sapp, M., Farrell, W., & Durand, H. (1995b). Cognitive-behavioral therapy: Applications for African-American middle school at-risk students. *Journal of Instructional Psychology, 22* (2), 169–177.

Sapp, M., Farrell, W., Hitchcock, K., & Johnson, J. (1999). Attitudes on rape among African American Male and Female College Students. *Journal of Counseling and Development, 77* (2), 204–208.

Sapp, M., Farrell, W., Johnson, J., & Ioannidis, G. (1997). Utilizing the PK Scale of the MMPI-2 to detect posttraumatic stress disorder in college students. *Journal of Clinical Psychology, 53* (8), 1–6.

Sapp, M., Farrell, W., Johnson, J., Kirby, R.S., & Pumphrey, K. (1997). Hypnosis: Applications for rehabilitation counselors. *Journal of Applied Rehabilitation Counseling, 28* (2), 31–37.

Sapp, M., & Hitchcock, K. (2001). Harvard group scale with African American college students. *Sleep and Hypnosis, 3* (3), 111–117.

Sapp, M., & Hitchcock, K. (2003a). Creative imagination, absorption, and dissociation with African American college students. *Sleep and Hypnosis, 5* (2), 90–99.

Sapp, M., & Hitchcock, K. (2003b). Measuring dissociation and hypnotizability with African American college students: A new dissociation scale – the general dissociation scale. *Australian Journal of Clinical Hypnotherapy and Hypnosis, 24* (1), 14–22.

Sapp, M., Ioannidis, G., & Farrell, W.C. (1995). Posttraumatic stress disorder, imaginative involvement, hypnotic susceptibility, anxiety, and depression. *The Australian Journal of Clinical Hypnotherapy and Hypnosis, 16* (2), 75–87.

Sapp, M., McNeely, R.L., & Torres, J.B. (1998). Death and dying of aged African Americans. *Journal of Human Behavior in the Social Environment, 1* (2/3), 229–315.

Sarason, I.G. (1984). Stress, anxiety, and cognitive interference: Reactions to tests. *Journal of Personality and Social Psychology, 46*, 929–938.

Sarbin, T.R., & Coe, W.C. (1972). *Hypnosis: A social psychological analysis of influence communication.* New York: Holt, Rinehart and Winston.

Sarbin, T.R. (1998). Hypnosis as a conversation: "Believed in imaginings" revisited. *Contemporary Hypnosis, 14*, 203–215.

Sarbin, T.R. (1999). *Believed-in imaginings: The narrative construction of reality* (pp. 15–30). Washington, DC: American Psychological Association.

Schiff, J. (1969). Reparenting schizophrenics. *Transactional Analysis Bulletin, 8*, 49–50.

Schiff, J. (1970). *All my children.* New York: Evans.

Schiff, J. (1975). *The cathexis reader.* New York: Harper and Row.

Schulman, B. (1985). Cognitive therapy and the individual psychology of Alfred Adler. In M.J. Mahoney & A. Freeman (Eds.), *Cognition and psychotherapy* (pp. 243–248). New York: Plenum.

Schultz, D. (1981). *A history of modern psychology* (3rd ed.). New York: Academic Press.

Schultz, D. (1990). *Theories of personality* (4th ed.). Pacific Grove, CA: Brooks/Cole.

Schultz, D., & Schultz S.E. (1992). *A history of modern psychology* (5th ed.). New York: Academic Press.

Schultz, D.P., & Schultz, S.E. (2001). *Theories of personality.* Belmont, CA: Wadsworth/Thomson Learning.

Seligman, M.E.P. (1975). *Helplessness: On depression, development, and death.* San Francisco: W. H. Freeman.

Shapiro, F. (1989). Efficacy of the eye movement of desensitization procedure in the treatment of traumatic memories. *Journal of Traumatic Stress, 2*, 199–223.

Shapiro, F. (1991). Eye movement desensitization and reprocessing procedure: From EMD to EMD/R – A new treatment model for anxiety and related traumata. *The Behavior Therapist, 12*, 133–135.

Shapiro, F. (1994). EMDR: In the eye of a paradigm shift. *The Behavior Therapist, 17* (7), 153–155.

Shapiro, F. (2001). *Eye movement desensitization and reprocessing: Basic principles, protocols, and procedures* (2nd ed.). New York: Guilford Press.

Sharf, R.S. (2004). *Theories of psychotherapy and counseling: Concepts and cases* (3rd ed.). Pacific Grove, CA: Thomson Brooks/Cole.

Sheehan, P.W., & McConkey, U.M. (1982). *Hypnosis and experience: The exploration of phenomena and process.* Hillsdale, NJ: Erlbaum.

Sherman, R., & Dinkmeyer, D. (1987). *Systems of family therapy: An Adlerian integration.* New York: Brunner/Mazel.

Shor, R.E. (1959). Hypnosis and concept of the generalized reality orientation. *American Journal of Psychotherapy, 13*, 582–602.

Shostrom, E.L. (Producer) (1965). *Three approaches to psychotherapy* (Part 3 – Albert Ellis) [Film]. Orange, CA: Psychological Films.

Shulman, B.H. (1984). *Essays in schizophrenia* (2nd ed.). Chicago: Alfred Adler Institute.
Siegel, S. (1983). Classical conditioning, drug tolerance and drug dependence. In Y. Israel & F.B. Smart (Eds.), *Research advances in alcohol and drug problems* (pp. 207–246). New York: Plenum.
Siegel, S. (1984). Pavlovian conditioning and heroin overdose: Reports by overdose victims. *Bulletin of Psychonomic Society, 22*, 428–430.
Silverman, M.S., McCarthy, M., & McGovern, T. (1992). A review of outcome studies of rational-emotive therapy from 1982–1989. *Journal of Rational-Emotive and Cognitive-Behavior Therapy, 10* (3), 111–175.
Simons, A.D., Murphy, G.E., Levine, J.L., & Wetzel, R.D. (1986). Cognitive therapy and pharmacotherapy for depression: Sustained improvement over one year. *Archives of General Psychiatry, 43*, 43–49.
Simpson, P.W., Bloom, J.W., Newlon, B.J., & Arminio, L. (1994). Birth-order proportions of the general populations in the United States. *Individual Psychology, 50* (2), 173–184.
Skinner, B.F. (1974). *About behaviorism*. New York: Knopf.
Skinner, B.F. (1987). Whatever happened to psychology as the science of behavior? *American Psychology, 42* (8), 780–786.
Skinner, B.F. (1988a). The operant side of behavior therapy. *Journal of Behavior Therapy and Experimental Psychiatry, 19*, 171–179.
Skinner, B.F. (1988b). Reply to Harnard. In A.C. Catania & S. Harnard (Eds.), *The selection of behavior: The operant behaviorism of B.F. Skinner: Comments and consequences* (pp. 468–473). Cambridge: Cambridge University Press.
Sloane, R.B., Staples, F.R., Cristol, A.H., Yorkston, N.J., & Whippler, K. (1975). *Psychotherapy versus behavior therapy*. Cambridge, MA: Harvard University Press.
Smith, C.L., Sapp, M., Farrell, W., & Johnson, J.H. (1998). Psychoeducational correlates of achievement for high school seniors at a private school: The relationship among locus of control, esteem, academic achievement, and academic self-esteem. *The High School Journal, 81* (3), 161–167.
Smith, M.L., Glass, G.V., & Miller, T.I. (1980). *The benefits of psychotherapy*. Baltimore: Johns Hopkins University Press.
Smithson, M. (2001). Correct confidence intervals for various regression effect sizes and parameters: The importance of noncentralized distributions in computing intervals. *Educational and Psychological Measurement, 61*, 605–632.
Smithson, M. (2003). *Confidence intervals*. Thousand Oaks, CA: Sage.
Soffer, J. (1993). Jean Piaget and George Kelly: Toward a stronger constructivism. *International Journal of Personal Construct Psychology, 6* (1), 59–77.
Spanos, N.P. (1986). Hypnotic behavior: A social psychological interpretation of amnesia, analgesia and "trance logic." *Behavioral and Brain Sciences, 9*, 489–497.
Spanos, N.P. (1991). A sociocognitive approach to hypnosis. In S.J. Lynn & J.W. Rhue (Eds.), *Theories of hypnosis: Current models and perspectives* (pp. 324–361). New York: Guilford Press.
Spanos, N.P., & Chaves, J.F. (Eds.) (1989). *Hypnosis: The cognitive-behavioral perspective*. Buffalo, NY: Prometheus Books.
Spiegel, H., & Connery, D.J. (1982). *The inner source: Exploring hypnosis with Dr. Herbert Spiegel*. New York: Holt, Rinehart, and Winston.

Spiel, O. (1956). The Individual Psychological Experimental School in Vienna. *American Journal of Individual Psychology, 12,* 1–11.

Spielberger, C.D., & Vagg, P.R. (Eds.) (1995). *Test anxiety: Theory, assessment, and treatment.* Washington, DC: Taylor and Francis.

Stampfl, T.G., & Levis, D.J. (1967). Essentials of implosive therapy: A learning-theory-based psychodynamic behavior therapy. *Journal of Abnormal Psychology, 72,* 496–503.

St. Clair, M. (2000). *Object relations and self psychology: An introduction.* Belmont, CA: Brooks/Cole.

Steiner, C. (1971). *Scripts people live.* New York: Grove Press.

Stepansky, P.E. (1983). *In Freud's shadow: Adler in context.* New York: Analytic Press.

Stevens, J.P. (2002). *Applied multivariate statistics for the social sciences* (4th ed.). Mahwah, NJ: Lawrence Erlbaum.

Sue, D.W., & Sue, D. (1990). *Counseling and the culturally different* (2nd ed.). New York: John Wiley and Sons.

Suinn, R.M. (2001). The terrible twos—anger and anxiety: Hazardous to your health. *American Psychologist, 56* (1), 27–36.

Suinn, R.M., & Richardson, F. (1971). Anxiety management training: A nonspecific behavior therapy program for anxiety control. *Behavior Therapy, 2,* 498–510.

Sullivan, H.S. (1953). *The interpersonal theory of psychiatry.* New York: W.W. Norton.

Sullivan, H.S. (1964). *The fusion of psychiatry and social science.* New York: W.W. Norton.

Sweet, A.A. (1995). Clinical notebook: A theoretical perspective on the clinical use of EMDR. *The Behavior Therapist, 18* (1), 5.

Teasdale, J.D., Fennell, M.J.V., Hibbert, G.A., & Amies, P.L. (1984). Cognitive therapy for major depression disorder in primary care. *British Journal of Psychiatry, 144,* 400–406.

Tellegen, A., & Atkinson, G. (1974). Openness to absorbing and self-altering experiences ("absorption"), a trait related to hypnotic susceptibility. *Journal of Abnormal Psychology, 83,* 268–277.

Thompson, B. (1992). Two and one-half decades of leadership in measurement and evaluation. *Journal of Counseling and Development, 70,* 434–438.

Thompson, B. (2002). "Statistical," "practical," and "clinical:" How many kind of significance do counselors need to consider? *Journal of Counseling and Development, 80,* 64–71.

Turk, D.C., Meichenbaum, D., & Genest, M. (1983). *Pain and behavioral medicine: A cognitive-behavioral perspective.* New York: Gilford Press.

Uba, L. (1994). *Asian Americans: Personality patterns, identity, mental health.* New York: Guilford Press.

Van Den Hout, M., & Merckelbach, H. (1991). Classical conditioning: Still going strong. *Behavioral Psychotherapy, 19,* 59–79.

Vernon, A. (1989). *Thinking, feeling, behaving: An emotional education curriculum for children grades 1–6.* Champaign, IL: Research Press.

Vogt, W.P. (1999). *Dictionary of statistics and methodology: A nontechnical guide for the social sciences.* Thousand Oaks, CA: Sage.

Wagstaff, G.F. (1981). *Hypnosis, compliance and belief.* New York: St. Martin's Press.

Wagstaff, G.F. (1991). Compliance, belief, and semantic in hypnosis: A nonstate sociocognitive perspective. In S.J. Lynn & J.W. Rhue (Eds.), *Theories of hypnosis: Current models and perspectives* (pp. 362–396). New York: Guilford Press.

Walen, S.R., DiGiuseppe, R., & Wessler, R.L. (1980). *A practitioner's guide to rational-emotive therapy*. New York: Oxford University Press.

Wallace, W.A. (1993). *Theories of personality*. Needham Heights, MA: Allyn and Bacon.

Warren, R., & McLellarn, R.W. (1987). What do RET therapists think they are doing? An international survey. *Journal of Rational-Emotive Therapy, 5* (2), 71–91.

Warwick, H.M.C., & Salkovskis, P.M. (1989). Hypochondriasis. In J. Scott, M.G. Williams, & A.T. Beck (Eds.), *Cognitive therapy in clinical practice: An illustrative casebook* (pp. 50–77). London: Routledge.

Watson, J.B. (1930). *Behaviorism* (Rev. ed.). New York: W.W. Norton.

Watts, R.E., & Holden, J.M. (1994). Why continue to use "fictional finalism"? *Individual Psychology, 50* (2), 161–163.

Wegner, D., & Wheatly, T. (1999). Apparent mental causation: Sources of the experience of will. *American Psychologist, 54,* 480–492.

Weinrach, S.G. (1995). Rational-emotive behavior therapy: A tough-minded therapy for a tender-minded profession. *Journal of Counseling and Development, 73* (3), 296–300.

Weishaar, M.E. (1993). *Aaron T. Beck*. London: Sage.

Wester, W.C. (1987). *Clinical hypnosis: A case management approach*. Cincinnati, OH: Behavior Science Center, Inc. Publications.

Wiener, N. (1948). *Cybernetics*. New York: Wiley.

Wilson, S.C., & Barber, T.X. (1981/1983). The fantasy-prone personality: Implications for understanding imagery, hypnosis, and parapsychological phenomena. In A.A. Sheikh (Ed.), *Imagery: Current theory, research, and applications* (pp. 340–387). New York: Wiley.

Wilson, T.G. (1989). Behavior Therapy. In R.J. Corsini & D. Wedding (Eds.), *Current psychotherapies* (4th ed., pp. 241–284). Itasca, IL: F.E. Peacock.

Wissink, L.M. (1994). A validation of transactional analysis in increasing self-esteem among participants in a self-reparenting program. *Transactional Analysis Journal, 24* (3), 189–196.

Wolf, F.M. (1986). *Meta-analysis: Quantitative methods for research synthesis*. Beverly Hills, CA: Sage.

Wolpe, J. (1958). *Psychotherapy by reciprocal inhibition*. Stanford, CA: Stanford University Press.

Wolpe, J. (1973). *The practice of behavior therapy*. New York: Pergamon Press.

Wolpe, J. (1997). Commentary on "Beyond the Efficacy Ceiling": Responses to an irrelevant subtitle. *Behavior Therapy, 28* (4), 613–615.

Woody, E., & Bowers, K.S. (1994). A frontal assault on dissociated control. In S.J. Lynn & J.W. Rhue (Eds.), *Dissociation: Clinical, theoretical and research perspectives* (pp. 52–79). New York: Guilford Press.

Woody, E., & Farvolden, P. (1998). Dissociation in hypnosis and frontal executive function. *American Journal of Clinical Hypnosis, 40,* 206–216.

Woody, E., & Sadler, P. (1998). On reintegrating dissociated theories: Comment on Kirsch & Lynn. *Psychological Bulletin, 123,* 192–197.

Woody, G.E., Luborsky, L., McClellan, A.T., O'Brien, C.P., Beck, A.T., Blaine, J., et al. (1983). Psychotherapy for opiate addicts: Does it help? *Archives of General Psychiatry, 40,* 1081–1086.

Wubbolding, R.E. (1991). *Understanding reality.* New York: Harper and Row.

Wubbolding, R.E. (1995). Reality therapy theory. In D. Capuzzi & D.R. Gross (Eds.), *Counseling and psychotherapy: Theories and interventions* (pp. 385–424). Englewood Cliffs, NJ: Merrill.

Wubbolding, R.E., Al-Rashidi, B., Brickell, J., Katitani, M., Kim, R.I., Lennon, B., et al. (1998). Multicultural awareness: Implications for reality therapy and choice theory. *International Journal of Reality Therapy, 17* (2), 4–6.

Yalom, I.D. (1980). *Existential psychotherapy.* New York: Basic Books.

Young, J.E. (1990). *Cognitive therapy for personality disorders: A schema focused approach.* Sarasota, FL: Professional Resources Exchange.

Zeig, J. (1980). *Teaching seminar with Milton Erickson, M.D.* New York: Brunner/Mazel.

Zimmerman, B.J. (1995). Self-efficacy and educational development. In A. Bandura (Ed.), *Self-efficacy in changing societies* (pp. 202–231). Cambridge, England: Cambridge University Press.

INDEX

A

ABCs of REBT, 117, 127
Abramson, L., 145
Acceptance, 108, 123, 127
Acquisition, 108
Activity Scheduling, 152, 156
Adaptability, 38
Adaptive child (AC), 177, 188
Adaptive regression, 94, 99
Adler, Alexandra, 34
Adler, Alfred, background of, 33–34
    See also Adlerian psychotherapy
Adlerian psychotherapy, 13, 14, 32–64
    critique of, 56–58
    Freud vs. Adler, 34–37
    key concepts of, 37–48
    therapeutic process of, 48–58
Adlerian therapists, 53, 55, 56
Adler, Kurt, 34
Adler School of Professional Psychology, 64
Adult ego states, 177–181, 195
Advances in Personal Construct Psychology, 172
African Americans, 25, 26, 29, 106, 109, 124
Agoraphobia, 76
Allen, B., 194
Allen, J., 194
Allen, W., 106
Alloy, L.B., 145
American Indians, 26–27, 109
American Journal of Clinical Hypnosis, The, 87
American Psychiatric Association, 139
American Psychological Association, 23
American Psychologist, 140
Amnesia, 7, 61
Amygdala, 30, 86
Anderson, A.K., 30
Anger, 119

Anglo-Saxon Americans, 24
Annoyance, 119
Antabuse, 76
Antidepressants, 141–142
Antisocial personality disorder, 61
Anxiety, 43, 44, 73, 74, 86, 118, 127
Anxiety disorders, 60, 73–75
Anxiety Disorders and Phobias: A Cognitive Perspective (Beck), 140
Anxiety management training (AMT), 76
Apomorphine, 76
Appalachian Americans, 24, 25
Applied behavior analysis, 66–68, 99
Applied value, 22–23
    Adlerian psychotherapy, 58
    behavioral therapy, 98
    cognitive-behavior modification (CBM), 163
    cognitive therapy, 156
    multimodal behavior therapy (MMBT), 136
    personal constructs psychotherapy, 172
    reality therapy, 210–211
    REBT, 125
    social learning theories, 110
    transactional analysis (TA), 195
Arbitrary inference, 70, 147, 156
Arbitrary rightness, 43
Aristotle, 42
Arlow, J.A., 37, 48
Arminio, L., 47
Asian Americans, 27–29, 106
Asians, 106, 109
Assertion training, 77, 99
Association for Behavioral Analysis, 102
Association for the Advancement of Behavior Therapy (AABT), 98, 101, 139
Attention deficit hyperactivity disorder, 93

Index

Attributional error, 147
Attribution theory, 43
Automaticity, 3, 6, 7, 16, 30, 93
Automatic thoughts, 153, 156
Autonomous personality dimension, 146
Aversive conditioning, 76–77, 78
Aversive counterconditioning, 76
Aversive stimulus, 76, 79
Aversive techniques, 78
Avoidant behavior, 114
Avoidant personality disorder, 61
Axelson, J.A., 23, 25
Axioms, of choice theory, 201–202

B

Banaji, M.R., 29, 30
Bandura, Albert, 3, 4, 71, 104, 105, 107–108, 116
Barabasz, A., 93
Barabasz, M., 93
Barber, Theodore X., 7, 65, 92, 93, 94
Bargh, J.A., 4
Barlett, F.C., 68
Barndollar, K., 4
Barrett, D., 7
Bartis, S.P., 93
Bartlett, F.C., 5
BASIC-ID, 72, 99, 130–136
Beal, D., 120
Beck, Aaron Temkin, 11, 12, 45, 58, 68, 70, 138
    See also Cognitive therapy
Beck Anxiety Inventory, 158
Beck Depression Inventory (BDI), 138, 141, 158
Becker, J., 66
Beck Hopelessness Scale, 142, 158
Beck Institute, 157
Beck, Judith, 140, 146
Beck Scale for Suicidal Ideation, 158
Beck's Depression Research Unit, 138
Beere, D.B., 84
Behavioral contracting, 80–81
Behavioral experiments, 152
Behavioral potential, 4, 105, 110
Behavioral rehearsal, 99, 156
Behavioral therapy, 12, 16, 98
Behavior modification, 12
Behavior Therapist, The, 87, 101
Behavior therapy, 65–102
    anxiety disorders and, 73–75
    approaches to, 66–72
    classical conditioning and, 75–77
    common characteristics of, 72–73
    critique of, 97–98
    extinction and, 77–78
    eye-movement technique and, 87–88
    guided imagery transcript and, 90–91
    hypnosis and, 91–96
    instrumental/operant conditioning and, 78–81
    progressive relaxation techniques and, 88–90
    self-control procedures and, 82–87
    therapeutic process of, 96–98
Behavior Therapy, 139
Beliefs, 36, 39, 41, 49, 50
Bergin, A.E., 3, 7
Berne, Eric, 38, 43, 44, 176
    See also Transactional analysis (TA)
Bibliotherapy, 82–84
Bilateral stimulation, 86, 87
Biofeedback, 12, 82, 99, 103
Birth order, 46–48, 58
Blame, 43, 69, 147
Blind spots, 43
Bloom, J.M., 47
Borderline personality disorder, 61, 146
Boundary work, 181
Bowers, K.S., 93
Breuer, Joseph, 35
Bridging, 132, 136
Broad-Spectrum Behavior Therapy, 136
Broks, P., 30

C

Catastrophizing, 156
Cautela, Joseph, 76
Center for Reality Therapy, 212
Challenging skills, Level III, 150
Charcot, Jean Marie, 6
Child, 180, 195
Child ego states, 177–181, 195
Children's actions, 44–45
Choice corollary, 167
Choice theory, 201–202, 204, 208–209, 211
Choice Theory: A New Psychology of Personal Freedom (Glasser), 200

Choice therapy, 13
Classical conditioning, 5, 16, 75–77, 99
Cognition and Behavior Modification (Mahoney), 139
Cognitions, 131–132
Cognitive and Behavioral Practice, 101
Cognitive-behavioral attributions, 69, 71, 147
Cognitive-behavioral hypnosis (CBH), 95–96
Cognitive-behavioral orientations, 12 table, 13 table
Cognitive-behavioral theories, 23, 71
Cognitive-behavioral therapies, 11, 12–13, 14, 15, 16, 22, 23, 68–71, 99
Cognitive-behavior modification (CBM), 159–164
  critique of, 163
  key concepts of, 159–162
  therapeutic process of, 162–163
Cognitive distortions, 71, 147, 156
Cognitive processes/behavioral actions, 5
Cognitive products, 5, 69
Cognitive propositions, 5, 69
Cognitive restructuring, 127
Cognitive shift, 156
Cognitive structure, 5, 69
Cognitive therapy, 138–158
  cognitive distortions in, 147
  cognitive model of depression and, 147–148
  critique of, 154–156
  depression and, 144–146, 147–148
  depression checklist, 148–150
  Diagnostic and Statistical Manual of Mental Disorders (DSM-IV-TR) and, 144
  hypothalamic-pituitary-adrenal (HPA) axis, 145
  key concepts of, 140–143
  multimodal behavior therapy (MMBT) and, 143–144
  personality theory and, 144
  psychoanalysis and, 143
  Rational emotive behavior therapy (REBT) and, 143
  therapeutic process of, 150–156
  treatments, 151–152
Cognitive Therapy and Research, 158
Cognitive Therapy, 139
Cognitive Therapy of Depression (Beck et al.), 139
Cognitive Therapy of Personality Disorders (Beck), 140

Cognitive triad, 147, 156
Cohen, J., 8, 9
Collaborative empiricism, 152
Comfort priority, 51
Commitment, 55
Commonality corollary, 167
Common sense, 38
Community feeling, 42, 58
Compensation, 45, 58
Compensation levels, 37
Competency, 190
Complementary transactions, 182, 183 fig., 195
Comprehensive cognitive-behavioral theories, 18
Comprehensiveness
  Adlerian psychotherapy, 56
  behavioral therapy, 97
  cognitive-behavior modification (CBM), 163
  cognitive therapy, 154
  multimodal behavior therapy (MMBT), 136
  personal constructs psychotherapy, 171
  reality therapy, 209
  REBT, 124
  social learning theories, 109
  transactional analysis (TA), 194
Concern, 118
Conditional assumptions, 146
Conditioning, 75–77, 78–81, 103–104
Confidence intervals, 9–11, 14, 15 table, 15
Confrontation, 52
Confusion, 43
Constant adult, 180
Constant child, 180
Constant parent, 180
Constellatory constructs, 166, 172–173
Constitution, United States, 25
Construct, 165, 166, 173
Construction corollary, 167
Constructive alternativism, 165, 173
Constructivism, 36, 59
Contamination, 180, 181 fig., 195
Contention scheduling, 6
Continuous reinforcement, 79, 80
Contracts, 80–81, 191
Contributions, 43
Control, locus of, 71, 105–106, 110, 188
Control priority, 51

Control theory, 199, 202, 211
Control Theory: A New Explanation of How We Control Our Lives (Glasser), 200
Control Theory in the Classroom (Glasser), 200
Control variables, 19
Coping imagery, 131, 137
Corey, G., 57, 187, 203, 205
Cormier, L.S., 79
Cormier, W.H., 79
Corollaries, 167
Corsini, R.J., 35
Coué, Emile, 160
Counseling skills, 49, 50, 52, 53–55
   Level I, 49, 96, 108, 124, 150, 153, 161, 170, 205, 206, 207
   Level II, 50, 96, 108, 124, 150, 153, 161, 170, 205, 206, 207
   Level III, 52, 53–55, 96, 108, 122, 143, 170, 171, 205
Counterconditioning, 76, 99
Covariance, 9
Covert behavioral therapy, 12
Covert desensitization, 99
Covert sensitization, 76–77, 78
Creating movements, 54
Critical parent, 178, 196
Crossed transactions, 182–183, 184 fig., 196
Cuban Americans, 27
Cues, 3, 104
Cultural groups, 24–29
Culture, 23
Cummings, Geoff, 11
Cunningham, L.M., 209

D

Dasgupta, N., 29
Davidson, P.R., 87
Debating, 127
Debriefing, 89–90, 91, 96
Decatastrophizing, 151, 156
Decentering, 151
Defense mechanisms, 43–44
Defensive external control individuals, 105–106
Defensive reactions, 133
d effect size, 3, 7, 8, 13, 14, 15
Deffenbacher, J.L., 161
Delirium, 61
Dementia, 61

Dependent personality disorder, 61
Dependent variables, 19, 20, 30
Depression, 82, 118, 140–143, 144–146, 147–148
   See also Antidepressants
Depression: Causes and Treatment (Beck), 138
Depression checklist, 148–150
Depression: Clinical, Experimental and Theoretical Aspects (Beck), 138
de Shazer, S., 49
Detecting, 127
Diagnostic and Statistical Manual of Mental Disorders (DSM-IV-TR), 60–62, 73–74, 125, 144
Dialectical behavior therapy (DBT), 68
Dichotomous thinking, 70, 147, 156
Dichotomy corollary, 167
Differential reinforcement, 80
DiGiuseppe, R., 120
Dinkmeyer, D.C., 44, 48, 52
Dinkmeyer, D.C., Jr., 44, 48, 52
Disappointment, 119
Discomfort anxiety, 127
Discomfort disturbance, 116
Discouragement, 59
Discrimination, 127
Disputing irrational beliefs, 120–122
Dissociation theory, 6, 30
Dissociative disorders, 60
Diversion, 152
Divorce, books on, 83
Dollard, John, 3, 4, 103–104
Douglas, L, 194
Draguns, J.G., 106
Dreams, 50
Dreikurs, Rudolf, 34
Drives, 3, 16
Dryden, W., 119
Dusay, J.M., 190
Dusay, K.M., 190
Dynamic therapy, 14
Dysthymic disorder, 145

E

Early recollections, 59
Eating disorders, 61, 83
Eclectic behaviorism, 72
Edwards, L., 94
Effectiveness of psychotherapy, 3–8

Effect sizes, 9, 15 table, 16
Ego anxiety, 127
Ego disturbance, 116
Egograms, 190, 191 fig.
Ego states, 177–181, 180 fig., 181 fig., 190, 196
Electra complex, 37
Ellis, Albert, 11, 45, 58, 68, 95, 153
   See also Rational emotive behavior therapy (REBT)
Elusiveness, 43
Embarrassment, 118
Emery, G., 140
Emotionality anxiety, 73, 74
Emotions, 117–119, 168
Empirical disputes, 120
Empirical validity, 22, 30
   Adlerian psychotherapy, 57
   behavioral therapy, 98
   cognitive-behavior modification (CBM), 163
   cognitive therapy, 155
   multimodal behavior therapy (MMBT), 136
   personal constructs psychotherapy, 171
   reality therapy, 209–210
   REBT, 125
   social learning theories, 109
   transactional analysis (TA), 194
Encouragement, 53, 59
Environmental determinism, 67
Epstein, Raissa Timofeyena, 34
Equipotentiality, 36
Erikson, M.H., 56
Ethical humanism, 127
Ethical humanist, 113
European Americans, 106
European Personal Construct Association (EPCA), 174
Excessive self-control, 43
Exclusion, 180, 181 fig., 196
Executive ego, 6
Existential psychotherapy, 41
Expectancies theory, 71
Expectancy, 3, 4, 16, 105, 110
Expectancy effect, 3
Experience corollary, 167
Exposure, 108
Exposure Therapy, 152
External control psychology, 201
Externalizing, 43

External locus of control, 188
Extinction, 77–78, 81, 99
Eye movement desensitization-reprocessing (EMDR), 22, 65, 84–87, 99
Eye movement technique (EMT), 65, 87–88, 99–100
Eysenck, Hans, 65

F

Fading, 100
Failure identity, 203
Fakouri, M.E., 50
Families/Stepfamilies, books on, 83
Family constellation, 46, 50, 59
Family modeling, 191
Family therapy, 189
Fan, X., 9, 10
Farrell, W., 124
Farvolden, P., 6
Faulty thinking, 52
Fechner, Gustav Theodor, 35
Feelings, 49, 67
Fictional final goal, 59
Fictional finalism, 42
Fictional goals, 42
Finalism/final cause, 42
Fisher, R.A., 9
Fish, J.M., 84
Fixed-role therapy, 168, 173
Fliess, Wilhelm, 37
Flooding, 13, 77, 100
Fragmentation corollary, 167
Frankl, Viktor, 78
Free association, 48
Free child (FC), 177
Freeman, A., 68
Freud's determinism, 36
Freud, Sigmund, 13, 34–37, 39–40, 41, 45, 48, 50, 56, 57, 140–141
Freud's seduction theory, 37
Friedberg, Fred, 88
Functional disputes, 121
Functionalism, 35

G

Game analysis, 188, 196
Games, 184, 185
Games People Play (Berne), 176

Gamma-amino butyric acid (GABA), 74
Garfield, S.C., 3
Generalized anxiety disorder (GAD), 74
Generalized expectancies, 105, 106, 110
Gestalt psychology/psychotherapy, 14, 35
Gilliland, B.E., 84, 201
Glasser Institute for Reality Therapy of the Education Training Center, 200
Glasser, William, 199–200, 201, 202–203, 205, 206, 208
    See also Reality therapy
Glass, G.V., 15
Global assessment of functioning scale (GAF), 62
Goals, 42
Goulding, M., 186–187, 189, 190
Goulding, R., 186–187, 189, 190
Graded Task Assignment, 152, 156
Greenblatt, R.L., 48
Greenwald, A.G., 29
Grieger, R., 115
Griffith, J., 49
Guided discovery, 142, 152
Guided imagery, 90–91, 100, 161
Guilt, 118–119

H

Hackett, G., 107
Hafner, J., 50
Haitians, 25
Hallucinations, cortical, 93
Hamburg, S.R., 7
Hammen, C., 74, 145
Harrington, G.L., 199
Harris, T., 187
Hazell, J., 194
Heckausen, J., 106
Hedonism, 115, 127
Herrnstein, R.J., 26
Heuristic value, 22
    Adlerian psychotherapy, 57
    cognitive-behavior modification (CBM), 163
    cognitive therapy, 155
    multimodal behavior therapy (MMBT), 136
    personal constructs psychotherapy, 172
    reality therapy, 210
    REBT, 125

social learning theories, 110
transactional analysis (TA), 194–195
Hilgard, E.R., 6
Hippocamus, 86
Hispanics, 106, 109
Histrionic personality disorder, 61
Hitchcock, K., 91
Hmong, 29
Holden, J.M., 42
Homework, 151
Horney, Karen, 39, 113, 138
Horwitz, A., 194
Hot cognition, 153, 156
Hull, Clark, 3, 104
Humanism, 115
Humanistic, 127
Humanistic psychotherapy, 14, 41
Husserl, Edmund, 36
Hypnosis, 7, 8, 12, 35, 65, 91–96, 100
Hypnotherapy, 12, 13, 14
Hypnotic regression, 94
Hypnotic relaxation, 94
Hypnotic responding, 6
Hypnotic types, 92–93
Hypothalamic-pituitary-adrenal (HPA) axis, 145
Hypothesis Testing, 151

I

Ideas: General Introduction to Pure Phenomenology (Husserl), 36
Idiographic/idiographic approach, 59, 67
I-E Scale (Internal (I)–External (E) locus of control scale), 106
Imagery-based recall, 161, 164
Imagery Reactor, 137
Imaginally-based therapy, 78
Imagination techniques, 12, 54
Immediacy, 53
Immediate exposure, 77
Implicit Association Test (IAT), 29, 30
Implosive therapy, 12, 13, 78, 100
Independent variables, 19, 20, 31
Indian Gaming Regulatory Act of 1988, 27
Indian Removal Act of 1830, 27
Individual corollary, 173
Individuality corollary, 167
Individual Psychology, 32, 36, 40–42, 45, 48–50, 55–57

See also Adlerian psychotherapy
Inferiority, feelings of, 59
Injunctions, 186–187, 196
Insight, developing, 52
Institute of Psychoanalysis (Vienna), 103
Intense exposure, 77
Internal dialogue, 127, 164
Internal locus of control, 71, 106
Internal-oriented people, 106
International Journal of Personal Construct Psychology, 172
International Journal of Reality Therapy, 200, 212
International Transactional Analysis Association, 197
Interpersonal trust, 106–107, 110
Interposition, 76
Intervening variables, 21, 22
Intrapsychic conflict, 36
Introspection, 35
In vivo desensitization, 76, 77
Irrational, 127
Irrational beliefs (IB), 114–115, 116–117, 120–122, 123
Irrationality, 113
Irrational jealousy, 119–120
Italian Americans, 25

J

Jacobs, A., 190
James, R.K., 84, 201
James, William, 35
Janet, Pierre, 6
Jealousy, 119–120
Jewish Americans, 25
Joines, V., 192
Journal of Cognitive Psychotherapy: An International Quarterly, 157
Journal of Constructivist Psychology, 173, 174
Journal of Individual Psychology, 57

K

Kalodner, C.R., 160
Karen Horney School, 113
Karpman, S., 185
Karpman's drama triangles, 185, 186 fig., 196
Kelly, George, 58, 104, 138
 See also Personal constructs psychotherapy

Kendall, Philip C., 68, 74, 145
Kirsch, I., 3, 4, 5, 6, 7, 92, 93, 103
Kirsch, James, 93
Klein, M., 177
Klerman, Gerald, 139
Kohut, Heinz, 192
Kopec, A.M., 120
Korzyski, A., 113

L

LaFontaine, L., 208
Lambert, M.J., 7
Lancaster, B.P., 20
Language differences, 209
Latin Americans, 27, 124
Lazarus, Arnold, 65, 72, 129, 131, 132, 133, 135
Lazarus, C.N., 131
Leahy, R.L., 68
Learned, helplessness, 72, 105, 145
Lewis, A.L., 177
Liebert, R.M., 104
Life positions, 187–188, 196
Life script, 176–177
Life script analysis, 188
Lifestyle, 38–39, 44, 49, 50, 56, 59
Lifestyle assessment, 59
Life tasks, 59
Linehan, Marsha, 68
Locus of control, 71, 105–106, 110, 188
Logical disputes, 120
Love/Intimacy, books on, 83
Love Is Never Enough (Beck), 140
Lynn, S.J., 3, 4–5, 6–7, 92, 93, 103
Lyons, L.C., 125

M

Magnification, 156
Mahoney, Michael, 139
Major attributional error, 43, 69
Maniacci, M., 32, 36, 40, 43, 55
Marger, M.N., 27, 29
Marshall, G.W., 106
Masculine protest, 39–40, 59
Maslow, Abraham, 201
Masson, J., 37
Maultsby, Maxie C., Jr., 113, 123
McClendon, R., 189

McGhee, D.E., 29
McNeely, R.L., 124
Meichenbaum, Donald, 68, 82, 159, 160, 161
Mental health, 211
Mental Health or Mental Illness (Glasser), 200
Mental retardation, 61
Merckelbach, H., 5, 75
Mesmer, Franz Anton, 35
Meta-analysis, 3, 8–11, 16
Metalsky, G.I., 145
Methodological behaviorism, 66
Mexican Americans, 27
Middle class social strata, 23
Miller, Neal, 3, 4, 103–104
Miller, T.I., 15
Mind in Action, The (Berne), 176
Mind reading, 70, 147
Misattributions, 70
Mistakes, basic, 58
Modality Profile, 137
Modeling, 13, 100, 108, 191
Moderator variables, 19, 21, 22
Modulation corollary, 167
Monoamine oxidase inhibitors (MAO), 141–142
Mood disorders, 60
Moreno, J.L., 189
Mosak, Harold H., 32, 34, 36, 39, 40, 43, 55
Mozdierz, G.L., 48
Multiaxial diagnoses, 60–62
Multicultural applications and limitations
   Adlerian psychotherapy, 56
   behavioral therapy, 97
   cognitive-behavior modification (CBM), 162–163
   multimodal behavior therapy (MMBT), 135
   personal constructs psychotherapy, 171
   reality therapy, 208–209
   REBT, 124–125
   social learning theories, 109
   transactional analysis (TA), 193
Multicultural counseling, 23, 31
Multimodal behavior therapy (MMBT), 72, 129–137
   bridging and, 132
   cognitions and, 131–132
   cognitive therapy and, 143–144
   coping imagery and, 131, 137
   critique of, 136
   key concepts of, 129–130
   structural profiles and, 130–131
   therapeutic process of, 134–136
   tracking and, 132–134, 137
Murray, C.A., 26
Muscular relaxation, 75
Musturbation, 127
Mutual assent, 190

N

Narcissistic personality disorder, 61
Nash, M.R., 94
National Institute of Mental Health (NIMH), 139
Native Americans, 26–27, 106
Natural child (NC), 177
Negative addictions, 211
Negative attribution, 69–70
Negative consequence, removal of, 79
Negative prediction, 70, 71, 147
Negative reinforcement, 79, 100
Neimeyer, Robert A., 171, 173
Neobehaviorism, 68
Neodissociation, 16
Neodissociation model of nonvolitional hypnotic responding, 6
Neo-Pavlovian model, of classical conditioning, 75
Neo-Pavlovian theory, 5
Neurotic Constitution, The (Adler), 36
Neurotransmitters, 141
Newlon, B.J., 47
Nomothetic, 59
Nomothetic approach, 66
Nonconscious, 133, 137
Nontraditional forms of behavioral therapies, 17
Nontraditional forms of cognitive-behavioral therapies, 12, 14
Norman, D.A., 5, 6
North American Personal Construct Network (NAPCN), 174
North American Society of Adlerian Psychology, 64
Nosek, B.A., 29, 30
Null hypothesis, 8, 14, 16
Nurturing parent, 178, 196

O

Object relations, 192
Object relation theory, 196

Observational learning, 4, 108, 110
Obsessive compulsive disorder (OCD), 74
Obsessive-Compulsive personality
  disorder, 61
Oedipal complex, 37
Okeke, B.I., 106
"Only if" statements, 51–52
Operant conditioning, 78–81, 100
Operant extinction, 81
Organ inferiority, 37, 59
Organizing corollary, 167
Overcorrection, 81
Overgeneralization, 71, 147, 156

P

Padesky, C.A., 140
Paining, 211
Panic attacks, 74
Paradoxical intention, 53, 78
Paranoid personality disorder, 61
Parent ego states, 179–181, 196
Parker, K.C.H., 87
Parsimony, 22
  Adlerian psychotherapy, 56–57
  behavioral therapy, 97–98
  cognitive therapy, 154
  multimodal behavior therapy (MMBT),
    136
  personal constructs psychotherapy, 171
  reality therapy, 209
  REBT, 125
  social learning theories, 109
  transactional analysis (TA), 194
Pashler, H.E., 7
Paul, G.L., 16, 129
PCP International Conferences, 174–175
Pearson product-moment correlation coefficient, 9
Pedhazur, E.J., 19
Perls, Frits, 35
Permeability, 166, 173
Personal construct psychology, 172, 175
Personal constructs psychotherapy, 165–175
  action strategies of, 168–169
  corollaries of, 167
  critique of, 171–172
  emotions and, 168
  key concepts of, 165–167
  therapeutic process of, 169–172
Personality disorders, 61

Personalization, 70, 147, 156
Person-centered psychotherapy, 14, 36, 57
Phelps, E.A., 30
Phenomenology, 36, 41, 42, 57, 59
Philadelphia General Hospital, 138
Piaget, J., 5, 68
Placebo effect, 3, 8, 16
Placebos, 7
Pleasing priority, 51
Poidevant, J.M., 177
Polarized thinking, 70
Polish Americans, 25
Positive addictions, 203, 211
Positive reinforcement, 79, 100
Positive stages, 203
Posttraumatic stress disorder (PTSD), 74, 84,
    87–88
Powers, R.L., 49
Powers, William, 202
Practical significance, 8, 16
Precision, 18, 22
Precision and Testability
  Adlerian psychotherapy, 57
  behavioral therapy, 98
  cognitive-behavior modification (CBM),
    163
  cognitive therapy, 154
  multimodal behavior therapy (MMBT),
    136
  personal constructs psychotherapy, 171–
    172
  reality therapy, 210
  REBT, 125
  social learning theories, 110
  transactional analysis (TA), 194
Preemptive constructs, 166, 173
Premack principle, 80, 100
Preston, John, 148
Primary drives, 3, 104
Primary priority, 51
Primary reinforcers, 79
Primary view of psychological disturbances,
    112, 128
Principal diagnosis, 61
Priorities, 50–51
Private logic, 38, 45–46
Prochaska, J.O., 194
Progression relaxation techniques, 88–90
Progressive relaxation, 100
Prompting, 100
Propositional constructs, 166, 173

Psychoanalysis, 35, 36, 45, 48, 143
Psychological Corporation, The, 158
Psychological hypnosis, 65, 91–94
Psychological insights, 116–117
Psychological interactionism, 116, 127
Psychological situation, 105
Psychology of Personal Constructs, The (Kelly), 175
Psychophysics, 35
Psychotherapy, beginnings of, 35
Psychotherapy research, 3–17
   effect size measures for traditional cognitive-behavioral therapies, 11–15
   meta-analysis, 8–11
   psychotherapy effectiveness, 3–8
Psychotic disorders, 61
Puerto Ricans, 27
Punishment, 81, 82, 100, 105
Push button technique, 54–55

Q

Quality School: Managing Students Without, The (Glasser), 200
Quality time, 202, 211
Quality world, 201, 211
Question, The, 49–50, 59

R

Racial categories, 24
Racial prejudice, 29–30
Rackets, 185–186, 196
Radical behaviorism, 66, 67, 100
Radical behaviorism/neobehaviorism, 67 table
Range corollary, 167
Range of convenience, 173
Rational, 128
Rational alternative disputes, 121
Rational Behavior Therapy, 113
Rational emotive behavior therapy (REBT), 58, 69, 112–125, 127, 143
   disrupting clients' irrational beliefs and, 120–122
   expanded ABCs of, 117
   historical developments of, 112–113
   hurt and, 119
   irrational jealousy and, 119–120
   key concepts of, 113–116
   major psychological influences of, 113
   nature of emotions and, 117–119
   psychological interactionism and, 116–117
   therapeutic process, 122–125
   two basic human disturbances and, 116
Rational-emotive imagery, 123
Rationality, 115
Rational jealousy, 120
Reactors, 131
Reality therapy, 13, 14, 199–212
   applications to mental health in, 203–204
   characteristics of, 205
   critique of, 209–211
   eight steps of, 206
   fourteen principles of, 208
   nondeterministic view of human nature and, 200–203
   therapeutic process of, 204–211
   WDEP system and, 207, 208, 211
Reality Therapy (Glasser), 199
Reattribution, 151, 157
Reciprocal determinism, 4, 71, 107, 110, 116
Reciprocal inhibitions, 75, 100
Recollections, early, 59
Redecision therapy, 196
Redefining, 151
Regression equation, 20
Regressive stages, 203
Regret, 118
Reinforcement, 4, 13, 79–80, 81, 82, 105, 110
Reinforcement value, 4, 105, 110
Reinforcing incompatible behaviors, 81
Relaxation therapy, 13
Remorse, 119
Reparenting, 190, 196
Research. *See* Psychotherapy research
Response cost, 81, 100
Response expectancies, 6, 7
Response set theory, of hypnosis, 92, 93
Restructuring of cognitions, 82
Retreat, 43
Richardson, F., 76
Role Construct Repertory Test, The (Rep Test), 168, 173
Role-playing, 54, 123
Rosenthal, R., 9
Rotter, Julian B., 3, 4, 71, 72, 104–105, 106, 107, 188
Rush, A. John, 139
Ryckman, R.M., 18

S

Sadness, 118
Sapp, Marty
   on Anglo-Saxon Americans, 24
   BASIC-ID and, 133–134
   creating movements and, 54
   on depression medications, 141
   evaluating theories of psychotherapy, 18
   on eye movement desensitization-reprocessing (EMDR), 84
   on hypnosis, 91, 93, 94
   Individual Psychology and, 32
   injunctions and, 187
   lifestyles and, 51
   meta-analysis and, 9, 11
   observational learning and, 108
   rackets and, 186
   Rational emotive behavior therapy (REBT) and, 124
   reality therapy and, 206, 209
   Role Construct Repertory Test, The (Rep Test) and, 168
   on test anxiety, 73
   on validity, 22
Sarason, I.G., 73
Sarbin, Theodore, 92
Schedules of reinforcement, 79
Schema, 157
Schemata, 5–6, 69, 70
Schemata theory, 68
Schiff, J., 190
Schizoid personality disorder, 61
Schizophrenia, 61
Schools Without Failure (Glasser), 200
Schulman, Bernard, 34
Schulz, R., 106
Script analysis, 196
Scripts People Live (Steiner), 177
Seasonal affective disorder (SAD), 145
Secondary drives, 3, 104
Secondary reinforcers, 79
Secondary transference, 170
Second-order BASIC-ID, 137
Seduction hypothesis/theory, 37
Segregation, 25, 26
Selective abstraction, 70, 147, 157
Self-affirmations, 164
Self-characterization, 173
Self-control, 43, 100
Self-control procedures, 82–87, 82–87
Self-control strategies, 12, 82
Self-disparagement, 43
Self-efficacy, 71, 107–108, 111
Self-efficiency, 105
Self-instructional training, 82, 160, 164
Self-interest, enlightened, 115, 127
Self-Management/Self-Enhancement, books on, 83
Self-monitoring, 82, 101
Self psychology, 192, 196
Self-punishment, 82
Self-reinforcement, 82
Self-talk, 159, 160, 164
Seligman, Martin E.P., 71, 105, 145
Sensate focus, 77, 101
Serotonin, 74
Serotonin reuptake inhibitors (SSRI), 142
Sexual disorders, 77
Sexual/identity disorders, 61
Shallice, T., 5, 6
Shame, 118
Shame-attacking exercises, 122, 127
Shaping, 101
Shapiro, Francine, 22, 65, 84, 85, 87
Shaw, Brian, 139–140
Short-term dynamic therapy, 48
Shulman, B.H., 43, 56
Sideshows, 44, 59
Simpson, P.W., 47
Sinn, R.M., 76
Skebu, B., 106
Skills/action strategies, Level III, 53–55
Skinner, B.F., 66, 67, 78, 104
Sleep disorders, 61
Smith, M.L., 15
Smithson, M., 14
Smyth, Larry, 87, 88
Social class, 23
Social dependent personality dimension, 146
Social interest, 42–43, 59
Sociality, 170
Sociality corollary, 167, 173
Social Learning and Clinical Psychology (Rotter), 104
Social learning theories, 3, 4, 71–72, 101, 103–111
   Bandura's, 107–108
   critique of, 109–110
   Dollard's, 104

Social learning theories (*continued*)
  interpersonal trust and, 106–107
  locus of controls of, 105–106
  Miller's, 103–104
  Rotter's, 104–105
  therapeutic process of, 108–110
Social phobia, 74
Social psychology, 36
Society for Free Psychoanalytic Research, 40
Society of Individual Psychology, 40
Sociocognitive theories, 71
Sociocognitive theory of automaticity, 4–5
Socioreligious ethnic groups, 24
Sociotrophy, 146, 157
Socratic method, 69, 153
Soft determinism, 36
Solution-oriented therapy, 49
Sorting, 168
Sour grapes rationalization, 44
Specific expectancies, 105
Sperry, L., 44, 48, 52
Spiegler, M.D., 104
Spielberger, C.D., 73
SPSS, 9, 10, 11
Stampfl, T.G., 77
Stations of the Mind (Glasser), 200
Stations of the Mind, Taking Effective Control of Your Life (Glasser), 200
Statistical significance, 8, 16
Steiner, C., 177
Stereotypes, 29, 30
Stewart, I., 192
Stoic philosophers, 128
Stress, 86
Stress disorder, 74
Stress hierarchy, 75
Stress inoculation training (SIT), 101, 160–162, 164
Stress management and relaxation, books on, 84
Strokes/stroking, 186, 196
Structural analysis, 196
Structural equations modeling, 22
Structuralism/structuralists, 35
Structural profiles, 137
Subjective reasoning, 153, 157
Subjective Units of Distress Scale (SUDS), 75–76, 85, 101
Substance-related disorders, 61
Successive approximation, 80

Sue, D., 29
Sue, D.W., 29
Suffering, 43–44
Suicide, 84, 142
Summarization, 50
Superiority priority, 51
Superiority, striving for, 40–41
Superordinate construct, 165–166, 173
Supervisory attentional systems, 6
Suppressor variables, 19, 20, 21
Sweet lemons rationalization, 44
Systematic desensitization (SD), 12, 75, 101

T

Task setting, 55
Technical eclecticism, 72, 129
Teleology, 44, 45, 59
Terminating/summarizing sessions, 55
Testability, 22
Test anxiety, 73–74
Theoretical eclecticism, 72
Theories, 18
Therapist, role of
  Adlerian psychotherapy and, 55
  behavioral therapy and, 96–97
  cognitive-behavior modification (CBM) and, 162
  cognitive therapy and, 152–153
  multimodal behavior therapy (MMBT) and, 134
  personal constructs psychotherapy and, 170
  reality therapy and, 205
  REBT and, 122–123
  social learning theories and, 108
  transactional analysis (TA) and, 193
Thinning, 79, 101
Thompson, B., 9, 10, 11
Thorndike, Edward Lee, 78
Three Approaches to Psychotherapy, The, 124
Time outs, 81
Token economy, 80, 81, 101
Topographical regression, 94
Torres, J.B., 124
Total behavior, 201, 202, 204, 205, 211
Tracking, 132–134, 137
Traditional forms of cognitive-behavioral therapies, 11, 16

Transactional Analysis in Psychotherapy (Berne), 176
Transactional Analysis Journal, 197
Transactional analysis (TA), 13, 14, 38, 57, 176–198
   action strategies of, 190–192
   analysis of psychological games and, 184–186
   Berne's approach to, 187–188
   Developmental perspective of human nature and, 177–179
   family therapy and, 189
   new developments within, 192
   redecisional theory of, 189
   script analysis and, 186–187
   structural analysis of, 179–181, 188
   therapeutic process of, 192–193
   transactions and, 181–184
Transference, 36, 48
Trauma, 59, 84, 85, 86, 88
   See also Posttraumatic stress disorder (PTSD)
Treatment transcripts, 88–90
Triadic reciprocality, 107

U

Ulterior transactions, 183–184, 185 fig.
Unconditional acceptance, 122
Unconscious conflicts, 78
United States of America Transactional Analysis Association, 197
U.S. Census data, 28 table

V

Vagg, P.R., 73
Validity, 22
Validity of cognition scale (VOC), 85
Van Den Hout, M., 5, 75
Variable reinforcement, 79
Vernon, A., 124
Violent Youth, books on, 84
Vocational psychology, 34

W

Watson, J.B., 66, 67
Watts, R.E., 42
WDEP system, 207, 208, 211
Websites, 64, 102, 158, 175, 197, 212
Wedding, D., 35
Wednesday Evening Group for the Vienna Psychoanalytic Society, 40
Wegner, D., 4
Weight Management, books on, 84
Weinrach, S.G., 124
Weishaar, M.E., 155
Weissman, Myrna, 139
Wertheimer, Max, 35
West Indies, 25
Wheatley, T., 4
White Anglo-Saxon Protestants (WASP's), 24
White ethnic Americans, 25
Wiener, Norbert, 204
William Glasser Institute, The (Los Angeles), 200, 212
William Glasser LaVerne College Center, 200
Wissink, L.M., 190
Wolf, F.M., 8
Wolpe, Joseph, 65, 75, 77, 85, 139
Women's Issues, books on, 84
Woods, P.J., 125
Woody, E., 6, 93
World War II, 20
Worry, 73, 74
Wubbolding, R.E., 200, 202, 203, 204, 206, 207
Wundt, Wilhelm, 35

Y

Young, Cornell, 26, 29, 30

Z

Zamansky, H.S., 93
Zimmerman, B.J., 107

Charles C Thomas
PUBLISHER • LTD.

P.O. Box 19265
Springfield, IL 62794-9265

Book Savings*   Save 10%, Save 15%, Save 20%

- Hargis, Charles H.—**TEACHING LOW ACHIEVING AND DISADVANTAGED STUDENTS.** (3rd Ed.) '06, 182 pp. (7 x 10), $34.95, paper.

- Adams, Dennis & Mary Hamm—**REDEFINING EDUCATION IN THE TWENTY-FIRST CENTURY: Shaping Collaborative Learning in the Age of Information.** '05, 208 pp. (7 x 10), $52.95, hard, $32.95, paper.

- Burke, Peter J. & Robert D. Krey—**SUPERVISION: A Guide to Instructional Leadership.** (2nd Ed.) '05, 462 pp. (7 x 10), 22 il., $89.95, hard, $63.95, paper.

- Kronick, Robert F.—**FULL SERVICE COMMUNITY SCHOOLS: Prevention of Delinquency in Students with Mental Illness and/or Poverty.** '05, 168 pp. (7 x 10), 19 il., $31.95, paper.

- Obiakor, Festus E. & Floyd D. Beachum—**URBAN EDUCATION FOR THE 21ST CENTURY: Research, Issues, and Perspectives.** '05, 262 pp. (7 x 10), 1 il., $52.95, hard, $35.95, paper.

- Hefzallah, Ibrahim M.—**THE NEW EDUCATIONAL TECHNOLOGIES AND LEARNING: Empowering Teachers to Teach and Students to Learn in the Information Age.** (2nd Ed.) '04, 378 pp. (7 x 10), 6 il., $77.95, hard, $55.95, paper.

- Karp, David R. & Thom Allena—**RESTORATIVE JUSTICE ON THE COLLEGE CAMPUS: Promoting Student Growth and Responsibility, and Reawakening the Spirit of Campus Community.** '04, 290 pp. (7 x 10), 1 il., 9 tables, $77.95, hard, $48.95, paper.

- Kuther, Tara L.—**GRADUATE STUDY IN PSYCHOLOGY: Your Guide To Success.** '04, 198 pp. (7 x 10), 14 il., $48.95, hard, $28.95, paper.

- Levinson, Edward M.—**TRANSITION FROM SCHOOL TO POST-SCHOOL LIFE FOR INDIVIDUALS WITH DISABILITIES: Assessment from an Educational and School Psychological Perspective.** '04, 300 pp. (7 x 10), 10 il., 3 tables, $61.95, hard, $41.95, paper.

- MacKinnon, Fiona J. D.—**RENTZ'S STUDENT AFFAIRS PRACTICE IN HIGHER EDUCATION.** (3rd Ed.) '04, 444 pp. (7 x 10), 1 il., $95.95, hard, $65.95, paper.

- Siljander, Raymond P., Jacqueline A. Reina, & Roger A. Siljander—**LITERACY TUTORING HANDBOOK: A Guide to Teaching Children and Adults to Read and Write.** '05, 204 pp. (8 1/2 x 11), 71 il., 16 tables, $32.95, spiral (paper).

- Welch, Paula D.—**HISTORY OF AMERICAN PHYSICAL EDUCATION AND SPORT.** (3rd Ed.) '04, 414 pp. (7 x 10), 62 il., $79.95, hard, $59.95, paper.

- English, Fenwick W.—**THE POSTMODERN CHALLENGE TO THE THEORY AND PRACTICE OF EDUCATIONAL ADMINISTRATION.** '03, 292 pp. (7 x 10), 19 il., 4 tables, $57.95, hard, $38.95, paper.

- Wehmeyer, Michael L., Brian H. Abery, Dennis E. Mithaug & Roger J. Stancliffe—**THEORY IN SELF-DETERMINATION: Foundations for Educational Practice.** '03, 338 pp. (7 x 10), 24 il., 27 tables, $66.95, hard, $46.95, paper.

- Denbo, Sheryl J. & Lynson Moore Beaulieu—**IMPROVING SCHOOLS FOR AFRICAN AMERICAN STUDENTS: A Reader for Educational Leaders.** '02, 288 pp. (8 x 10), 5 il., 1 table, $70.95, hard, $47.95, paper.

- Nicoletti, John, Sally Spencer-Thomas & Christopher M. Bollinger—**VIOLENCE GOES TO COLLEGE: The Authoritative Guide to Prevention and Intervention.** '01, 324 pp. (7 x 10), 5 il., $74.95, hard, $51.95, paper.

- Wiseman, Dennis G. & Gilbert H. Hunt—**BEST PRACTICE IN MOTIVATION AND MANAGEMENT IN THE CLASSROOM.** '01, 228 pp. (7 x 10), 10 il., $54.95, hard, $37.95, paper.

- Sandeen, Arthur—**IMPROVING LEADERSHIP IN STUDENT AFFAIRS ADMINISTRATION: A Case Approach.** '00, 226 pp. (7 x 10), $49.95, cloth, $32.95, paper.

---

5 easy ways to order!

PHONE: 1-800-258-8980 or (217) 789-8980

FAX: (217) 789-9130

EMAIL: books@ccthomas.com
Web: www.ccthomas.com

MAIL: Charles C Thomas • Publisher, Ltd. P.O. Box 19265 Springfield, IL 62794-9265

Complete catalog available at ccthomas.com • books@ccthomas.com

Books sent on approval • Shipping charges: $7.50 min. U.S. / Outside U.S., actual shipping fees will be charged • Prices subject to change without notice

*Savings include all titles shown here and on our web site. For a limited time only.